POSITIVE LAW AND OBJECTIVE VALUES

Positive Law and Objective Values

ANDREI MARMOR

CLARENDON PRESS · OXFORD
2001

OXFORD
UNIVERSITY PRESS
Great Clarendon Street, Oxford OX2 6DP

Oxford University Press is a department of the University of Oxford.
It furthers the University's objective of excellence in research, scholarship,
and education by publishing worldwide in

Oxford New York
Athens Auckland Bangkok Bogotá Buenos Aires Cape Town
Chennai Dar es Salaam Delhi Florence Hong Kong Istanbul Karachi
Kolkata Kuala Lumpur Madrid Melbourne Mexico City Mumbai Nairobi
Paris São Paulo Shanghai Singapore Taipei Tokyo Toronto Warsaw
and associated companies in Berlin Ibadan

Oxford is a registered trade mark of Oxford University Press
in the UK and in certain other countries

Published in the United States
by Oxford University Press Inc., New York

First published 2001

British Library Cataloguing in Publication Data
Data available

Library of Congress Cataloging in Publication Data
Data available

ISBN 0–19–826897–1

1 3 5 7 9 10 8 6 4 2

Typeset by Hope Services (Abingdon) Ltd.
Printed in Great Britain
on acid-free paper by
Biddles Ltd., Guildford and King's Lynn

Preface

LAW is founded on social conventions. Social conventions determine what counts as law and how law is to be created, modified, and annulled. This thesis about the conventional foundations of law forms the topic of the first part of the book. In Chapter 1 I suggest a distinction between two main kinds of social conventions, coordination and constitutive, arguing that the latter kind is far more important for the explication of the conventional foundations of law. The fact that law is largely founded on constitutive conventions also explains why the law is partly, and in a very limited way, an autonomous social practice.

Unlike many other conventional practices, however, law is an authoritative institution, imposing on its putative subjects obligations and other normative demands which are often backed by threats and violence. The question of whether the normative–authoritative nature of law can be reconciled with its conventional foundations is closely examined in Chapter 2. I argue that the normativity of constitutive conventions is conditionally mandatory, and that the concept of conditional normativity explains how the law, like other conventional practices, engenders reasons for action. The normativity of law, however, is also claimed to be unique in several respects: first, the law is supposedly the only authoritative institution which imposes normative demands on its putative subjects regardless of their wilful participation. Secondly, allegedly, the law must be held to claim its supremacy over any other normative domain. Thirdly, the law, unlike many other conventional practices, enforces its normative demands by the use of force and the threat of violence. A careful analysis of these points, however, reveals that, properly construed, none of them threatens the conventionalist thesis.

In Chapter 3 I explore some of the implications of the conventional foundations of law on the debate between two main versions of legal positivism, the so-called 'exclusive' and 'inclusive' theses. I argue that inclusive legal positivism, which was meant to form a middle ground between traditional positivist theories and Dworkin's anti-positivism, is not a tenable position. There is no such middle ground. Inclusive legal positivism, I argue, is irreconcilable with both the conventional foundations of law and its essentially authoritative nature.

The next two chapters go on to defend the exclusive version of legal positivism from two different perspectives. Chapter 4 is devoted to an analysis of Dworkin's interpretative challenge. One of Dworkin's main arguments against legal positivism is based on the following two premisses: first, determining what the law is in each particular instance results from an interpretative reasoning; secondly, that interpretation necessarily involves evaluative considerations. Therefore, the argument concludes, it follows that determining what the law is always depends on evaluative considerations. The chapter focuses on the first premiss, examining three possible arguments in support of it: a semantic argument, an epistemic one, and Dworkin's theory of legal principles. I argue that none of these arguments succeeds. Neither semantic nor epistemic considerations can support the idea that determining what the law is always follows from an interpretation. I also argue that there are no legal principles of the kind Dworkin envisaged.

In Chapter 5 I consider in some detail the essential relationship between authority and authorship suggesting that there is no authority without authorship. Legal authority, I argue, must be attributable to persons who can form a judgement on how others ought to behave and communicate such a judgement to their putative subjects. This personal conception of authority has been recently criticized by Jeremy Waldron, and earlier by H. L. A. Hart in his discussion of Austin's jurisprudence. I argue that Waldron's impersonal conception of authority fails because it ignores the crucial distinction between theoretical and practical authorities. Hart's criticisms of Austin's personal conception of authority, however, are defensible only to the extent that they target Austin's rather crude definitions of sovereignty.

The conventional foundations of law and law's relative autonomy raise some difficult questions about the objectivity of law, morality, and the relations between them. The next three chapters are devoted to an analysis of various aspects of objectivity. The theory of objectivity I propose here is grounded on the distinction between objectivity and metaphysical realism, a distinction explained in Chapter 6 and further explored in the following chapters. In Chapter 6 I employ the example of interpretation in the realm of works of art to exemplify three different concepts of objectivity, none of which is committed to metaphysical realism.

Chapter 7 concerns four different questions about the objectivity of law. First, are there objective criteria about the identification of law? Can we have objectively correct (and incorrect) answers to the question what the law is on each particular issue? The distinction between objectivity and realism, I show here, is particularly helpful in alleviating some of the traditional worries about the objectivity of law in this respect. Secondly, there is a question about law's objective merit: can we say that particular laws are objectively correct or incorrect, right or wrong? An answer to this question partly depends on the issue of the autonomy of law. It depends on the question of whether legal right and wrong necessarily reduces to moral worth. On the basis of the theory of social conventions articulated in the first part of the book, I argue that there are certain standards of evaluation distinctively legal in character, not reducible to moral values. The third question concerns another sense of objectivity which is particularly interesting in the legal case. It is the kind of objectivity which is concerned with the avoidance of bias, partiality, favouritism, and such. My main concern here is to analyse the relations between objectivity in this sense, which I call judicial objectivity, and neutrality and equality. Finally, I consider a familiar question about the possible objectivity of legal theory, arguing that though legal theory is evaluative in many respects, it does not necessarily depend on moral conceptions.

Despite the fact that various aspects of the objectivity of law do not necessarily depend on the objectivity of morality or of values in general, the objectivity of values is a pressing issue for anyone interested in a critical perspective on law and other social institutions. The last chapter takes this issue up directly and suggests an account of the objectivity of values, arguing that values are relational properties. Needless to say, this is only a tentative and partial account. Within the confines of one chapter the objectivity of values cannot be discussed in sufficient detail and depths. The main purpose of this chapter is to show that when objectivity is detached, as it should be, from a commitment to metaphysical realism, an objective stance about values seems to be more convincing than its subjectivist alternatives, particularly with respect to the rational motivation for valuing.

The essays included in this book, some of which have been previously published and others written especially for it, have been written during five or six years. During these years I have been troubled by four main issues: the nature of social conventions, legal authority, interpretation, and objectivity. Together these issues form the main concerns of this book and provide the basis on which I try to defend a relatively strong or 'exclusive' version of legal positivism.

Naturally my views on some of these issues have changed over the time and therefore some of the essays published here are substantially revised. In particular, some of the views I published about objectivity I no longer hold. At one time I thought that careful inquiries about the nature of 'truth' may greatly facilitate the discussion about objectivity, particularly with respect to the objectivity of values. I now tend to think that this is not the case, and that the objectivity of values need not rely on any fancy theory of 'truth'. The intuitive idea that propositions are rendered true or false by their correspondence with how things really are suffices, I think, for purposes of establishing the metaphysical objectivity of values.

Many friends and colleagues have commented on drafts of these essays during the years and I am grateful to them all. A particular dept of gratitude I owe to Joseph Raz, whose comments and criticisms of most of the chapters included in this book were invaluable. I have benefited greatly from comments on various parts of the book suggested by Jules Coleman, Jeremy Waldron, Alon Harel, Chaim Gans, Scott Shapiro, Leslie Green, Martin Stone, David Enoch, Charles Larmore, and Meir Dan-Cohen. Elizabeth Garrett read substantial parts of the manuscript and suggested invaluable improvements of style and editing. I am also grateful to the Cegla Institute at Tel Aviv University and the University of Chicago Law School for financial support and research assistance.

Acknowledgements

Chapter 1 is a revised version of 'Legal Conventionalism', published in *Legal Theory*, 4 (1998), 509.

Chapter 4 is a revised version of 'The Separation Thesis and The Limits of Interpretation' which appeared in the *Canadian Journal of Law and Jurisprudence*, 12 (1999), 135.

Chapter 5 appeared under the title 'Authorities and Persons', in *Legal Theory*, 1 (1995), 337. The version published here is revised and somewhat extended.

An article version of Chapter 3 is due to be published in the collection edited by Jules Coleman and Scott Shapiro, *The Oxford Handbook of Jurisprudence and the Philosophy of Law*.

Material in the first two sections of Chapter 7 is drawn from part of my 'An Essay on the Objectivity of Law' which appeared in B. Bix (ed.), *Analysing Law: New Essays in Legal Theory* (Oxford, 1998), 1.

I am grateful to all these publishers and editors for their permission to use the material in this book.

Table of Contents

1
Constitutive Conventions

THERE are two questions I would like to address in this chapter. The first and main question is, whether there are Rules of Recognition, along the lines suggested by H. L. A. Hart. The second question concerns the age-old issue of the autonomy of law. One of the main purposes of this chapter is to show how these two issues are closely related. The concept of a social convention is the thread holding these two themes tightly knit in one coil. Basically, I will argue that a novel account of social conventions can be employed to re-establish Hart's thesis about the Rules of Recognition, and that this same account shows why, and to what extent, law is partly an autonomous practice.

RULES OF RECOGNITION

H. L. A. Hart's thesis about the existence of the Rules of Recognition has become one of the main dogmas taught to jurisprudence students for decades. It is also, undoubtedly, one of the main theses presented in *The Concept of Law*.[1] Basically, it maintains that in each and every modern legal system, there are 'social rules', as Hart called them, which are followed by the pertinent legal community (particularly judges), and these rules define the sources of law. Namely, the rules identify those facts or events which are taken to yield the established ways of the creation, modification, and annulment of legal standards in the relevant legal system.[2]

The idea that there are, as a matter of social fact, rules of recognition, had not been the main worry of Hart's critics for quite some time. It was the further, conceptual thesis of Hart and other legal positivists, which engendered the main controversies, namely, that the concept of legal validity is exhausted by reference to the rules of recognition. According to this conceptual thesis, a norm is legally valid if, and only if, it derives its validity from one of the sources of law identified by the rules of recognition. Dworkin's main critical

This chapter is a revised version of my article 'Legal Conventionalism', published in *Legal Theory*, 4 (1998), 509–31. I am grateful to Jules Coleman, Chaim Gans, Leslie Green, Alon Harel, Stephen Perry, Joseph Raz, Scott Shapiro, Martin Stone, and Ben Zipursky for their comments on drafts of this essay.

[1] Hart, *The Concept of Law*, mainly ch. 5.

[2] Hart further assumed that in each and every legal system, eventually one Rule of Recognition can be identified, which subsumes, in a hierarchical ordering, all the rest. This further assumption we need not share here, and I shall henceforth assume that nothing substantial is lost if we hold the more plausible assumption that the rules of recognition are not necessarily hierarchically structured.

efforts in the 1970s, for instance, aimed to show that this conceptual thesis is groundless, since the law comprises numerous norms whose legal validity cannot be traced to the sources of law identified by the rules of recognition.[3] In other words, it was not the existence of the rules of recognition, but their importance for the explication of the concept of legal validity, which was the focus of most of the controversy at the time.

Hart's thesis about the existence of rules of recognition is, nevertheless, problematic. Dworkin, for one, seems to have changed his mind recently, and he now certainly claims that there are no rules of recognition at all. But even before this shift occurred, both fellow positivist and non-positivist critics noticed serious problems about Hart's thesis, and it is worth noting what those difficulties are.

We cannot tell whether there are rules of recognition or not, unless we know what kind of rules they are. In *The Concept of Law*, Hart offered a detailed explanation of the nature of these social rules. It is here, in the characterization of the rules of recognition as 'social rules' that the difficulties lie. The idea of a 'social rule' is actually a term of art in *The Concept of Law*, and it is based on Hart's *practice theory of rules*, to which we must turn for a moment.

THE PRACTICE THEORY OF SOCIAL RULES

We encounter an enormous variety of rules in our lives. In a modern society, people follow many kinds of rules enacted by public or private institutions. But there is also a great variety of rules people follow, sometimes without being very much aware of it, which have no institutional origins. These are mostly social rules; the rules we follow in numerous contexts which have no particular origin in the enactment of an individual or an institution. Although there is undoubtedly an enormous diversity of such social rules, Hart's practice theory of rules was meant to capture the essence of them all, in the following definition.

A social rule, say R, exists in society S, Hart maintained, if and only if the following conditions are present:

1. There is a regularity of behaviour according to R, in S; namely, most members of S regularly conform to R.
2. Most members of S manifest a normative attitude towards R, which Hart called 'acceptance'.

The idea of 'acceptance' basically consists of two components:

[3] Dworkin, *Taking Rights Seriously,* mainly chs. 2–4.

a. For most members of S, the existence of R constitutes reasons for action in accordance with R.
b. The existence of R is employed by members of S both as grounds for criticizing deviant behaviour and as a justification for exerting social pressure on other members of S to conform to R.

In *The Concept of Law,* Hart presented this account of social rules as a general explication of the nature of social rules. In this generalization Hart had been clearly wrong, as he himself came to admit years later. In the posthumously published Postscript to *The Concept of Law*[4] Hart conceded some of the critical points raised against his account, both by Raz and Dworkin, and he suggested a considerable modification of the practice theory of rules, to which I shall come in a moment. In order to understand this modification, however, we must briefly dwell on the two main reasons which have been provided for the inadequacy of Hart's original account. Though differently formulated, I believe that these criticisms are shared both by Raz and Dworkin.[5]

First, it has been noted that Hart's account of social rules seems to be incapable of distinguishing between an instance of following a rule, and that of following a generally accepted reason.[6] This is a crucially important distinction, both for any reasonable account of the concept of a rule, and particularly, for the question of whether there are any rules of recognition as Hart envisioned. As we shall shortly see, it is the upshot of Dworkin's recent criticism of the rules of recognition that at best they are generally accepted reasons, but not rules at all.

Consider, for example, the distinction between the rules of a game, namely, those rules which define the moves one is entitled to make, or what constitutes winning or losing the game, etc., and generally accepted strategies within the game.[7] Strategies are principles of action which are generally accepted as reliable guides of conduct, but they are not considered or acted upon as rules of the game. Hart's account of social rules, however, seems to apply both to

[4] Hart, *The Concept of Law*, 2nd edn., Postscript.

[5] See Dworkin, *Taking Rights Seriously*, and Raz, *Practical Reason and Norms*. There is some unclearness about the question whether Hart thought that the practice theory of rules applies to morality as well. In any case, it is clear enough that it cannot apply to moral rules. Rules of morals and similar domains need not be practised in order to be valid. Hart's requirement for a regularity of behaviour as a basis for the rule's existence simply does not apply to such spheres as morality. We often hold moral rules to be valid despite the fact that they are not practised in the pertinent community, or anywhere else.

[6] 'Following a reason' may sound rather awkward, and perhaps it is. I use this unusual term (instead of, for example, 'acting on a reason') not only to emphasize symmetry, but also because I intend to refer to those cases where people act according to a reason with some generality. Generality is actually twofold: both referring to the kind of reasons and to the occasions in which those reasons are taken to apply.

[7] The distinction, as well as the game example, was first suggested by Warnock, in *The Object of Morality*, 43–6.

rules and strategies. In both cases we would have a regularity of behaviour, and a normative attitude of 'acceptance' as the latter is defined by Hart.

The point that Hart's original account misses here is delicate but important. Hart thought that the normativity of a social rule consists in the fact that the rule is considered to constitute a reason for action. Though this is clearly correct, it is not a sufficient characterization of a rule's normativity. Rules constitute reasons for action in a special way, namely, in that they are taken to replace something which would have applied to the circumstances had there not been a rule governing it. It is, of course, extremely difficult to articulate what this 'something' that the rules are there to replace really is. I tend to think that there are different elements of practical reasoning which different kinds of rules are there to replace, but we need not go into this complicated matter here.[8] Suffice it to say that Hart's practice theory of rules, even if basically correct, requires a crucial addition. It must be construed so as to allow for the distinction between following a rule and following a generally accepted reason. Otherwise, Hart's theory of the rules of recognition remains open to the charge that there are actually no such rules at all, but only generally accepted reasons for compliance with the decrees of various institutions, which may or may not be good reasons, but they are not rules at all.

Secondly, and more importantly, both Raz and Dworkin have noted that Hart's original account of the normativity of social rules is largely vacuous. There is simply nothing in the practice theory of rules to explain the kind of reasons people would have for following a social rule. Hart's account leaves one wondering what prompts people to regard a rule as a reason for action. Simply pointing to the fact that there *is* a regularity of behaviour, which seems to be suggested by Hart as part of the reason for following a social rule, is clearly the wrong answer. It is only in special and unique circumstances that the reason for following a rule partly consists in the fact that others follow it too. Namely, in those cases where the rule in question is a social convention. But not all the social rules are conventions, of course.[9]

It is in this last point, that Hart found the anchor for his modified account. In the Postscript to *The Concept of Law,* Hart basically conceded these critical observations and inferred the obvious conclusion: the practice theory of rules, he claimed, is not a general account of social rules, as such, but only of one subcategory of social rules, namely, social conventions. Since it should

[8] Joseph Raz, for instance, in his famous analysis of mandatory rules in *Practical Reason and Norms* claimed that such rules are there to replace the balance of the first-order reasons which would have applied to the circumstances. Mandatory rules, Raz claims, are a combination of first-order reasons for action, and exclusionary reasons, namely, reasons not to act on certain types or excluded reasons. The question whether this or a similar account can be applied to the rules or recognition or not will be taken up in detail in Chapter 2.

[9] For example, at least intuitively, we would not think of the moral rules we adhere to as a species of conventions. We tend to follow many social rules because we believe that they capture some truths about the ways we ought to behave.

have been clear from the start that the rules of recognition are conventions, this late concession has no effect on Hart's main insights about the rules of recognition. As he put it in his own words: 'the theory remains as a faithful account of conventional social rules which include . . . the rule of recognition, which is in effect a norm of judicial customary rule existing only if it is accepted and practiced in the law-identifying and law-applying operations of the courts.'[10]

Thus, according to Hart's modified version, the rules of recognition are social conventions, and the original practice theory of rules is presented as an account of the concept of social convention. However, a crucial element has been succinctly added to the original definitions, and this is the idea that a necessary *reason* for following a rule which is a social convention consists in the fact that others follow it too. The fact that there is a regularity of behaviour according to R, provides a crucially important reason for members of S to regard R as a reason for action and to follow it too.

This late modification did not convince Dworkin, however. He clearly rejects Hart's suggestions about the conventionality of the rules of recognition:

> On my view, there is no fully shared rule of recognition at all: the supposed convention, that the American Constitution is the supreme law of the land or that Parliament is the supreme lawgiver in Britain, can only be described as conventionally accepted if we ignore the fact that what those abstract formulations mean to some lawyers, as guides to identifying true, concrete propositions of law, is very different from what they mean to others.

And in the sequel:

> So Hart's picture of law, as fixed by a conventional rule of recognition, cannot be sustained even for Anglo-American legal systems, except by making the convention so abstract that it becomes: law must be identified by the right tests for identifying law. And then there is no longer any point to calling that a *convention*.[11]

It should be said that Dworkin's current position about the rules of recognition was formulated long before Hart's Postscript became publicly known. At least as early as the mid-1980s, when *Law's Empire* was published, it was clear enough that Dworkin was no longer willing to assume that there are any *conventions* about the recognition of the law, even with respect to the most limited and humdrum instances that we would call 'easy cases'. There are instances of widespread agreement amongst an 'interpretative community' about what counts as law, and there are even paradigms of law, but none of this amounts to the existence of social conventions, as Hart would have it. According to Dworkin, such interpretative starting points, or 'raw material',

[10] Hart, *The Concept of Law*, 2nd edn., 256.

[11] Dworkin, 'Hart's posthumous reply', unpublished manuscript (circulated at his Oxford seminar in 1997).

never amounts to more than a local and tentative convergence of beliefs and attitudes, which may well be widely shared, but again, it never amounts to more than that; namely, widely shared beliefs and attitudes. Such beliefs do not constitute a conceptual framework for the understanding of law, and they are never secure from challenge by better interpretations which would rule them out of existence by the sheer power of interpretative reasoning.[12]

Dworkin's objection to the existence of rules of recognition, however, is seriously impeded by two recurrent mistakes underlying his conception of conventionalism. He has always assumed that conventions manifest a pattern of agreement. In view of this consensus basis of conventions, the existence of a social convention is essentially incompatible with substantial controversies about its content. Both assumptions, however, are misguided. Conventions, as we shall see in detail below, have no such consensual basis. It is not anything like tacit agreement, or an implicit consensus, that brings about the existence of a social convention. On the contrary, social conventions tend to emerge precisely in those cases where an agreement is difficult or impossible to reach. The fallacy in Dworkin's second assumption is even clearer. A controversy over the content of a rule of recognition does not prove that there is no such a rule. Even when there are several ways of understanding a rule (or anything else for that matter), there must be something there that people can understand differently and argue about. There are different ways of understanding the American Constitution, and there are different ways of understanding its normative supremacy, but none of this controversy would have been intelligible in the first place, if such conventions were indeed 'so abstract that [they] become: law must be identified by the right tests for identifying law'. The apparent plausibility of Dworkin's argument stems, perhaps, from a confusion between the question of whether there is a rule, and the different question of whether we can agree on the formulation of the rule. It may well be the case that there is no general agreement on the appropriate formulation of a rule of recognition, but this does not entail that no such rule exists.[13]

In other words, it is not the controversial nature of the rules of recognition which render them problematic. It has been noted many times that social conventions need not be uncontroversial in order to exist and fulfil their functions as conventional rules.[14] Dworkin's recent position, however, indicates that there is another criticism hidden there, and I would like to suggest that it presents a much more serious challenge. The 'rules of recognition', Dworkin seems to be claiming, are, at best, generally accepted reasons, but they are not rules, and hence they are not conventions either. Although Dworkin himself hardly provides any arguments to support this claim, I believe that a closer

[12] Dworkin, *Law's Empire*, 91.

[13] I am indebted to Ben Zipursky for mentioning this possibility to me.

[14] On what can and what cannot be controversial about conventions I will have much more to say in Chapter 3.

look at the contemporary philosophical analyses of conventions may well reveal some reasons to side with Dworkin on this question. These reasons, however, have nothing to do with the controversial nature of the rules of recognition.

A FIRST LOOK AT SOCIAL CONVENTIONS

When H. L. A. Hart published *The Concept of Law*, little philosophical attention had been paid to the analysis of the concept of social convention. There were, of course, important discussions about the conventionality of language, but little attention had been paid to trying to understand what conventions are. This changed dramatically, however, and only about a decade later, with the publication of David Lewis's pioneering book, *Convention: A Philosophical Study*.[15] Lewis defined the purpose of his project as an attempt to respond to Quine's objection to the conventional basis of language. Quine argued that the supposed conventions of language cannot be much like the standard instances of conventions, since conventions are agreements, and of course, we have never agreed with one another to abide by the conventions of language. Quine's assumption, Lewis argued, was simply wrong: conventions are not agreements since they are rules which emerge as practical solutions to recurrent coordination problems.

A typical coordination problem arises, according to Lewis, when several agents have a particular structure of preferences with respect to their mutual modes of conduct: namely, that between several alternatives of conduct open to them in a given set of circumstances, each and every agent has a stronger preference to act as the other agents will, than his own preference for acting upon any one of the particular alternatives. Most coordination problems are easily solved by simple agreements between the agents to act upon one more or less arbitrarily chosen alternative, thus securing uniformity of action amongst them. However, when a particular coordination problem is recurrent, and agreement is difficult to obtain (mostly because of the large number of agents involved), a social rule is very likely to emerge, and this rule is a convention. Conventions, in other words, emerge as solutions to recurrent coordination problems, not as a result of an agreement, but as an alternative to such an agreement, precisely in those cases where agreements are difficult or impossible to obtain.[16]

Lewis's analysis of conventions in terms of solution to recurrent coordination problems embodies remarkable advantages; quite apart from the fact

[15] Lewis, *Convention: A Philosophical Study*.

[16] It is worth keeping in mind that the solution of a coordination problem—unlike other types of game-theory situations—does not call for a sanction-based solution. More on this in Chapter 2.

that it is capable of explaining the emergence of conventions without relying on the need for agreement, it also explains two important intuitions largely shared about the unique features of social conventions. First, there is an important sense in which conventions are regarded as *arbitrary* rules. One of the most basic intuitions about conventions we have is that if a rule is a convention, then there must be at least one other alternative rule that people could have followed instead in order to achieve the same purpose. Second, an equally strong intuition is that our reasons for following a rule which is a convention are strongly linked to the fact that others follow it too. Therefore, it is typically thought that there is no point in following a conventional rule if it is not actually practised by the pertinent community.

Now, both of these two intuitive features of conventional rules are nicely explicable by Lewis's analysis. Beginning with the second, we can see that according to Lewis's analysis, the whole point of a conventional rule is to secure uniformity of action amongst a number of agents. After all, it is precisely the point of a coordination problem that each and every agent's dominant preference is to act just as the other agents will. Hence, the relevant agents would have no reason to abide by the conventional rule if they thought that others would not abide by the same rule too. Thus, the rationale of conventions as solutions to coordination problems easily explains why the reason to follow a convention hinges on the fact that others follow it as well.

Lewis's analysis can also explain why, and to what extent, conventional rules are rightly considered arbitrary. It is the basic structure of a coordination problem that there are at least two alternatives of conduct available to the agents in question: between these alternatives, the agents have a stronger preference for uniformity of action, as compared to their preference for any one of the particular alternatives open to them. Thus, from the agents' own perspective, the choice between any one of the relevant alternatives is pretty much arbitrary since they would like to abide by whichever option secures uniformity of action amongst them.

These, and some other advantages that I can not mention here, quickly turned Lewis's analysis of conventions into the mainstream, almost a textbook philosophical account of the concept of social conventions. Although several philosophers criticized Lewis on certain details of his definition, the core idea that conventions are solutions to recurrent coordination problems, has been widely shared ever since.[17] Remarkably, however, with few notable exceptions,[18] legal philosophers have paid very little attention to this mainstream philosophical account of social conventions. This *is* remarkable, since it is clear that Hart's account of the 'conventional' rules of recognition does

[17] Gilbert in her book *On Social Facts* suggested an alternative account of social conventions. My reservations about her alternative I have expressed in 'On Convention'.

[18] Postema, 'Coordination and Convention at the Foundations of Law'. See also Raz, '*Facing up*: A Reply'.

not square easily with Lewis's analysis of the concept of social conventions. If Lewis is basically right about what conventions are, the rules of recognition would not seem to be conventions at all.

There are two main problems that come immediately to light. First, it would be very difficult to maintain that the rules of recognition are *arbitrary* rules. Some of them may be. But thc *fundamental* rules of recognition of a legal system certainly would not be regarded by the members of that legal system as arbitrary at all. For the US judges, jurists, and the public at large, the normative supremacy of the American Constitution is not merely one arbitrarily chosen alternative among several other rules of recognition which would be equally acceptable. The same is true of the British rule of the supremacy of Parliament, and numerous similar examples. After all, the rules of recognition define what the law is in a given community, and this is clearly a matter of utmost political importance. It matters a great deal to all of us who makes the law, and how it is to be enacted. Thinking of such rules of recognition in terms of arbitrariness would certainly strike most jurists and politically conscientious people as a crazy idea. There seems to be nothing arbitrary about the fact that Americans opted for the kind of Constitutional structure that they have and continuously maintain. Americans obviously believe that their fundamental rules of recognition, embodying the supremacy of their Constitution, Federalism (selective) adherence to Common Law, and so forth, reflect political choices of great importance. How can this political dimension be reconciled with the conception of rules of recognition as arbitrary solutions to recurrent coordination problems?

And here we come to the second and main problem in applying Lewis's analysis to the rules of recognition: the rules of recognition do not seem like solutions to recurrent coordination problems at all. Perhaps some of the more technical rules of recognition can be so regarded, but the fundamental rules of recognition of the legal system do not seem to be closely tied to the solution of coordination problems. The political choices they embody are far more complex and manifold than the basic structure of a coordination problem. Admittedly, the analysis of coordination problems has advanced considerably in the last few decades, and a great deal of complexity and richness has been added to Lewis's original account. Nor should we assume that coordination problems are typically simple or of one particular kind. Complexities notwithstanding, the basic idea of a coordination problem remains the same: securing some form of uniformity of action where such uniformity is in the best interest of the parties involved, and it is recognized by them as such. I do not believe that this is the rationale of most of the rules of recognition. Consider, for instance, the basic idea of Federalism in the USA. The Federal structure of the US legal system is instantiated by a set of rules of recognition that US judges, lawyers, and numerous other officials follow. These rules have a purpose, a political rationale, which originated in the famous political compromise of the Independence, and was reshaped by subsequent political events, like the Civil War and the New Deal. But these reasons and political solutions which underlie the rationale of the rules of recognition which instantiate the idea of Federalism have little to do with the structure of a coordination problem. The problem to be solved was not the need to coordinate the political power of the states and the Federal government. It was the more pressing political question of whether the emerging states should yield their political independence to a central government at all which generated the famous Federalist compromise. Federalism, and the rules of recognition it instantiates, is a delicate and subtle compromise between conflicting claims to authority, and not a solution to a coordination problem.

My guess is that these, or similar thoughts, may have led Dworkin (and, presumably, many others) to conclude that the alleged rules of recognition are not conventions at all, but, at best, generally accepted reasons. The supremacy of the American Constitution is a widely shared political conviction, Dworkin maintains, and not a conventional rule. Our discussion so far seems to suggest that if Lewis is basically correct about what social conventions are, Dworkin may well be quite right about the alleged rules of recognition: they don't look like conventional rules at all. I want to suggest, however, that such a conclusion is premature. A closer look at the nature of social conventions is necessary at this point. Such an analysis will reveal that Lewis's conception is much more limited in scope than has been generally assumed. An alternative, or rather additional, account of conventions can show why the rules of recognition are conventions after all.

A CLOSER LOOK AT SOCIAL CONVENTIONS

Let us begin with a refinement of the notion of 'arbitrariness' which is characteristic of conventional rules. There is, indeed, an important sense in which rules which are conventional are arbitrary: we think that if, say, R is a conventional rule, there must be at least one other rule, say R′, that could have been followed instead, achieving the same purpose.[19] This is clearly manifest, for example, in those cases where we are familiar with different rules solving the same type of coordination problem. In most of the Commonwealth countries people drive on the left side of the road, and in most others, they drive on the right. The choice between these two options seems to be pretty much arbitrary; both rules solve the same kind of coordination problem. Hence the

[19] I am not assuming here that conventional rules necessarily serve a particular purpose. My doubts about such functionalist explanations of conventions will be spelled out in the sequel, mainly the last section. For the time being, however, Lewis's framework should suffice for the illustration of the arbitrariness of conventions.

rule is, in a sense, arbitrary. But it is crucially important to be precise about what 'arbitrariness' means here. Some philosophers were quick to conclude that 'arbitrariness' is equivalent to indifference, and this is not so.[20] People need not be indifferent as to the choice between the conventional rule they actually follow, and any other rule they could have followed instead. In order to show that 'arbitrariness' does not imply 'indifference', a formal definition of the arbitrariness of social conventions may prove useful.

The following is the definition I propose:

Given that A is the main reason[s] for members of a population, P, for following a rule, R, in circumstances C, R is an arbitrary rule if and only if:

there is at least one other rule, R′, so that if most members of P were complying with R′ in circumstances C, then for all members of P, A would be a sufficient reason to follow R′ instead of R. The rules R and R′ are such that it is normally impossible to comply with them concomitantly in circumstances C.[21]

Now consider the following example, which is a typical case of what Lewis called an 'imperfect' coordination problem. Cellular phones are abundant in my country and most people use them regularly. These phones, however, tend to be somewhat unpredictable, and many conversations are cut off in the middle. So now we face a standard (recurrent and multiple) coordination problem: who should resume the call—the original caller, or the receiver? For obvious reasons, it would be preferable to have a social convention whereby the original caller is expected to resume the call if the conversation is prematurely cut off (at least we can be sure that she knows the number). Nonetheless, if for some obscure reason, a convention evolves whereby it is the receiver of the call who is expected to resume it in such cases, then despite the clear preference of the alternative rule, most of us would be better off complying with the convention which is actually practised. That is, of course, as long as the reasons for having a convention in the first place are more important for us than the reason for preferring an alternative course of action.

So we can see now that conventional rules are arbitrary, even if we are far from indifferent as to the choice between R and R′. Furthermore, we can also see that the notion of arbitrariness admits of degrees. Conventions can be more or less arbitrary. We could say that a conventional rule is completely arbitrary if it is true that the agents are indeed completely indifferent as to the

[20] See, for example, Gilbert, *On Social Facts*, 340–1.

[21] I have presented and defended this definition in my article 'On Convention'. There is, however, one clarification that I should mention here: the reason[s], 'A', which motivates people to comply with the rule R in the first place, need not be independent of the conventions themselves. I may have no reason whatsoever to play chess if there is no such conventional game to play. If I do have a reason to play chess, surely it depends on the fact that there is such a game that I can actually play. The importance of this point (which goes against Lewis's definition) will only become apparent later on.

choice between R and R′; and the rule would be less and less arbitrary, as we move away from complete indifference, up to the point where the preference of uniform conformity is just slightly stronger than the preference of a particular option.

Thus far, the story goes pretty much along the lines suggested by Lewis's original account.[22] There are two modifications, however, that need to be considered. The first is modest, but important. It concerns the question of whether it is necessary that people be aware of the arbitrary nature of the rule they follow in order for that rule to be a social convention. Lewis thought that the answer is affirmative. He insisted on a condition of *common knowledge* regarding the arbitrariness of the rule in question.[23] Yet I think that Tyler Burge has convincingly demonstrated that Lewis erred here.[24] People can be mistaken about the conventional nature of the rules they follow. To mention just one of Burge's examples, imagine a small, completely isolated linguistic community, none of whose members ever heard of anyone's speaking a different language. Now suppose that the people in this community believe that the language they speak is the only possible language in the world. They think that there are no humanly possible alternatives to speaking their language. Nevertheless, we would have no inclination to deny that their language is as conventional as any other language. As Burge put it, 'they are simply ignorant or wrong about the nature of their activities'.[25]

The second, and much more important modification of Lewis's account concerns the scope of his thesis. I do not wish to doubt that Lewis's account of conventions is at least partly correct, and in many cases, illuminating. Undeniably, numerous conventions emerge as solutions to recurrent coordination problems and this explains their entire rationale. Doubts arise, however, with respect to the generality of this thesis, and now I would like to substantiate these doubts. I would like to argue that there is another type of conventional rules, arbitrary in the sense I have defined, which cannot be explicated by Lewis's account. These are the *constitutive conventions* of autonomous social practices.[26]

When we claim that a conventional rule functions as a solution to a recurrent coordination problem, the following condition must obtain: it should be entirely possible for us to describe the precise nature of the coordination problem, and the relevant agents' preferences, antecedent to the existence of the conventional rule in question. In other words, there must be a coordination *problem* first, followed by its solution in the form a conventional rule. Furthermore, if Lewis's analysis is not be thought of as rather vacuous and

[22] See Lewis's account of imperfect coordination problems in Lewis, *Convention: A Philosophical Study*, at 76–80.

[23] See Lewis, ibid. at 75.

[24] Burge, 'On Knowledge and Convention'.

[25] Ibid. at 250.

[26] I have presented the basic argument about constitutive conventions in my 'On Convention'.

unhelpful, the coordination problem we diagnose must be pretty well structured. 'Here we are, let's do something' is not a coordination problem in the relevant sense. Otherwise, just about anything *we* do could be described as a solution to a coordination problem.

Now the problem is that this obvious condition is not met by numerous conventional practices we are familiar with. Take the rules constituting the game of chess, for example. (Just about any structured game would do, of course). It seems rather awkward to claim that the rules constituting the game of chess are solutions to a recurrent coordination problem. Antecedent to the game of chess, there was simply no problem to solve. Of course, once the game is there to play, and it is played, it may give rise to certain coordination problems which might then be settled by additional conventions. But chess itself, as a game of a particular kind, is not a solution to a problem of coordination. 'Let's have a competitive intellectual game', or something like this, is not a coordination problem along the lines suggested by Lewis. If it were, then 'Let's have a just Constitution' would also be a coordination problem, and of course, it is not. Thus, the problem is this: either we stick to the idea of a coordination problem as a fairly structured set of conditions and preferences, in which case, numerous conventions could not be described as solutions to such problems, or else we think of a coordination problem as something rather loose, applying to any set of circumstances where some form of collective action is pertinent, in which case, just about any rule we follow would be an instance of following a convention.

Have we not reached the point of a useless quarrel over definition? In order to dispel this impression, let me concede the following. Perhaps it is not so important whether the emergence of a game like chess can or cannot be described as a solution to some coordination problem or other. Even if it can be so described, namely, even if chess somehow emerged as a solution to some loose form of a coordination problem, I would argue that in the case of chess, this is not illuminating. The uniqueness of such conventional practices, like playing chess, would be completely missed if we analyse them along the lines suggested by Lewis. In the case of a coordination convention, such as the telephone-call-resuming convention, the whole point of the rule consists in the solution of the coordination problem which engendered it. The reason for having this convention is the same reason people would have for following it in each particular instance. On the other hand, it would be ridiculous to maintain that the whole point of playing chess consists in the solution of a coordination problem between the players. People who play chess follow the rules of the game because by doing so they can engage in an activity they regard as, say, intellectually rewarding. Whatever the reason for having the game might be, or whatever 'problem' it was invented to solve, would have little bearing on the reasons people have for playing it. Once the game is there to play, it establishes, as it were, its own point.

It is a typical feature of conventions constituting such practices as the game of chess, that they partly constitute the point or value of the activity itself, and it is in this sense that we can talk about autonomous practices: namely, that the point of engaging in them is not fully determined by any particular purpose or value which is external to the conventions constituting the practice. In such cases, it is the practice itself which provides its own point, as it were, and at least some of its own standards of evaluation. The purpose, point, or value, of an autonomous practice is partially set by the conventions constituting the practice. This is true not only of games, such as chess, but of numerous other social practices constituted by social conventions, such as practices of etiquette, conventions of fashion, and artistic genres. The point of the conventions constituting, for example, the genre of opera, is not to solve a coordination problem (whose problem would that be, anyway?), but it is precisely the point of constituting a distinct, partly autonomous, genre. The conventions constituting the practice of opera themselves define, to a considerable extent, what is the point of operas, and what would make sense to say about them.

All this is just a rough sketch, and great deal more needs to be said about conventions constituting autonomous practices. I hope that the following observations, even if far from comprehensive, prove useful.

Constitutive conventions are systematic

One distinguishing mark of constitutive conventions, in contrast to the coordination conventions explained by Lewis, is that the former, but not necessarily the latter, typically come in systems. There must be a system of conventional rules to establish a social practice, that is, some cluster of rules intertwined in a more or less complex structure. This is a feature which stems from the constitutive function of such conventions, from the fact that they constitute a practice.[27]

Furthermore, it should be kept in mind that conventions, by themselves, do not constitute social practices. A social practice does not consist in a set of rules, although it is constituted by rules. It is the whole 'grammar' of the activity constituted by the conventions which makes it an activity of a certain kind.[28] If there is a social practice, then there are a lot of things that it makes sense to say about that practice. And, of course, a lot of things that it does not make sense to say about it. As Wittgenstein famously remarked, 'Grammar

[27] The systematic nature of constitutive rules was first observed by J. Searle, in his *Speech Acts*, at 33–42. Although I certainly draw here on Searle's distinction between constitutive and regulative rules, I am not sure that I want to subscribe to his basic idea that these are two separate types of rules. Others have claimed, and perhaps they are right about this, that all rules have both constitutive and regulative functions. See also Chapter 2, n. 8.

[28] On this particular point, see the very intriguing article of Hubert Schwyzer, 'Rules and Practices'.

tells what kind of object anything is.'[29] Consider, for instance, the genre of (contemporary) theatre. It is an artistic genre constituted by a set of conventions, distinguishing, among other things, theatre from other conventionally established genres of stage performances. Thus, a great many things which normally take place in a theatre performance are instantiations of recognized conventions. However, such conventions also establish a whole grammar which is appropriate for this particular genre. We know, for instance, that it makes perfect sense to praise (or to complain) about the dramatic aspects of a theatre show, but that it makes no sense to complain, for example, that theatre performance is not competitive enough, or that it is a bad show because it does not manifest physical strength. Such values as competitiveness and physical strength are not associated with the intrinsic values of theatre. If they were, it would have been a different social practice.

Partial autonomy

More importantly, however, we should realize that the autonomy of social practices is always partial. All social practices are related to general human concerns of one kind or another. Even the game of chess, which is probably one of the most autonomous practices we are familiar with, is, nevertheless, closely related to such general human concerns as winning and losing, competitiveness, intellectual superiority, and the like. The autonomy of chess, however, consists in the fact that the conventions constituting the practice are *radically underdetermined* by those general values and human concerns that they instantiate. There is, after all, an indefinite number of potential practices which could instantiate those same general human concerns which are instantiated by chess. The latter is just one option, arbitrarily chosen, as it were.

Most social practices, however, are less autonomous than chess is. Consider, once again, distinct artistic genres, like opera, for example. Operas instantiate general musical and dramatic values, which are themselves related to more general artistic human concerns. In this respect, the autonomy of operas is rather limited and partial. Nonetheless, there are certain values, standards of appraisal, and concerns which are distinctly operatic, so to speak. The conventions which establish the genre of opera also define, to some extent, its own intrinsic values, and a considerable extent of its grammar; they define a great deal of what it makes sense to say about operas.

Thus, in each social practice constituted by conventions, there is a mixture of general concerns these practices are there to serve or instantiate, and values associated with the practice in ways which are constituted by the conventions constituting the practice itself. Different practices can be more or less autonomous, according to the specific combination of such values.

[29] Wittgenstein, *Philosophical Investigations,* section 373.

The dynamic aspect of constitutive conventions

Constitutive conventions are prone to change. In this they differ markedly from coordination conventions. The latter serve specific functions in a specific set of circumstances, and hence, as long as the circumstances remain constant, the convention is unlikely to change. As we noted above, in the case of a coordination convention, the reasons for having the convention in the first place, and the reasons for following it in each particular instance, are basically the same. Hence the relative stability of such conventions.[30] On the other hand, conventions constituting autonomous practices constitute a whole grammar of, *inter alia*, evaluative concerns which might then affect the point, and consequently the content and shape of the constitutive conventions themselves. In other words, constitutive conventions tend to be in a constant process of interpretation and reinterpretation which is partly affected by external values, and partly by those same values which are constituted by the conventional practice itself. The rapid changes which occurred in the conventions of the visual arts in the course of the twentieth century provide a dramatic example of this process. Some of the pressure for change came from external influences of a rapidly changing world, such as mass industrialization, the development of new techniques, etc. However, some of the pressure for change came from new interpretations of those old values which were thought to be constitutive of the genre. Artists have gradually realized, for instance, that the point of a painting need not be achieved by a figurative composition; once this dramatic shift occurred, in the form of Cubist and mainly abstract paintings, the constitutive conventions of painting also underwent a considerable change. So, just as the constitutive conventions establish the values associated with the practice, so changes in those values tend to change the conventions which initially constituted them. We may safely assume that the more a given practice tends to be interpretative, the more likely it is that such changes will occur.

Division of labour

It is typical of constitutive conventions that we tend to have a very partial knowledge of them. Most of us, for example, are aware of the fact that there are conventions constituting distinct genres of theatre, but I confess that my knowledge of the content of those conventions is very partial, and I suspect that some theatre patrons know even less. We know, however, that others know what those conventions are. There are, in this field, as in many others, experts, or perhaps better, practitioners. But the dividing line between the

[30] It is true, of course, that if the coordination convention does not instantiate the optimal solution to the relevant coordination problem, a certain pressure may build up to move towards the optimal solution. But once the optimal equilibrium has been reached, there would be no further inherent pressure for change.

practitioners, whose practice determines the conventions, and others, who are more or less aware of them, is not a sharp one. To the question, Whose convention is it?, there is rarely a simple answer. What we would normally see is a kind of division of labour: a core of practitioners, whose practices and self-understandings determine, to the greatest extent, what the convention is, and additional groups of people in outer circles, whose knowledge of the convention is much more partial, and whose influence on its content is relatively marginal. But again, the distinction between the relevant populations is not a hard and fast one; a complex division of labour may obtain, whereby even those groups who are relatively farther removed from the inner circle do affect, albeit in limited way, the shape and content of the relevant conventions.

Perhaps the clearest example of this actually obtains in the case of the law. Most people are only faintly aware of the rules of recognition of their country, and, mostly, they rely on their lawyers to know what those conventions really are. Even within the legal circles, however, some groups are more important than others. Judges, and perhaps to a similar extent, legislators, play the crucial role. The rules of recognition, as noted by Hart himself, are, first and foremost, the conventions of judges, particularly in the higher courts. But in fact, other legal officials can also play various roles in determining the content of the rules of recognition. The practices of police officers, accountants, tax collectors, city councilors, etc., all contribute something to what the rules of recognition are. So once again, the image I suggest is one of a division of labour, taking place in concentric circles; the closer one is to the centre, the greater effect one has on what the convention is; and vice versa, of course. Generally speaking, however, most of us are, most of the time, in the outer circles and we rely on others who know better; namely, on those whose practice it is.

Note, by the way, that none of this is expected to obtain in the case of coordination conventions. Coordination conventions are there to solve a particular recurrent coordination problem. Such conventions cannot be expected to solve the coordination problem if people are largely ignorant about their content. To be sure, I am not trying to suggest that people must be aware of the existence and nature of the coordination problem which gave rise to the emergence of the convention. But they must be aware of the solution, otherwise the convention cannot fulfil its function as such a solution.

The condition of efficacy

A final clarification before we return to the rules of recognition. We have already noted the widespread assumption that the reasons for following a social convention are strongly tied to the fact that others also adhere to the same rule. Consequently, it is typically the case that there is no point in following a conventional rule which is not actually followed by the pertinent community. Let us call this the condition of efficacy. We have also seen that this condition of efficacy is easily explicable by Lewis's analysis: if it is the point of a convention to solve a recurrent coordination problem, then the assumption is that for each and every agent, uniformity of action is preferable to any other alternative course of action. The dominant preference of each agent is simply to act in coordination with the other agents in the relevant circumstances. However, if the condition of efficacy is not met, the alleged convention can no longer fulfil its original function, and hence there is no reason to follow it. Now the question that arises is whether there is an alternative explanation of the condition of efficacy for those social conventions which are not coordination conventions. Or should we claim that the condition of efficacy does not hold with respect to constitutive conventions?

I think that the former option should be pursued, since the explanation is clear enough: it consists in the idea of a social practice. Conventional rules can constitute a social practice only if the rules are actually followed. Conventions, unlike moral rules for example, do not exist in the abstract: 'it ought to be that it ought to be that *p*' normally entails that 'it ought to be that *p*', whereas 'it ought to be that it is a convention that *p*' does *not* entail that 'it is a convention that *p*'. Only practised conventions are conventions.

Does this mean that the reasons for following a set of constitutive conventions consist in the fact that others follow it too? Not necessarily. People's reasons for engaging in a conventional practice cannot merely be explained as a desire for uniformity of action. (Some people go to the opera just because others go there too, but they would normally try to conceal this embarrassing explanation for their action.) It is normally the values inherent in the practice which explain people's reasons for engaging in it. Yet people sometimes engage in a conventional practice for no reason at all, or for various obscure reasons which have little to do with the point of the practice itself. This should come as no surprise; we have already seen that there is an important difference between constitutive conventions and coordination conventions in this respect. In the latter case, the reasons for following the convention in each particular instance are closely tied to the reasons for having the convention in the first place, viz. the solution of the pertinent coordination problem. In the case of constitutive conventions, no such close relationship necessarily exists.[31]

Nevertheless, in both cases, the condition of efficacy holds true. Conventional rules exist only if they are actually practised by the pertinent community. It is the practice of following the rule which makes it a convention in the first place.

To be sure, I am not trying to suggest that the idea of a social practice is very clear. For example, suppose that John and Sarah go to the cinema every

[31] The normativity of conventions is explained in Chapter 2.

Tuesday evening; does this constitute a social practice? I guess not. But now, suppose that they just add more people to this habit of going to the cinema on Tuesday evenings, say, their neighbours; would it become a social practice just by getting the sufficient number of people? I am still inclined to say 'no'. But what would be missing here? One is inclined to reply that what is missing is the idea that the Tuesday cinema habit is a social practice, and not just a happy coincidence of personal habits. Now, this may not be as silly or circular an answer as it sounds. Social practices exist when there is a custom of following a rule. The idea of a custom, however, is not to be confused with something like 'a lot of people doing the same thing'. There is no custom of drinking water, although most people drink water very often. The contrast here is not like the one between an aria and a chorus, but rather it is analogous to the difference between making noise and playing music. A lot of people making the same noise does not make it music. A social practice has a history, a set of values it instantiates, and a sense in which the fact that others follow the same rules is, in itself, crucially significant.

THE RULES OF RECOGNITION REVISITED

I think that by now we have most of the pieces of the puzzle at our disposal, and we just need to put them in place. The rules of recognition, I would like to show, are (by and large) constitutive conventions, establishing partly autonomous practices of identifying the sources of law. Now, some of the worries about the conventionality of the rules of recognition mentioned earlier can easily be relieved; others require more careful treatment.

First, however, let me give an illustration of the kind of recognition conventions I have in mind. Consider the following example. Common Law jurisdictions have a well-defined set of rules establishing the doctrine of precedent. Now, whereas precedent is a conventionally recognized source of law in Common Law jurisdictions, it is not such a recognized source of law in some other jurisdictions, e.g. France and Germany. Even in France and Germany, however, one can observe certain patterns of legal arrangements and legal decisions which resemble precedent. The lack of a doctrine of precedent in German law does not entail, in practice, a total lack of deference to higher courts' decisions on part of the lower courts. The hierarchical structure of the court system, and the possibility of appeals, by themselves, dictate a certain amount of precedent-like behaviour, so to speak, in the actual practice of the French and mainly the German courts.

In other words, a hierarchical structure of courts always creates some pressure towards precedent-like behaviour. Nevertheless, despite this almost universal phenomenon, the fact is that in some jurisdictions a well-defined doctrine of precedent has evolved, while in others it is not only lacking, but is doctrinally denied. Different rules of recognition are practised in similar circumstances in these two types of jurisdictions. Furthermore, the practices established by these rules of recognition embody a whole grammar of descriptive and evaluative judgements. The doctrine of precedent does not only consist in a set of rules that courts follow; it consists in a whole cluster of behavioural and argumentation patterns characteristic of them, and a great many things that it makes sense to say, or doesn't make sense to say, within and about the various aspects of the practice.

Now this is, I think, a good illustration of the partial autonomy of conventional practices. On the one hand, there is a set of circumstances calling for some form of precedent-like practice; on the other hand, it is evident that these circumstances, and the needs emergent from them, are not definitive of the practices emergent from them. The conventional practice, in other words, is underdetermined by the external needs which give rise to its emergence. The constitutive conventions themselves constitute part of the practice's point, many aspects of its grammar, and some of the values associated with it.

What is it that explains the difference, then? One option would be to maintain that what we face here is a standard coordination problem, differently solved by these two different legal systems. But there is an obvious difficulty with this suggestion, since it would actually present the French and German legal systems with an unsolved coordination problem. If the pressure for precedent-like behaviour on part of the courts stems from coordination needs, and only the Common Law countries have a developed precedent practice, Continental systems would seem to be in a pathetic predicament: here there is an obvious problem of coordination, and the Germans or the French have declined to develop the conventions for solving it! Quite an unlikely scenario. The real difference lies, of course, in the respective histories of these different legal system.[32]

There is a general lesson here, which most of Hart's commentators seem to have missed. Conventionalism in any social domain inevitably calls for Historicism. In this respect, Conventionalism is markedly at odds with traditional Functionalist explanations of social practices. On this Functionalist *v.* Historicist dichotomy, Conventionalism sides with the latter. In order to explain a conventionally established social practice—that is, in the case of constitutive conventions, as opposed to simple coordination conventions—one must always consult history. This is just another way of putting the idea of the partial autonomy of social practices. Even if there are relatively well-definable needs that a social practice is there to solve, as in the case of legal precedent, the practice which is actually constituted by conventions is nor-

[32] As every amateur legal historian knows, the roots of the Continental system's decline to follow the practice of precedent are in the French Revolution and the rigid doctrine of separation of powers it engendered.

mally underdetermined by those external needs. The practice's development, and its emergent grammar, are largely determined by historical contingencies.

How far can we generalize the precedent example, that is, as a general model for the conventional rules of recognition? I think that we can do this pretty much all the way down. However, this requires us to take stock of previous sections, and dispel some of the worries we had initially encountered. First, there was the problem that the rules of recognition do not look like solutions to recurrent coordination problems. We have dealt with this problem at length. We saw that constitutive conventions do not emerge as solutions to coordination problems at all. One main concern remains, however, with respect to the arbitrariness of conventional rules. Can we reconcile the moral-political aspect of the rules of recognition with their arbitrary-conventional nature?

Two clarifications already mentioned bear on this point. First, we have noted that a given rule can be arbitrary, in the relevant sense, even if it is not recognized as such by the pertinent community. People need not be aware of the arbitrary nature of the rule they follow, for that rule to be a convention, and arbitrary in the relevant sense. A legal community can be wrong, or ignorant, about the real character of the rules of recognition they follow.[33]

Secondly, and this is the crux of the matter, we saw that the condition of arbitrariness does not imply the idea of indifference. A rule can be arbitrary, in the sense we have defined, even if it reflects moral or political convictions. And the same is true in other areas, of course. Opera, theatre, and even the game of chess, instantiate evaluative convictions, and this evaluative dimension does not impair the conventional foundation of such practices. The crucial question is not whether the rules of recognition reflect political convictions, but whether those same convictions provide sufficient reasons for acting in accordance with the rule, even if the rule in question is not followed by others. By saying that the rule is conventional, we suggest a negative answer only to this last question. Suppose that a German judge genuinely believes that the doctrine of precedent, for example, is superior to any other conceivable alternative, morally, politically, or otherwise. Would it not be rather absurd to maintain that she has to abide by this doctrine even if it is not practised by her fellow judges in Germany?

One could insist, of course, that the doctrine of precedent is not only a conventional set of rules of recognition in the Common Law systems, but also, a political ideal in itself, worthy of respect, regardless of practice. One would then have to say, among other things, that the French and German legal

[33] But not the content, of course. I am certainly not trying to suggest that a whole legal community can be wrong about the content of the rules of recognition. On the contrary; I have elsewhere argued at some length that the conventional foundations of law make it impossible for a whole community of lawyers to misidentify their law. See Marmor, *Interpretation and Legal Theory*, ch. 5.

systems are morally or politically deficient in their lack of respect for this doctrine. Perhaps so; but then, of course, one is no longer talking about the rules of recognition.

To sum up so far: the condition of arbitrariness, essential to the idea of a social convention, is not at odds with the moral or political content of the rules of recognition. Rules of recognition do reflect, as they must, political convictions which have been shaped by the history of the relevant legal system. Their conventionality consists in the essential link between the reasons for following the relevant rules and the fact that those are the rules which are actually practised in the community. This is perfectly consistent with the definition of arbitrariness of conventions I suggested in the previous section.

Another problem, however, seems to emerge here. Can conventional rules of recognition give rise to a judicial *obligation* to follow the rule? If the rule of recognition is only a social convention, why should a judge feel that she is obliged to follow the rule, if she could follow a different rule that she considers, for example, morally superior. As Leslie Green observed, Hart's 'view that the fundamental rules [of recognition] are "mere conventions" continues to sit uneasily with any notion of obligation', and this Green finds troubling, because the rules of recognition point to the 'sources that judges are *legally* bound to apply'.[34]

In the next chapter, I will have much more to say about these and similar concerns. For now, let me explain, briefly, why I think that this particular worry is a spurious one. From a moral or political point of view, the rules of recognition, by themselves, cannot be regarded as the sources of the obligation to follow the law. Whether judges, or anybody else, should or should not respect the rules of recognition of a legal system is purely a moral issue that can only be resolved by moral arguments (concerning the age-old issue of political obligation). And this is more generally so: the existence of a social practice, in itself, does not provide anyone with an obligation to engage in the practice. The rules of recognition only define what the practice is, and they can say nothing on the question of whether one should or should not engage in it. But of course, once one does engage in the practice, playing the judge, as it were, there are *legal* obligations defined by the rules of the game.

In other words, Green should not be worried by the notion of a *legal* obligation to follow the rules of recognition. The judge in a soccer game is equally obliged to follow the rules of his game, and the fact that the game is conventional poses no difficulty from this, let us say, 'internal player's' perspective. But again, the constitutive rules of soccer cannot settle for me the question of whether I should play soccer or not. Similarly, the rules of recognition cannot settle for the judge, or anyone else for that matter, whether they should play by the rules of law, or not. They only tell the judges what the law *is*.

[34] Green, 'The Concept of Law Revisited', at 1697.

The analogies between law and games that I have been using throughout this chapter, call for many more clarifications and caveats. Let me conclude this chapter, however, with one such proviso. Unlike games, such as chess or soccer, which are relatively isolated from general human concerns, and hence autonomous to a very considerable extent, law is certainly much more closely related to numerous practical concerns. Law's relative autonomy is much more limited and partial than that of games and artistic genres. The dimension of partial autonomy is best seen as a continuum, whereby games like chess are one extreme, being perhaps one of the most autonomous social practices, and law on the other extreme, as probably one of the least autonomous practices we are familiar with. (Artistic genres would be somewhere in the middle, closer to games than to law, I would guess.) If I am right about this, a methodological question arises here: why bother about this issue at all? Why should we care about the autonomy of law, if we initially admit that it is very limited and partial?

The main answer to this question cannot be given here, since it concerns the issue of the objectivity of law which is complicate enough to deserve a separate essay.[35] But I can suggest three related observations here. First, as I have tried to show in some detail above, the autonomy of law (as of other social practices) is a consequence of its conventional foundations. Law is partly autonomous because it is conventional, and not the other way around. Secondly, we must keep it in mind that Conventionalism is a significant doctrine only if it is not maintained across the board. It is significant precisely because not everything is a matter of social conventions. In our case, it is mainly the contrast between law, which is claimed to be conventional, and morality, which is not, that is of particular interest. Finally, and this is a point I have already mentioned, but would like to re-emphasize. Conventionalism, properly understood, strongly supports historicism as opposed to functionalism. There are a lot of 'isms' in this sentence, so let me be clear about what I mean here.

Lewis's account of social conventions is basically a functionalist explanation. It explains both the emergence of conventions and their rationale in terms of a specific function conventional rules are there to fulfil (viz. of solving a particular coordination problem). I have tried to argue here that this explanation is too impoverished; a great many conventions are not fully explicable in such functional terms. Historical contingencies, and the emergent constitutive conventions, play a crucial role in determining the shape and content of the social practices we encounter. Functionalism without history is like a novel's basic plot without the narrative. The narrative is written by history, and it shapes the plot much more than functionalists would like to admit. The partial autonomy of social practices is simply the consequence of this narrative-dependent plot.

[35] See Chapters 6 and 7.

Perhaps this connection between Conventionalism and Historicism that I attribute to the legal positivism espoused by H. L. A. Hart would surprise many of Hart's critics.[36] Perhaps it is not only the critics' fault. Hart, like Wittgenstein before him, was probably aware of the Historicism entailed by Conventionalism, but both of them paid too little attention to history to make this explicit enough.

Be this as it may, I hope I have said enough to show that Hart's theory about the rules of recognition still deserves to be considered very seriously. I have also tried to show that Hart's theory is basically correct, although between the original practice theory of rules, and the explicit Conventionalism of the Postscript, I have tried to substantiate the latter.

[36] Not all of them; Leslie Green, for example, has made this point very convincingly, though I think that he failed to notice the conventionalist foundation. See Green, 'The Concept of Law Revisited', at 1698ff.

2
Conventions and the Normativity of Law

THE idea that the law is founded on social conventions suggests a very close analogy between the law and other conventional practices, such as games and artistic genres. But such analogies are limited, of course, and it is on those limits that I want to focus in this chapter. In particular, it is possible to doubt the analogy on grounds pertaining to the unique features attributed to the normativity of law. Unlike games and artistic genres, the law is an authoritative institution, imposing on its subjects normative demands that other, conventionally constituted practices do not seem to impose. The law claims to be a legitimate authority; it purports to create obligations to comply with its demands; the law imposes its demands on its subjects regardless of their wilful acceptance of its authority; it claims normative supremacy over all other normative domains; and all this is actually enforced by means of threats, coercion, and sheer force. How do these various aspects of law's normativity relate to its conventional foundations? This is, basically, the complex question I want to discuss in this chapter.

CONVENTIONS AND REASONS FOR ACTION

The question about the normativity of law is a difficult one to define, and legal philosophers often refer to a number of things when they discuss the normative aspect of law. At the very least, however, the idea that law is a normative social practice suggests that the law purports to give rise to reasons for action, and that at least some of these reasons are obligations (in a sense yet to be defined). The claim I want to address in this section is that even this minimal conception of the normativity of law is irreconcilable with its conventional foundations. It has been claimed that conventions cannot, by themselves, create obligations.[1] True, people often say that they do something (or refrain from doing it) *because* the action is prescribed by a convention. We spell convention 'convention' and not, say, 'convension' because the spelling conventions of English prescribe this particular spelling. When I meet an acquaintance I greet her because of the convention prescribing such behaviour. When people play chess, they move the bishop diagonally because this

I am grateful to Leslie Green, Joseph Raz, Eric Posner, Alon Harel, and Chaim Gans for helpful comments on drafts of this chapter.

[1] Ronald Dworkin has advanced this claim in various forms. See, for example, his *Taking Rights Seriously*, ch. 3, and *Law's Empire*, ch. 4. Recently, Leslie Green published an article advancing this claim very explicitly. See Green, 'Positivism and Conventionalism'.

is how the chess rules define the moves of the game. Conventional rules guide much of our daily behaviour. Upon reflection, we would normally think of such conventions as at least part of our reasons for action. Under normal circumstances, invoking the existence of a convention is a good explanation for one's action, and actions can certainly be explained as instances of following a convention.

None of this should be denied. Nor is it denied that the existence of a conventional rule can indeed be *a* reason for action. The critique here is threefold: First, it is claimed that conventions can never constitute a *complete* reason for action, and I think that this is correct. Second, it is claimed that conventions cannot engender *obligations*, or *exclusionary reasons*, and this, I think, is a mistake. Finally, and consequently, it is claimed that conventions cannot be at the foundations of law because they cannot explain the normative aspect of the rules of recognition. I will take up these points in turn.

Let us begin with coordination conventions. Admittedly, such conventions do not seem to be obligatory in any straightforward sense, partly, at least, because they do not seem to create, by themselves, the reasons for action. Spelling conventions, for example, are only required if there is an underlying reason for uniformity of spelling. Similarly, we only need the conventions of the road because we care about our safety and wish to avoid accidents. Generally, coordination problems emerge only where the preferences of the parties concerned include a dominant preference for coordinated behaviour. Without such an underlying, dominant, preference, there is simply no coordination problem to begin with.[2] Therefore, a coordination convention which exists to solve a recurrent coordination problem can only create auxiliary reasons for action. The primary reason for action is always the reason which initially calls for the coordinated behaviour in the relevant circumstances.

Similar, though somewhat more complicated considerations apply to constitutive conventions as well. Before the reasons for following a particular constitutive convention come into play, there is always an open question about the reasons for participating in the relevant practice. For example, if I decline to greet my friends, or move the bishop in straight lines while playing chess, there is a sense in which one appropriate response to criticism could be that I just do not want to 'play the game'. In other words, the reasons for following the convention are always parasitic on other, underlying reasons, those which render committed participation in the practice intelligible, desirable, worthwhile, or perhaps even obligatory.[3] Thus, in both types of conventions, we should distinguish between the primary reasons for action, which are not, by themselves, created by the existence of the conventions, and

[2] I will qualify this statement in the sequel.

[3] Note that I talk about reasons for committed participation in the practice; it is not being assumed here that avoiding participation in the practice is always a feasible option. More on this later in the chapter.

the auxiliary reasons which are engendered by the conventional rules. In the case of coordination conventions, the primary reasons are those due to which the coordinated behaviour is required in the first place. In the case of constitutive conventions, the primary reasons are those which would render the participation in the relevant practice desirable, intelligible, etc. Generally speaking, conventions would have little bearing on answering such a question as 'why should I do it?'; conventions typically determine the ways in which something is done, answering the 'how', rather than the 'why' question. An instance of following the greeting convention assumes that one values such things as politeness and civility. The greeting convention, by itself, does not provide the reason for greeting anybody. The underlying reasons for greeting an acquaintance are those which follow from values we associate with politeness and civility; the greeting convention only tells us how to go about participating in the practice, assuming we have reasons to participate. A similar structure applies to the chess example: in following the bishop's move convention, there is a presupposition that one wishes to play chess.

In these latter cases, however, there is an interesting and important complexity involved. As we have seen in the previous chapter, constitutive conventions *partly* constitute the point of the practice itself and some of the values inherent in it. The conventions constituting an artistic genre, for instance, partly determine the specific values of that genre, what counts as excellence or failure in the genre, what should be appreciated in it, and so on. Hence there is some kind of circularity which is typically involved in such reasoning. On the one hand, constitutive conventions would not by themselves constitute the reasons for participation in the practice; they only define what the practice is. On the other hand, the reasons one may have for participating, that is, the reasons for playing the game, as it were, would normally rely on those values which are constituted by the conventions constituting the practice.

So the reasoning here is partly circular, but not entirely. As we have seen in the previous chapter, the autonomy of conventional practices is always limited and partial. Even the most autonomous social practices instantiate certain general human concerns which are external to the values constituted by the conventional practice. (Competitive games are about winning and losing; etiquette is about politeness and civility, and so forth.) Therefore, one does not face the danger of a vicious circularity: it would have been a vicious circle, had it been the case that the sole reason for following a convention P, consists in the fact that P constitutes a value V, and V is the reason for following P. But this is never the case. The reasons for participation in a social practice constituted by conventions are complex and mixed, comprising values which are external to the practice and those which are partly constituted by it.

The essential point remains, however, that even in the case of constitutive conventions, complexities notwithstanding, the conventions themselves never constitute a complete set of reasons for action. The answer to the question why should one follow a given convention must, eventually, also appeal to some set of primary values and reasons which are not prescribed by the convention but presuppose its very point of existence.[4]

Thus, to sum up so far: conventions typically engender auxiliary reasons for action, determining the ways in which one should go about doing things which are supposedly valuable, either antecedently of the conventions themselves, as in the case of coordination conventions, or just given the availability of the conventional practice, as in the case of constitutive conventions.

Now it is time to consider the second question, namely, whether conventions can be mandatory norms. For the sake of the argument, let us assume that mandatory norms must constitute both primary and exclusionary reasons for action, along the lines suggested by Joseph Raz's illuminating (though somewhat controversial) account.[5] Following a mandatory norm, or complying with a duty, is not simply an instance of acting on the balance of reasons. Mandatory norms purport to create a very unique structure of reasons, comprising reasons of two kinds: mandatory norms prescribe primary, or first-order reasons for action, and second-order, exclusionary reasons, that is, reasons not to act on certain types of potentially conflicting reasons. This unique combination of reasons for action and exclusionary reasons is the structure of practical reasoning we have in obligations. Being under an obligation, Raz maintains, means that one has primary reasons for action *and* exclusionary reasons, that is, reasons not to act on certain types of conflicting reasons.

Assuming, then, that mandatory norms do have such a unique function in our practical reasoning, let us turn to the question of whether conventions can be mandatory norms. Our previous analysis, suggesting that conventions typically create auxiliary reasons for action, might be taken to imply that the answer is negative. But this is not necessarily so. Once again, the case of coordination conventions is simpler.

Coordination conventions would be mandatory norms, that is, obligatory, when the norm subjects have *an obligation to solve the coordination problem* which initially gave rise to the emergence of the relevant convention. This simple solution may have been obscured by the prevalent discourse of game-theoretical analysis. Game theories typically formulate the structure of coordination problems in terms of the subjective preferences of the parties

[4] A word of caution: it is not being assumed here that constitutive conventions must have a point, in terms of a particular function they are there to fulfil. I have argued against such a reductionist view in the previous chapter, and I am not withdrawing that argument here. See the definition of *arbitrariness* in Chapter 1.

[5] See Raz, *Practical Reason and Norms*. The fact that Raz's account of mandatory norms is controversial will not affect the force of the following arguments. Raz presents the strongest plausible interpretation of mandatory norms; therefore, even if some weaker version can be substantiated, it would only make it easier to maintain that conventions can be mandatory norms.

concerned, whereby the agents would all actually prefer the coordinated course of action over other potential alternatives. However, this emphasis of subjective preferences is misguided. People often have a *reason* to solve a recurrent coordination problem, regardless of their subjective preferences.[6] Sometimes those reasons are straightforward instances of duty. The conventions of the road provide a good example. Such conventions are there to solve coordination problems that *ought* to be solved, regardless of the subjective preferences of the particular individuals involved. Avoiding collisions and accidents which are likely to occur without the coordinated driving on the roads are objectives we ought to seek. Like any other type of duty, such 'ought' easily lends itself to Raz's analysis of exclusionary reasons. Therefore, if there is a convention which has emerged to solve such problems, there is a duty to comply with the convention, and the convention is a mandatory norm.

It is important to realize that this analysis need not rest on a general assumption that whenever there is a duty to x, and y is a means to achieving x, one has a duty to y. As a generalization, the assumption is probably false. Suppose, for example, that Sarah promised to meet Leslie at the cinema and that she could only make it there on time if she took the first taxi cab she could get hold of. Is Sarah under an obligation to take the particular taxi cab she encountered? Is she under an obligation to let herself be driven by that particular driver? These are difficult questions, but we need not try to solve them. As opposed to such examples, the coordination convention case is much simpler, since there is a clear connection between the problem that needs to be solved and its solution in the form of a conventional rule following. After all, the whole point of a coordination convention is to function as a solution to such problems. If a convention emerged to solve a particular recurrent coordination problem which we have a duty to solve, the transitivity of the duty is straightforward enough.[7]

Needless to say, not all coordination conventions emerge as solutions to such coordination problems that need to be solved as a matter of duty. It would be safe to assume that a great many, perhaps most, coordination conventions are not mandatory norms. Yet some of them are, and there seems to be nothing in the nature of coordination conventions to preclude this possibility.

The case of constitutive conventions is similar but somewhat more complicated. To begin with, such rules typically have a dual function, both constitutive and regulative.[8] On the one hand, constitutive conventions define what

[6] Cf. Raz, '*Facing up*: A Reply'.

[7] I am grateful to Leslie Green for discussing this issue with me. Green believes, however, that there are more difficulties here than I assume.

[8] In a trivial sense all rules which are actually practised are constitutive, in the sense that they constitute the particular practice of following that rule. This point may have alluded Searle in his

the relevant practice is; at the same time, however, they also prescribe modes of behaviour within the practice, and in this they manifest a regulative function. The question we should address is, whether this regulative function of constitutive rules can be seen as a form of mandatory prescription, and what is the sense in which people 'ought' to follow such rules.

Notably, we often encounter constitutive conventions formulated in terms of straightforward mandatory norms. 'Move the bishop diagonally', or 'One ought to move the bishop diagonally' are formulations we are quite likely to encounter when, for example, a novice is instructed how to play chess. However, the formulation of such utterances is misleading. What such rules really assert is something like this: If you want to play chess, this is how it is done. As we have already seen above, such an 'if clause' is a necessary, albeit mostly implicit, prologue to each and every set of constitutive conventions. This 'if clause', however, also provides the key to our understanding of the normativity of constitutive conventions. Such rules are *conditionally mandatory*, that is, they resemble mandatory norms in all but one crucial respect: the 'ought' such rules prescribe engenders reasons for action only on the condition that one is initially committed to participating in the practice constituted by these same conventions. Committed participation in the practice conditions the normative, reason-giving, aspect of the rules which both define what the game is and prescribe how one should go about engaging in it.[9]

Perhaps an analogy with the way in which decisions operate in our practical reasoning may prove helpful here. Consider, for example, Raz's own analogy of mandatory norms with the idea of a decision.[10] It is an essential part of the idea of a decision that one deliberately forgoes future deliberation on the overall balance of reasons. The whole point of a decision is one's need to end a process of deliberation. Such a process can come to an end, however, only if one decides to end it, that is, one decides a future course of action whereby at least certain types of reasons are excluded from further consideration as potential reasons for or against the relevant action. The analogy is,

original definition of the distinction between constitutive and regulative rules. (See his *Speech Acts* at 33–42; and compare Raz, *Practical Reason and Norms*.) Not all rules or conventions, however, constitute a social practice in the *thick* sense I have outlined in the previous chapter. This may suggest that the distinction between regulative and constitutive conventions is not a logical or categorical distinction between two distinct *types of rules*, as it is a distinction between two major functions rules can have in our lives. Presumably, one and the same rule (or perhaps we had better say rule formulation) can form a basically regulative function in one context or society, and in another context, it can form part of a set of constitutive rules. In this respect, the view presented here is closer to Raz's than to Searle's.

[9] Cf. Raz, *Practical Reason and Norms*, at 122–3; Raz makes a similar point here, but instead of pointing to the conditional nature of constitutive conventions he stresses the 'artificial' nature of the values which such practices as games manifest. I find this notion of 'artificial' values, however, too limited and I doubt that we can ascribe it to other conventionally constituted practices, such as artistic genres or etiquette. The relative artificiality of such values stems from the partial autonomy such practices manifest, as explained in the previous chapter.

[10] Raz, 'Reasons for Action, Decisions, and Norms'.

however, that decisions also involve a kind of 'if clause', namely, a prior decision to make a decision; every decision presupposes a second-order decision to make a decision.[11] Similarly, every instance of following a constitutive rule, or convention, involves, or rather, presupposes, a second-order decision to participate in the practice as it is constituted by those conventions.

The nature of this second-order decision to participate in the relevant practice can vary considerably. One may have a particular reason, or set of reasons to participate in a given practice; one may have no particular reason but only a slight preference; or one may even have a duty to participate. Presumably, these different types of reasons would normally affect the nature of the 'ought' which is prescribed by the constitutive conventions. However, it should be noted that the connection between one's reasons to participate in the practice and the nature of the reasons to follow the constitutive rules of the practice is not necessarily a direct or straightforward one. Two chess players, for example, may indulge in the game, strictly following the rules of chess, even if their initial reasons for playing the game diverge considerably. I will return to this point later in the discussion.

People's reasons to participate in a social practice constituted by conventions can be moral reasons, and as such, they can sometimes amount to a moral obligation. It would be safe to assume that there are conventional practices in which people ought to participate as a matter of moral duty. This should not obscure our previous point, however, that the normativity of constitutive conventions is always conditional. In other words, it may well be the case that we have a moral duty to follow a constitutive convention, but in such cases, the duty is conditioned by the existence of the conventional practice and the underlying obligation to participate in it. Constitutive conventions could not in themselves amount to mandatory norms, but for one who ought to be a committed participant in the practice which is constituted by those conventions.

But now the question arises whether we can explain the normative nature of the rules of recognition, assuming that the obligatory nature of such rules is entirely conditional on the underlying reasons for participating in the practice of law? Some commentators have thought that we cannot. Of course they are right if they regard Conventionalism as an answer to the question: why should we have law in the first place? As we have just seen, constitutive conventions, by themselves, cannot answer such questions. Legal Conventionalism, however, properly construed, does not make such a claim. Conventions should not be invoked in order to answer the question of why we should have law and legal systems, but only to answer the question of what counts as law in any given society. Social conventions cannot explain the point of law and

[11] I assume here that there is a distinction between decision and choice; not every choice amounts to, or follows from, a deliberate decision.

its functions in our society. Law is conventional only in the sense that its rules of recognition are social conventions, and the function of such conventions is to determine the recognized criteria of legal validity, that is, to answer the question of what counts as law as opposed to other normative domains.

A complete philosophical account of the normativity of law comprises both an explanatory and a normative-justificatory task. The explanatory task consists of an attempt to explain how rules or conventions can give rise to reasons for action, and what kinds of reasons are involved. The task of justification concerns the elucidation of the reasons people *should* have for acknowledging law's normative aspect; it is the attempt to explain the legitimacy of the authority of law or, at least, the conditions law should meet in order to be a legitimate authority. Conventionalism, as I understand it, plays an important role in the explanatory aspect of the normativity of law. It has little bearing on the task of justifying the normativity of law. The reasons for acknowledging the authority of law cannot derive from social conventions.

The rules of recognition are, by and large, constitutive conventions. Now, as we have just seen, the rationale of constitutive conventions always comprises the 'if clause'; merely pointing to the fact that there are such conventions cannot explain why people would have any reason to follow the conventions. Such reasons come into play only if the subjects already have a reason to play the game, as it were. But the essential point is that they *need not have the same reasons* for playing the game. Once a game is there to be played, all that is needed in this respect is a very general understanding of its point. Once people share such a rough and general grasp of the point of the game, they may play it for a host of different, even conflicting reasons, and some of them may participate for no reason at all. This, I think, is basically the case with the law as well.

The constitutive conventions of law, the rules of recognition, determine in each particular society what the law is, what counts as law. Such conventions only define what the rules of the game are. Admittedly, in order to prevail as a conventional practice, the practitioners, and to some lesser extent, the population at large, must share some common understandings about the general point of the conventions, such as, what they are for, and what is, by and large, the point of such a practice; for example, that the law is an authoritative institution, and that it purports to regulate social behaviour. Similarly, we may safely assume that chess would have been a very different social practice if chess players, and others, thought of chess not as a competitive game but, say, as something like a religious rite.[12] Some general and common understanding regarding the purpose of the practice is constitutive of what the practice is. Beyond this vague point of consensus, however, it does not matter for the purposes of rendering the normative aspect of the practice intelligible, why

[12] See, for example, Schwyzer, 'Rules and Practices'.

particular people engage in it. It should matter, of course, for each one of them. People's reasons for following the convention can only be rendered complete, and eventually, intelligible, if their reasons for participating in the practice are taken into account. But a practice constituted by conventions can flourish even if the practitioners' reasons for participating in the practice diverge radically. Some people, judges included, may think of law as the embodiment of morality. Others, and again, judges included, may think of the law in terms of their religious convictions. And still others may think of law in purely selfish terms, like the Holmesian 'bad man', or any other variant of such an attitude.[13]

The essential point is, however, that whatever the reasons for peoples' participation in the practice may be, such reasons need not form part of the explication of the normativity of the practice. The concept of legal normativity simply does not depend on the kind of reasons people have for their participation in the practice of law, although it is true that people would normally have such reasons, and that those reasons cannot be dictated by the rules of recognition themselves. In other words, the rules of recognition, like any other type of constitutive conventions, only define what the practice is. They only tell us what counts as law in our society. As such, namely, as constitutive rules, they also define the legal validity of norms; which is simply to say that they define the rules of the game. This leaves open the question of why people should practise the law of their country; of why they should play the game, as it were. Yet as long as enough people, particularly practitioners, do play the game, for whatever reasons for doing so they may have, the practice will exist as a normative practice. In *this* respect, the normativity of law is exactly like the normativity of any other social practice constituted by conventions. Chess players assume the normativity of the rules of the game, but those rules are not there to settle for the players whether they should play the game or not. They only define what the game is. Similarly, the rules of recognition only define what 'the legal game' is, and as long as legal practitioners play by those rules, they assume, but only for the purposes of the game they play, that those rules are obligatory. Whether judges, other practitioners, or laymen, have any moral or other reasons to play the game or not, is a totally separate question. Surely, there are better reasons to 'play' the law than to play chess, but those reasons cannot be prescribed by the social conventions themselves.

[13] Many legal philosophers seem to hold the view that judges, at least in their official roles, must be presumed to be committed to a particular normative point of view. Often arguments concentrate on the question whether this judicial point of view is necessarily moral or not. I do not share this view about the uniqueness of the judicial point of view about the normativity of law. The only uniqueness I see about the official judicial perspective on law's normativity is, that judges (and other legal officials) must see themselves as *committed* participants, which is only to say that they really play the game; but the normative grounds of such commitments need not be unique or monolithic.

None of this implies, however, that there are no significant differences between the normativity of law and that of chess, or other familiar social practices constituted by conventions. I will look at some of these differences in the next section.

CONVENTIONS AND LEGAL AUTHORITY

One of the main aspects of the normativity of law concerns its unique authoritative nature. Law is a *de facto* authority. Any legal system in force imposes authoritative demands on it subjects. Furthermore, as Joseph Raz insightfully claimed, it is a necessary feature of law that it claims to be a legitimate authority.[14] Any particular legal system may fail in its claim to legitimacy, of course, but it is essential to law that it make such a claim on its subjects. This is, actually, the main difference between H. L. A. Hart's famous example of the gunman situation and the law.[15] Unlike the gunman who threatens you with 'your money or your life', and cares little or not at all about the legitimacy of his claim, the law claims your money, your freedom, or even your life, as a legitimate demand, one that you ought to respect. Very much like the gunman, though, the law cares very little about your actual consent, or willingness, to be subject to its authoritative demands (though it may claim that you ought to consent). Furthermore, it claims supremacy over other normative domains, and enforces such claims coercively, often by sheer force.

Now, these aspects of the authoritative nature of law would seem to move the legal practice miles away from the game analogy. I do not wish to dispute this here. The question is, whether such allegedly unique features of the authority of law threaten the thesis about its conventional foundation. I will consider each one of these points in turn, namely, law's essential claim to legitimacy, its authoritative nature, its encompassing reach, its claim to supremacy, and finally, its coercive aspect.

Authority and legitimacy

Law is an authoritative institution. I will take as much for granted. But what makes it essential for law to claim *legitimate* authority over its subjects? Robert Paul Wolff says that '[A]uthority is the right to command and correlatively, the right to be obeyed. It must be distinguished from power, which is the ability to compel compliance, either through the use or the threat of force.' I think that he is right:[16] Any practical authority, as such, must be

[14] Raz, 'Authority, Law and Morality'.

[15] Hart, *The Concept of Law*, 80.

[16] *In Defense of Anarchism*, 4. Wolff is quite wrong, however, to associate authoritative prescriptions with commands, but this should not be a matter of concern here. See Raz, *The Authority of Law*, ch. 1.

assumed to make a claim to its legitimacy. Law's claim to legitimacy simply follows from its authoritative nature. Let me explain.

Practical authorities exist, or are presumed to exist, in order to make a practical difference with respect to their putative subjects' reasons for action. Authorities may fail in achieving this, of course, but it is the essence of a practical authority that it aims to make such a difference. In other words, it is the essence of a practical authority that it claims to produce, what Hart famously called, partly *content-independent* reasons for action.[17] That is to say, for the authorities' subjects, it must be practically significant that whatever they have been prescribed to do by the authority has been actually prescribed by the authority, and not by reason alone.

Isn't this essential feature of authorities, then, sufficient to explain why authorities, as such, must make a claim to their legitimacy? Not quite. The possibility that something like sheer force can ground an authority's claim to make such a practical difference should be explored. In other words, why isn't the gunman a practical authority *vis-à-vis* his victim? He is certainly there to make a practical difference, but this is a difference he aims to achieve by sheer threat of violence, not by virtue of a claim to legitimacy. Now, there are two intuitive rejoinders here which seem to present themselves, but neither is quite convincing. One would be to maintain that simply as a matter of linguistic intuition, we just do not regard the gunman as a practical authority. But such linguistic intuitions are notoriously inconclusive. Linguistic intuitions tend to emerge from habits of thought which may be groundless or mistaken. Perhaps a more promising line of thought is suggested by Hart's own account of the example, which maintains that the difference between the gunman and a practical authority consists in the nature of the obligation to comply which we associate with each type of situation. Though the gunman can *oblige* his victim to comply with his demand, it is not the kind of demand we would consider as constituting an *obligation* to obey. But in the context of our present concerns (which is different from Hart's), the distinction leaves our question unanswered. Hart simply assumes that the gunman is not an authority; his distinction between 'oblige' and 'obligation' cannot explain why we are justified in assuming as much. True, unlike the law, the gunman does not claim to create an obligation for his victim; but it still leaves open the possibility that he is an authority.

If, as I believe, we do have a reason *not* to regard the gunman as a type of authority, this must derive from the particular role authorities are assigned in our practical reasoning. In other words, we associate authorities with a claim to legitimacy because it explains their rationale in our practical reasoning. There is simply no need to explain why it makes sense to succumb to the

[17] Hart, *Essays on Bentham*, ch. 10. A more detailed account of this aspect of practical authorities is provided in Chapter 6 below.

gunman in authoritative terms; the practical reasoning here is rendered transparent by the expected pay-offs of the available courses of action imposed by the gunman's threat. On the other hand, it would be impossible to explain the rationale for following a decree of an authority, unless we assume that it has been issued on the grounds that—in some sense, not necessarily moral—the putative subjects ought to do what the authority prescribed. Borrowing Raz's terminology, we could say that authorities must be presumed to rely on their assessment of the relevant 'dependent' reasons, that is, reasons which are taken to apply to their putative subjects.[18] The gunman's decree is not regarded as authoritative because it makes no claim to have based the decision on dependent reasons, on reasons which would have applied to its subject regardless of the command backed by a threat.

In other words, in the gunman case, we are simply expected to act on the balance of reasons created by the threat. In such cases we do not need to invoke the idea of an authority; it would play no role in the explanation of our practical reasoning. Authorities are only called for when action on the balance of reasons is either not a transparent matter, or else, for some reason impossible or self-defeating. Authorities, in other words, are there to fulfil a constructive function in practical reasoning, and this function is basically their inherent claim to legitimacy. The law's essential claim to legitimacy, then, simply derives from its authoritative nature.[19]

Once this point has been clarified, the only question which remains for us to explore right now is whether there are any reasons to doubt that conventionally constituted practices can be authoritative. It is actually difficult to see why there should be such doubts. True, most social practices constituted by conventions are not authoritative in their nature. But quite a number of them are. Some conventional practices, besides the law, that is, do manifest authoritative structures, even rather complex ones. Consider, for example, the complex authoritative structures of so called 'primitive' tribal societies, which are, of course, very close to a rudimentary form of a legal system. Other examples are the authoritative structure which is manifest in patriarchal families; the authoritative nature of scientific communities, professional guilds, and the like; and even in a relatively loose conventional practice such as fashion, there are figures of authority who determine the current trends in fashion for the rest of the population.

Law, however, is claimed to be unique in its authoritative nature in three respects: first, it may be thought that the law is the only authoritative institution which claims an encompassing reach, that is, imposing its demands on its subjects regardless of their wilful participation. Secondly, the law claims to be

[18] Raz, 'Authority, Law and Morality'.

[19] Once again, note that this matter of legitimacy need not be of the moral kind. Authorities are often needed to solve practical problems which have little, if anything, to do with morality.

the supreme authority of the land. Finally, the law enforces its claim to authority by coercion and sheer force.

Involuntary membership

Surely one idea people have in mind when they say that the law is not like a game is that games we need not play. The law, on the other hand, imposes its authority on its subjects regardless of their consent or wilful participation. The legal community is a very 'generous' club where membership is automatically gained by birth (or even earlier), and rescinded by death (and not even then). (And mind you, this involuntary membership is rather costly.) It would be a mistake, however, to think that this feature is unique to law. Involuntary membership is a feature of many other social practices which manifest authoritative structures. Examples such as mentioned above would do to clarify this point. Numerous conventional social practices can be authoritative, even oppressive, and membership in them is no more a matter of choice than it is with regard to the law. We are born and raised into numerous conventional practices shaping our cultures, and a great deal of the process of our socialization during childhood and adolescence consists of reconciling ourselves to the authority of such practices. Consider, for example, cultures (luckily getting rarer these days) which manifest relatively strict conventions of etiquette and fashion. Such cultures typically comprise elaborate conventions determining what is 'right' or 'proper' dress for certain occasions, and people who deviate from such conventions are harshly criticized. Membership in such a 'fashion community' is no more a voluntary club than the law is.

The only difference I see here is, that since the law is a highly institutionalized practice, with sophisticated means of communication, enforcement, and coercion, its disregard of wilful participation is perhaps more conspicuous and transparent compared with other social practices. But again, a great many practices constituted by social conventions can be both authoritative and impose their authority on their subjects regardless of their consent.

But now the following question emerges here: how can we reconcile the non-voluntary aspect of membership in the legal community, with the contention I stressed earlier, that the normativity of law is conditional on the availability of reasons for committed participation in the practice? What is the point of such conditional normativity of a practice if one has no choice but to participate in it? The answer to this puzzle consists in the general truth that the need for reasons does not entail the actual possibility of choice. The fact that one needs a good reason to do A simply does not entail that avoiding A must be a feasible option.

Suppose, for example, that Sarah faces a choice between doing A or B, and suppose further that unknown to her at the time, option B is actually not feasible. Had Sarah chosen to opt for B, there is simply no way she could have actually done it. Now, the fact is that Sarah considers all the relevant reasons, and then decides to opt for doing A. Surely her decision based on a particular reason to do A instead of B is not, in any way, rendered unintelligible *qua* a reason-based decision by the fact that Sarah had no real choice here. Now let us modify the example, and suppose that Sarah actually knows all this in advance; she knows that B is an option that she could not actually carry out in the circumstances. What difference would it make? She could, of course, realize that there is no point in deliberating about the issue at all, no need to come to a decision. But suppose she nevertheless wants to reach a decision. Sarah thinks that there is a reason for her to prefer A over B, even if she knows that B is not a feasible option. Would it not make perfect sense for her to come to a decision in such circumstances? For example, suppose that Sarah is offered an opportunity to embark on a criminal career, say, of becoming a thief, though the truth is that she could not really become a thief even is she tried. Now Sarah decides to decline the offer, *because* she believes that there is a moral reason to avoid theft, and she believes that it is this moral reason which guides her actions. This is in spite of the fact that she knows that being a thief is not the kind of activity she could actually carry out, even if she tried. Despite the fact that in a practical sense, Sarah could never really become a thief, and she knows this, her decision to refrain from theft is based on reasons condemning theft as such.[20] Similarly, even if most people most of the time have no practical possibility of avoiding the law's reach, it may still be the case that their reasons for complying with law's demands have nothing to do with this lack of choice. They may simply believe that it is good to be *committed* participants in the legal practice.

But what about the other way round? Can one make a reason-based decision to reject the normativity of the law, knowing full well that it is practically impossible to escape from the law's reach? Let us return, for a moment, to the deliberation of whether to become a thief, that is, knowing that one could not actually carry out a decision to embark on such a career, even if one tried. Suppose, then, that John is faced with this dilemma, and, like Sarah, he also knows that becoming a thief is not the kind of activity he could really carry out. Could John, nevertheless, decide to become a thief? Would such a decision make any sense? John could decide *to try* to become a thief, knowing full well that he is bound to fail. But of course, he cannot rationally decide *to become* a thief. Nevertheless, in one important sense, John's decision favouring the theft option is practically significant, in that he may feel estranged or alienated from the alternative he is left with. And this is what would normally happen with those who reject or cast-off the normativity of the law. They

[20] It is true that under such circumstance, observers tend to doubt the authenticity of the decision; they may think that the decision is biased, or not quite genuinely guided by the proclaimed reasons. But this is beside the point.

would remain participants in the legal practice of their country due to a lack of feasible alternatives; but they are *alienated participants*. Generally speaking, people can deliberately alienate themselves from various aspects of their lives even when those aspects are not choosable in any straightforward sense.[21]

The supremacy of law

Another problematic aspect of the authoritative nature of law consists in its alleged claim to supremacy. It is a widely shared view, particularly, but not exclusively, amongst legal positivists, that the law must be assumed to make a claim to its supremacy over all other normative realms.[22] Even when the law recognizes its own limits *vis-à-vis* other normative domains, those limits are self-imposed by the law: the law claims to be the final arbitrator of its own domain. Now this is a complicated issue, and we should proceed here with caution. Perhaps it is correct to raise serious doubts about the possibility of such a unique claim to normative supremacy based on social conventions. After all, the existence and particular content of social conventions is basically a contingent matter, and it would be groundless to assume that whenever such conventions exist, they must take up a particular shape, namely, embodying such a claim to normative supremacy. In other words, if law is based on social conventions, we should be able to envisage the possibility of a legal system which does not make a claim to normative supremacy. Thus, the main question I wish to raise is whether this claim to supremacy is really a feature of law, as such, or of something else instead, that is, of the modern state, or the modern conception of political sovereignty.

Historically, legal positivism is a doctrine about the nature of law which has been closely associated with modern conceptions of political sovereignty. Legal positivism emerged, as early as Hobbes propounded it, hand in hand with the modern conception of the state, as a uniform embodiment of political sovereignty, claiming monopoly over the use of force in the society, and supremacy over church, Natural Law, local customs, and in general, all other normative realms. Hobbes is a good example. He was one of the very first political philosophers (alongside Bodin, perhaps) to have conceived of political sovereignty in terms of a claim to absolute normative supremacy of the

[21] See, for example, Frankfurt, *The Importance of what we Care about*, ch. 2.

[22] See Raz, *Practical Reason and Norms*, 150, and *The Authority of Law*, 116–20. See also John Finnis, *Natural Law and Natural Rights*, 267, who explicitly takes it for granted that the law must essentially make such claim. Raz, by the way, argues that law's claim to supremacy is entailed by its claim to comprehensiveness, by which he means that the law claims authority to regulate *any type* of behaviour. However, I find it difficult to see the relation of entailment here. The law can only claim the authority to regulate any type of behaviour if it presupposes its supreme authority, that is, its supremacy over all other normative sources or domains. Comprehensiveness presupposes the claim to supremacy. But perhaps these are only two sides of the same coin.

sovereign. Despite Hobbes's lack of popularity at the time, much of the modern conception of the state emanated from his political theory. The fact that he was also one of the first legal positivists is no coincidence.[23] Legal positivism emerged, in large part, from this novel idea of the state as the supreme political sovereign.

From a historical perspective, then, the idea that law is the manifestation of political sovereignty and that as such it must claim supremacy over other normative domains, is a hallmark of legal positivism, closely linking the latter with the modern conception of the all powerful, sovereign state.[24] But the question is whether history notwithstanding, this link is necessary or not. And I don't think that it is.

Let us remain within the bounds of history, for a little while yet. Those who maintain that the law must, as a matter of its essence, claim such supremacy over other normative domains, face a very serious problem regarding the history of law. It is arguable that medieval legal systems, for example, had no such claims to supremacy. On the contrary: positive law was seen as an exception to customs, traditions, religion, and in general, social practices long in force. Thus the law, as a relatively exceptional normative source, could only intervene within the narrow space left open by these other normative sources. It is not the perfection of law itself which changed all this after the Renaissance, but the profound changes which have occurred in the political sphere, and the emergence of the modern state. First emerged the idea of the state, with *its* political claim to normative supremacy, and then came the associated idea of law as the instantiation of this sovereignty, its essential tool. With this conception of state sovereignty came the idea, or rather the confusion, that law itself must claim such a supremacy over other normative domains.

The typical source of this confusion stems from the fact that the original Hobbesian idea of the essential supremacy of the political sovereign, instantiated by the law as its tool, has been gradually turned on its head.[25] Hobbes's idea was that political sovereignty must be absolute, acknowledging no limits and claiming supremacy over all other normative domains. Later philosophers, however, realizing that Hobbes confused here the need for finality in a political regime with the need for a final *human* authority, have replaced

[23] Notably, Locke's explicit rejection of Hobbes's absolutism about the political sovereignty was based on Locke's deep commitment to Natural Law convictions. On the major role of Natural Law in Locke's political thought, see, for example, Simmons, *The Lockean Theory of Rights*.

[24] Legal positivism's most conspicuous flourishing in the nineteenth century coincided, and not accidentally, with the rising notion of the Nation State. It is no accident that legal positivism flourished in the nineteenth century in Germany, as it was there that the idea of the unified Nation State struggled to gain dominance over separatism and medieval political structures. In Germany of the nineteenth century, more than in England or anywhere else, legal positivism went hand in hand with the political aspiration of the emergent Nation State.

[25] By this I do not mean to imply that Hobbes's original idea was correct.

Hobbes's personal conception of authority with the law.[26] Assuming, contra Hobbes, that the very idea of political sovereignty derives from the law, it seemed natural to conclude that it is the law which must be seen as the final authority, acknowledging no limits and claiming its supremacy over other normative realms.

There are several confusions involved here, some of which will be discussed in Chapter 5. For our present purposes, however, it is sufficient to realize that the argument is not valid, even if its premisses are true. Even if we assume (as we should not) that political, state sovereignty must be absolute, and we grant that sovereignty itself derives from the law, it simply does not follow that the law is, essentially, the supreme normative domain or that it must make a claim to such supremacy.

There are two potential senses in which it can be claimed that political sovereignty *derives* from the law: legitimacy and identity. In one sense, it may be argued, again, contra Hobbes, that the legitimacy of political sovereignty derives from the law. Legality is conceived, in this sense, as a precondition for the legitimacy of political authority. In another sense, it could be argued that the very possibility of identifying the political sovereign, as such, depends on the law. As Hart, for example, famously argued, we can only tell who the political sovereign is by considering the rules of law. Political sovereignty rests in an office and the office is constituted by the law.[27]

Whether any of these arguments are correct or not remains to be seen. But even if both are correct, the conclusion we discuss here does not follow. Assuming that A has an essential feature, say F, and that A's legitimacy derives from B, does not entail the conclusion that B also possesses the feature F. And the same holds for identity. Even if A is essentially an F, and A can only be recognized as such according to some features of B, it simply does not follow that B is also an F.

Be this as it may, the essential point is that the very idea of a legal system which does not claim supremacy over all other normative realms is anything but a contradiction in terms. It is easy to envisage an imaginary legal system, which operates alongside other normative domains in the society, and basically fulfils those same functions we associate with modern legal systems. Suppose, for example, that in our imaginary society, there are deeply entrenched traditions concerning the regulation of certain professional guilds, and their unique commercial customs. Suppose it is also a well-entrenched tradition in this society that those unique commercial customs and practices are beyond the law's reach. Finally, suppose that this generally recognized limit on the law's reach stems from a general social convention, and not from any explicit or implicit self-imposed legal doctrine. In other

[26] See for example Jean Hampton, *Hobbes and the Social Contract Theory*, at 98–9.
[27] Hart, *The Concept of Law*, chs. 3–4.

words, the members of our imaginary society think of this limit on law's authority as an external limit, imposed on the law, not by it.[28]

Surely, such a legal system is not necessarily doomed to failure. Nor do I believe that this is the main issue here. The point would be, that regardless of this society's self-understandings, such a limit on the authority of law only makes sense if we assume that it is an instantiation, albeit a tacit one, of law's claim to supremacy, not its refutation. Law is limited, the argument under consideration would hold, not because it need not claim supremacy, but because the law itself recognizes its limit. But this sounds like a bad argument, reminiscent of Austin's notorious doctrine of 'tacit commands'. How exactly, we should ask, does the law recognize its own limit in such a case, when the community's self-understandings, including the legal community's practices and self-understandings, suggest otherwise.[29] When no one has asked you anything your silence can hardly amount to tacit consent.

Coercion

Throughout human history the law has been known as a coercive institution, enforcing its practical demands on its subjects by means of threats and violence. Even within the legal positivist tradition, however, the coercive aspect of the law has given rise to fierce controversies. Early legal positivists, such as Bentham and Austin,[30] have maintained that coercion is an *essential* feature of law, distinguishing it from other normative domains. Legal positivists in the twentieth century have tended to deny this, claiming that coercion is neither essential to law, nor, actually, pivotal in the fulfilment of its functions in society.

There are several issues entangled here, and we should carefully separate them. To begin with, John Austin's famously discredited thesis that each and

[28] This, of course, is not a very imaginary example. Interesting empirical research has been conducted in recent years showing that very sophisticated legal systems have long existed in specific commercial and social environments which have very little to do with the authority of the state. The legal system regulating the international diamond industry, for example, emerged in a particular commercial environment, maintaining its uniqueness and separation from domestic law, wherever the industry exists, largely disregarding state law or state sovereignty. Similar forms of non-state law are abundant in other industries and commercial spheres. See, for example, Ellickson, *Order without Law*. Supporters of the supremacy thesis would claim, of course, that such instances of opting out from state law only manifest specific privileges granted by the state law to unique legal systems. This is exactly the point that I think that we have good reasons to doubt: the monopolization of law by the state is a relatively recent historical development, and not an essential aspect of the law itself.

[29] Here is another example: I venture to speculate that the relations between the law in the USA and its capitalist system manifests a subordination of law to capitalism and not vice versa. Capitalism in the USA, I think, poses a limit on the law, delineating certain invisible contours to its reach, in a way that renders American law's claim to supremacy limited by its capitalist system. Needless to say, the law can transform capitalism in the USA, shape its content and operation, but I think it cannot, at least in the present context, abolish capitalism or disregard it.

[30] And we could add Oliver Wendell Holmes to this list; see his famous 'The Path of Law'.

every legal norm, as such, must comprise a threat backed by sanction, involves at least two separate claims: in one sense, it can be understood as a thesis about the concept of law, maintaining that what we call 'law' can only be those norms which are backed by sanctions of the political sovereign. In a second, though not less problematic sense, the intimate connection between the law and the threat of sanctions is a thesis about the normativity of law. Basically, it is a reductionist thesis, maintaining that the normativity of law consists in the subjects' ability to predict the chances of incurring punishment or evil.

In addition to this particular controversy, there is the further question, concerning the relative importance of sanctions for the fulfilment of the functions of law in society. Kelsen, for instance, maintained that the monopolization of violence in society, and the law's ability to impose its demands by violent means, is the most important one of law's functions in society.[31] Contemporary legal positivists, like Hart and Raz, deny this, maintaining that the coercive aspect of law is much more marginal than their predecessors have assumed. Once again, the controversy here is actually twofold: is coercion *essential* to what the law does? And even if it is not deemed essential, how important is it compared with other functions law fulfils in our lives?

Let me begin with a few observations about the latter issue, which may prove useful for our discussion about the relations between the normativity of law and its coercive aspect. Joseph Raz suggested a very interesting argument, purporting to show that coercion is neither essential to what the law is, nor very important to its functions in regulating social behaviour.[32] The argument is based on the following thought experiment: imagine that there is a world of angels. Their world is exactly like ours, only that the angels differ from us humans in that they simply do not need any external incentives to perform what they are told to do (or, know to have reason to perform?!). In other words, the society of angels simply does not require any sanctions whatsoever. Would those angels, nevertheless, need something like a legal system? Very plausibly, the answer is yes. They would need social institutions very similar to what we call law in our society. The angels would need public means of solving recurrent coordination problems they encounter; they would also need institutions of conflict resolution determining facts and settling problems of interpretation; often enough, they might need to be told what ought to be done in certain circumstances, where morality or prudence remain indeterminate or otherwise inconclusive. And so on. Therefore, Raz concludes, we can see that the functions of law in our lives are not dominated by the need for coercion; coercion is certainly not essential to law, nor is it as important as normally assumed.[33]

[31] Kelsen, *General Theory of Law and State*.

[32] *Practical Reason and Norms*, 159–60.

[33] Perhaps the conclusion Raz himself intended to draw from this thought experiment is more limited than the view I attribute to him here.

This argument, however, is somewhat inconclusive, for two main reasons. First, it is far from clear how the *rationality* of the imaginary angels in our thought experiment should be defined. Would those angels, for example, encounter Prisoners' Dilemma situations? If the answer is affirmative, it would be difficult to show that the angels need no sanctions to overcome problems of opportunism. If we assume, on the other hand, that angels are so rational, or altruistic, that they have no incentive to defect in PD situations, the very relevance of the example becomes highly questionable. First, because the example becomes too imaginary, so to speak. The further our angels are removed from the human condition, the less clear it becomes what we are supposed to learn from the example. More importantly, however, the relevance of the example would become doubtful because, as we shall see in a moment, the law plays a much greater role in solving problems of opportunism, like PD situations, than in solving coordination problems.

Be this as it may, the fact that we can imagine a social institution, very similar to law, without any coercive aspect whatsoever, may prove that coercion is not an essential feature of law, that is, in some abstract or conceptual sense. However, such a thought experiment can hardly settle the question of whether coercion is a major aspect of law in our society. I think that the coercive aspect of law is actually much more important than Hart and Raz seem to have assumed. The effective ability to impose sanctions is a major service the law provides for its subjects. The law is not always the most efficient sanction provider, but often it is. The crucial importance of this service, and its scope, may have alluded some critics because not enough attention has been paid by legal philosophers to the distinction between law's function in solving coordination problems, and law's function in solving problems of opportunism, like Prisoner's Dilemma situations.[34] One major difference between these two types of situations is that the former, but not the latter, can be solved without the incentive provided by sanctions. Therefore, if we forget the ubiquity of PD situations the law deals with, and focus exclusively on coordination problems, a distorted picture emerges, whereby the law can fulfil most of its important functions in society without the tool of sanctions. It is now a widely shared view, however, that most of law's functions in the spheres of private and commercial law concern the resolution of PD type situations and other similar types of problems of opportunism. Such situations call for a sanction-based solution, and very often, the law turns out to be the most efficient sanction provider (typically, when reputation sanctions in the market are bound to fail).

The service of providing sanctions is not exclusively needed in the contexts of private or commercial law. Important aspects of the criminal law also deal with problems of opportunism, most importantly, in the production of pub-

[34] One notable exception is Green's article, 'Law, Co-ordination, and the Common Good'.

lic goods. Other, similar examples have been discussed extensively in the literature, and need not be enumerated here. Suffice it to say that the effective provision of sanctions is a major function of law in our culture due to the prevalence of recurrent PD types of situations. Furthermore, it should be kept in mind that both opportunism and coordination problems are often solved by extra-legal social institutions (e.g. social conventions, the market, etc.). Nevertheless, the law plays a greater role in resolving problems of opportunism than in solving recurrent coordination problems. Most recurrent coordination problems in our lives tend to be solved by the emergence of social conventions. Because there is no inherent conflict of interests involved in a coordination problem between the relevant agents, solutions for such problems are easier to obtain without the services of the law. Reputation sanctions provided by market forces, however, needed for the solution of PD type situations, are harder to come by, due to the ubiquity of information problems and other familiar forms of market failure.

The provision of sanctions, then, is a major function of law in our society, and even if the coercive aspect of the law is not conceptually essential to it, it is a very important aspect of the law which should not be underestimated. Nevertheless, it remains an open question whether sanctions form part of the normativity of law, and it is now time, long overdue perhaps, to consider this issue.

Austin's reductionist account of the normativity of law, maintaining that the normative aspect of law simply consists in the subjects' ability to predict sanctions, was discussed extensively, and fiercely criticized, by H. L. A. Hart. I have only one crucial point to add to Hart's detailed criticisms.

Hart's fundamental objection to Austin's reductionist account of law's normativity is, on Hart's own account, 'that the predictive interpretation obscures the fact that, where rules exist, deviations from them are not merely grounds for prediction that hostile reactions will follow . . . but are also a reason or justification for such reaction and for applying the sanctions.'[35] Now, this emphasis on the reason-giving function of rules is surely correct, but perhaps not enough. Supporters of the predictive account could claim that it only begs the further question of *why* people should regard the rules of law as reasons or justifications for actions. If it is *only* because the law is an efficient sanction-provider, then the predictive model of the normativity of law may turn out to be correct after all. In other words, Hart's fundamental objection to the predictive model is actually a result of his vision about the main functions of law in society, holding, contra Austin and Kelsen, that those functions are not exclusively related to the ability of the law to impose sanctions.[36]

[35] *The Concept of Law*, 82.

[36] Stephen Perry has suggested a similar argument but for a different purpose. He also seems to have claimed that Hart's own account of the normativity of law depends on his theory about law's main functions in society. Perry, however, uses this point to argue that such a dependence

Now, as I argued above, I think that law's functions in our culture are more closely related to its coercive aspect than Hart seems to have maintained. But we should certainly refrain from endorsing Austin's or Kelsen's position that providing sanctions is law's only function in society. Solving recurrent and multiple coordination problems, setting standards or role models for desirable behaviour, proclaiming symbolic expressions of communal values, resolving disputes about facts, and such, are important functions which the law serves in our society, and those have very little to do with law's coercive aspect and its sanction-providing functions. Furthermore, even where the law's function concerns its role as a sanction provider, it is often not along the lines suggested by Austin. As Hart correctly pointed out, Austin seems to have been guided exclusively by the model of the classical provisions of the criminal law, which normally state a duty to refrain from a certain type of action, 'or else . . .'; The provision of sanctions for the solution of problems of opportunism functions in a very different way. In such cases, sanction is provided by the law as a public and collective instrument which enables people to achieve certain goals they could not otherwise achieve without defeating their own endeavours. Unlike the case of the classical criminal law provisions, however, the law does not purport in such instances to set the goals themselves. These are two very different ways, then, in which prediction of sanctions would figure in people's reasons for action, and I think that Hart was quite right to insist upon this difference.[37]

Nevertheless, it should be realized that Hart's fundamental objection to the predictive model of the normativity of law is ultimately based on his own account of law's essential functions in our society, and not solely on the truth about the nature of rules, as such. Hart quite correctly maintained that most of the law's subjects are not exclusively interested in the possibility of prediction of sanctions. Our interests in the law, as its putative subjects, are much more diverse and complex. However, this diversity follows from the diversity of the law's functions in our lives, and not merely from the fact that legal rules purport to give rise to reasons for action.

on an account of law's functions actually shows why Hart's theory of law is not, and cannot be, general and descriptive as he famously maintained. Once we are in the business of accounting for law's functions, Perry maintains, we are inevitably engaged in a normative theory which must rely on evaluative, moral, judgements, of the kind insisted upon by Ronald Dworkin. I must admit that I find this last move perplexing. Functions, like other aspects of social institutions, can be both explained and evaluated from critical perspectives. Perry never explains why any attempt to explain the functions of a social institution necessarily involves a critical assessment of it. I can say, for example, that the function of chairs is that people sit on them; sitting is what chairs are for. I can then go on to suggest that chairs are actually not so good, as sitting on them for hours a day tends to create back problems often resulting in pain. Needless to say, the functions of law are much more complex and difficult to account for, but not, essentially, different; in both cases, we can either explain what the function is, or criticize it, or both. See Perry 'Interpretation and Methodology'; for a more detailed criticism of Perry's view, see Chapter 7.

[37] Hart explained this difference in terms of the distinction between duty-imposing *v.* power-conferring rules. See *The Concept of Law*, chs. 2 and 3.

ON WHAT LEGAL CONVENTIONALISM IS NOT

This last point should also be kept in mind when we consider the theoretical limits of legal conventionalism. Let me conclude this chapter with a few remarks on what legal conventionalism is not. First and foremost, legal conventionalism is not a doctrine about the legitimacy of legal authority. Some legal philosophers, Dworkin amongst them, have thought that conventionalism is an initially plausible, albeit eventually wrong, answer to the question of why we should hold the law a legitimate institution.[38] But the truth is that conventionalism is not even an initially plausible answer to the question of what makes the law morally or otherwise legitimate. Whenever people follow a conventional rule, it always makes sense to ask them why they should follow the rule. Questions about the legitimacy of law pertain to this 'why' question, and they cannot be answered by pointing to the fact that there are social conventions determining what the law is. The fact that legal practice is based on social conventions can form part, but only a part, of the reasons people may have for granting law's legitimacy; but it cannot form the grounds for such an answer.

Even more confused is the doctrine which associates conventionalism with the essential function of the law in society. The predominance of game-theoretical analysis of social conventions, and the widely shared view that social conventions only emerge as solutions to recurrent coordination problems, has given rise to the view which seeks to equate the function of law in society with the function of coordination conventions. Legal conventionalists of this brand claim that achieving coordination is what law fundamentally does in our society.[39] The problem is that not everything which is green is an apple, and some apples are not even green. Coordination problems can be solved by countless means; the emergence of a social convention as a solution to a recurrent and multiple coordination problem is only one option, and it is an option which typically evolves in a considerable period of time. Often we need the law (or some other public instrument) to solve multiple recurrent coordination problems precisely because social conventions have not yet emerged, and we would rather have the solution now than wait. It is just puzzling, however, and simply groundless, to maintain that coordination is all that the law does. If it were the case that the law is mostly there to solve complex coordination problems in our lives, it would have been a much more

[38] *Law's Empire*, ch. 4; Dworkin defines the question as one about the 'justification of the use of collective force', which he sees as the essential evaluative question about law's legitimacy.

[39] Leslie Green claims that 'all but a few of its original proponents have now either abandoned this theory or qualified it out of existence'. See Green, 'Positivism and Conventionalism', 42. Nevertheless, most of Green's article is devoted to the refutation of this 'abandoned' theory. Green is not necessarily wasting his time, though. Some theories are never abandoned thoroughly enough.

benign and much less violent institution than it actually is. The law is not a signpost. Its functions in our society are numerous and complex; solving recurrent coordination problems is only one of them, and not necessarily the most important one.

Similar considerations apply to the widespread assumption which associates legal conventionalism with the general concern with law's stability and predictability. Once again, Dworkin shares this misconception, claiming that conventionalists are primarily concerned with the question of 'why past politics is decisive of present rights' and that they think that the answer consists in the 'ideal of protected expectations'.[40] An ideal it may be, but not one which is more closely associated with legal conventionalism than with any other theory about the nature of law. Nor is it the only ideal which anyone who cares to think about it ever thought that is exclusive of law's merit. In order to function effectively, the law must be, to some extent, predictable and stable. We need not invoke legal conventionalism to explain as much. Nor would there be any reason to ascribe conventionalism the absurd view that protecting expectations is the only value law should promote in our lives. Law is a very complex phenomenon. Its functions in society, or the reasons for acknowledging law's legitimacy, just cannot be reduced to one simple idea.

[40] *Law's Empire*, 117.

3
Exclusive Legal Positivism

MOST contemporary legal positivists share the view that there are conventional rules of recognition, namely, conventions which determine certain facts or events that are taken to yield established ways for the creation, modification, and annulment of legal standards. These facts are the *sources of law* conventionally identified as such in each and every modern legal system. The purpose of this chapter is to consider some of the conceptual relations between the conventionally identified sources of law and the idea of legal validity. In particular, I will strive to defend here a 'strong' or 'exclusive' version of legal positivism, mainly against its 'inclusive' or 'incorporatist' rivals.

The kind of exclusive positivism I have in mind would basically hold that legal validity is exhausted by reference to the conventional sources of law: all law is source based, and anything which is not source based is not law. This formulation is, of course, much too crude and we shall have to refine it as we go along. For the time being, however, it suffices for the purpose of defining the main controversies about legal validity, and these are basically about the relations between law and morality. Exclusive positivism denies, whereas inclusive positivism accepts, that there can be instances where determining what the law is, follow from moral considerations about that which it is there to settle.[1] Contemporary anti-positivists, like Dworkin, claim that determining what the law is *always* requires such moral considerations about what the law should be, and thus they reject the sources thesis as incoherent.

Though both anti-positivists and inclusive legal positivists share the view that there are close relations between morality and legal validity, they differ on the grounds of these relations. Dworkin, for example, maintains that the dependence of legal validity on moral considerations is an *essential* feature of law which basically derives from law's profound interpretative nature. Inclusive positivism, on the other hand, maintains that such a dependence of legal validity on moral considerations is a contingent matter; it does not derive from the nature of law or of legal reasoning as such. Inclusive positivists claim that moral considerations affect legal validity only in certain cases, namely, in those which follow from the rules of recognition which

I am indebted to Jules Coleman, Joseph Raz, Alon Harel, and Scott Shapiro for helpful comments and criticisms.

[1] The phrase in the text 'what the law is' can refer to two possible things: which norms are legally valid, and what it is that the law actually prescribes in particular instances. I believe that exclusive positivism is committed to the view that moral and other evaluative considerations do not affect both these aspects of legality. In this chapter, however, I will concentrate on legal validity. In the next chapter I will argue that it is rarely the case that we understand a legal rule without knowing how to apply it to specific cases.

happen to prevail in a given legal system. In other words, the relevance of morality is determined in any given legal system by the contingent content of that society's rules of recognition. As opposed to both these views, exclusive legal positivism maintains that a norm is never rendered legally valid in virtue of its moral content. Legal validity, according to this view which I will strive to defend here, is entirely dependent on the conventionally recognized sources of law.

A FIRST LOOK AT THE SOURCES THESIS

Why should we think that legal validity is exhausted by reference to the conventionally identified sources of law? Why can it not be the case that moral considerations determine what the law is? There are two basic arguments supporting the sources thesis which I will strive to defend here. The first argument derives directly from the conventional foundation of law articulated in Chapter 1. The second argument was presented by Joseph Raz, and it derives from the authoritative nature of law.

Before we proceed, however, a few clarifications about the concept of legal validity are called for. To begin with, it should not be assumed that legal validity is coextensive with the membership of norms in a legal system. The latter is more restricted; norms can be legally valid even if they do not belong to the legal system in which they are applied. Norms of public international law can be valid in a certain legal system, even if they do not belong to it. Similarly, according to familiar provisions of private international law, it is often the case that the legal norms of a foreign country are legally valid with regards a given dispute, and bear on its legal consequences. These foreign norms, however, do not gain membership in the legal system which applies them.

Could it be said, then, that the legally valid norms are those norms which judges (and other officials) are legally bound to apply? This would seem to be a mistake. Judges may be legally bound to apply norms and other considerations which are not, by themselves, legally valid, and vice versa; there may be legally valid norms judges are not bound to apply (e.g. because the issue is not justiciable).

It seems that the best way to define legal validity is by its affinity with truth. This is partly suggested by the fact that validity is a phase-sortal concept: norms can either be legally valid, or not. Legal validity, like truth, does not admit of degrees. (I am neither denying, nor suggesting, that legal validity is logically bivalent, or that it excludes the possibility of indeterminacy. I am only suggesting here that legal validity does not admit of degrees.) Thus, we can say, uncontroversially, I hope, that a norm, say N, is legally valid in a system S, at time T, if and only if, the proposition—'According to the law of system S, at time T, N', is true. Part of what is entailed by the conventional foundations of the law is that the truth conditions of propositions of this kind are reducible to truths about social conventions combined with truths about particular facts or events.

This brings us to the first argument for the sources thesis. The argument is based on the conventional foundations of law and the essentially constitutive nature of the conventions of recognition. In Chapter 1 I have argued that an essential element of such a social practice like law is that it is founded on *constitutive conventions*, namely, on a set of conventions which determine what the practice is and how one goes about engaging in it.

Why could it not be the case, then, that such conventions also constitute ways of recognizing law simply by moral or political considerations? Basically, this cannot be the case because there is nothing the conventions could constitute there. There is no role constitutive conventions can play in determining that people should act according to moral reasons. Politics, morality, ethics, and similar considerations bear on our practical reasoning regardless of conventions. Constitutive conventions can make a difference only by determining specific ways in which such moral, political, and other types of concerns become part of law, that is, part of a conventionally established social practice. And this is precisely what the conventions of recognition do: they constitute practices of making law, changing it, applying it to novel cases, and the like.

Actually, this is not so simple. Conventions do play significant roles in shaping some of our moral conceptions, particularly with respect to the so-called *thick* moral concepts. The content of such thick concepts as 'shame', 'chastity', 'politeness', etc., is partly determined by social conventions. I do not wish to deny this. The point here is different, namely, that constitutive conventions have no role to play in determining that we should act according to moral reasons. Moral and other practical reasons are there to be acted upon, regardless of conventions. Conventions can constitute part (but only a part!) of what it means to act morally in this or that situation. But they cannot constitute reasons for acting according to reasons.

It is easy to misunderstand the constitutive function of the conventions of recognition by assuming that such a function is essentially motivated by an epistemic concern with certainty about the law. A widespread view attributed to positivism is that unless law is conventionally identified, it would be uncertain. Such uncertainty would be a serious problem, it is claimed, either because it would defeat the law's rationale in rendering certain all that which morality and prudence leave fuzzy or controversial, or else the law would face difficulties in fulfilling its putative social or moral-political functions.[2] Both

[2] It should be admitted that Hart's own characterization of the rules of recognition in the fifth chapter of *The Concept of Law*, emphasizing their role in solving the problem of uncertainty in the recognition of law, could certainly give rise to this interpretation. Hart's account, however,

these concerns about the certainty of law are beside the point. The function or point of constitutive conventions does not consist in rendering certain, or unequivocal, aspects of our lives which would otherwise remain uncertain and fuzzy; their point is to constitute a social domain which is valuable and worth engaging in. The constitutive conventions of theatre, for example, are not there to render more certain and concrete some pre-existing but vague conception of theatre, which had been there before the conventions were in place, as it were. Without the constitutive conventions, there is no theatre (nor concept of theatre). And without the constitutive conventions of recognition, there is no practice of law. Thus, by claiming that the rationale of the constitutive conventions of law is to determine ways in which moral and political reasoning become part of law, we need not think that the function of such conventions is to turn something vague and fuzzy into something more certain and concrete. It is not the preoccupation with certainty that matters here, but the idea of a social practice which is constituted by conventions. The conventions determine what the practice is; their function is constitutive and not epistemic.

I venture to guess that some critics have made this mistake because they tend to confuse the function of the rules of recognition, which is constitutive of what counts as law, with the various social and political functions of the law itself, which is a different issue altogether. It is certainly true that amongst the numerous functions and purposes of law in our society, it serves many which have an epistemic character. Certainty and predictability are among the values law is able to enhance in numerous areas, and part of its legitimacy can be derived from such epistemic functions it serves (that is, of course, to the extent that the law is legitimate). But none of this bears on the particular role of the rules of recognition, which is, again, constitutive and not epistemic.

So now we can return to the main argument. Conventions, I have argued, cannot determine ways of making law simply by moral and political arguments, because there is no constitutive function they can possibly have there. Conventions cannot constitute reasons for acting according to moral reasons; they can only shape the particular ways in which actions (or opinions, etc.) form a well-structured social practice.[3]

Perhaps I should add that there is no coordinative function conventions can fulfil here either. A coordination convention in the realm of moral-political reasoning can only determine *who* it is that we should listen to when

is ambiguous. According to one possible, and to my mind, plausible interpretation, we can read Hart's idea about the epistemic aspect of the rules of recognition as a historical speculation, suggesting that the emergence of those rules was driven, in large part, by the need of certainty in the identification of law. According to another interpretation, which is less plausible, enhancing certainty is the function or rationale of such rules. See also Hart's Postscript, 251.

[3] I don't want to deny, of course, that there are particular moral and political concerns which are created by the existence of certain legal institutions.

we must reach an agreement on how to act, and we cannot reach it on our own, as it were. But then the convention does not make law depend on moral considerations. On the contrary, it makes it depend on the decision of the agent (or some other decision procedure) who has been assigned by the convention to determine the outcome in such cases. In other words, it seems to me that under the assumption that the rules of recognition are coordination conventions inclusive positivism fairs even worse. The entire rationale of coordination conventions is to secure some uniformity of action in face of uncertainty or controversy as to other agents' possible actions. Such uncertainties are solved by the emergence of social conventions which indicate a particular course of action, either the one which would seem salient to most participants, or else one which just happens to evolve due to contingent circumstances. Conventions could not solve such coordination problems, however, if they prescribed that the relevant agents should act according to the right reasons which apply to them. After all, the coordination problem had supposedly arisen precisely because the agents haven't had enough assurance about the other agents' likely actions. In other words, coordination problems arise either when the reasons for action are themselves indeterminate under the circumstances or when the agents are uncertain that others will follow the right reasons. In such circumstances the coordination problem cannot be solved by indicating that the agents should act according to the right reasons.

The essential point, however, is this: conventions cannot constitute a practice which consists in the expectation that people who engage in the practice do what they would have reason to do regardless of the practice. Now, it is true that the constitutive conventions themselves are prone to be affected by the values inherent in the practice which is constituted by them. But this is a historical process which involves a gradual change of the conventions themselves. From a historical perspective, constitutive conventions tend to be under constant interpretative pressure, which is partly due to external needs and values of a changing world, and partly due to novel interpretations of those same values which are inherent in the practice. But this is always a slow, gradual, almost invisible process that takes place over time, and it results in changes of the conventions themselves.[4] Evaluative considerations, good and ingenious as they may be, do not, by themselves, constitute conventions, even if they are sound principles. Even if people realize that 'It ought to be that it is a convention that P', it simply does follow that 'It is a convention that P' (though in due course, a P convention may emerge). In other words, the dynamic aspect of conventionally constituted practices, like law and artistic genres, does not undermine their conventional foundation. And once we admit the conventional foundation of law, it no longer makes sense to say

[4] With one major exception: a revolution. Accounting for revolutionary changes of legal systems is a serious challenge for conventionalism, but I cannot hope to face it here.

that the law can be identified as such on the basis of moral or political considerations alone.

Let us turn now to the second argument for the sources thesis, suggested by Raz and based on his conception of authority.[5] The basic insight of Raz's argument is that the law is an authoritative social institution. The law, Raz claims, is a *de facto* authority. However, it is also essential to law that it must be held to *claim legitimate* authority. Any particular legal system may fail, of course, in its fulfilment of this claim. But the law is the kind of institution which necessarily *claims* to be a legitimate authority.[6] Now, it is a necessary condition of an authority's legitimacy that it be able to prescribe for its subjects reasons for action that the subjects would be better off complying with, as compared to their attempts to act on those reasons directly, without the mediation of the authority's directive. This is what Raz calls the authority's essential mediating role. Hence it follows that for something to be able to claim legitimate authority, it must be of *the kind of thing* capable of claiming it, namely, capable of fulfilling such a mediating role.

What kinds of things can claim legitimate authority? There are at least two such features necessary for authority capacity, and each one of them is sufficient to support the sources thesis: first, for something to be able to claim legitimate authority, it must be the case that its directives are *identifiable* as such, namely, as authoritative directives, without the necessity to rely on those same reasons which the authoritative directive is there to replace. If this condition is not met, namely, if it is impossible to identify the authoritative directive as such without relying on those same reasons the authority was meant to rely on, then the authority could not fulfil its essential, mediating role; it could not make the practical difference it is there to make. Note that this argument does not concern the efficacy of authorities. The point is not that unless authoritative directives can be recognized as such, authorities could not function effectively. The argument is based on the rationale of authorities within our practical reasoning. Authorities are there to make a practical difference, and they could not make such a difference unless the authority's directive can be recognized as such without recourse to the reasons it is there to decide upon.

Second, but this is an argument I will not attempt to substantiate here, for something to be able to claim legitimate authority, it must be the case that the authority is capable of forming an opinion on how its subjects ought to behave, distinct from the subjects' own reasoning about their reasons for action. In other words, a practical authority, like law, must be basically personal authority, in the sense that there cannot be an authority without an author.[7]

[5] See Raz, *Ethics in the Public Domain,* ch. 9.

[6] In Chapter 2 I argued that law's claim to legitimacy necessarily follows from its authoritative nature.

[7] This conclusion is defended in Chapter 5.

Now, it is not difficult to see that this conception of legal authority entails the sources thesis, since it requires that the law, *qua* an authoritative resolution, be identifiable on its own terms, that is, without having to rely on those same considerations which the law is there to settle. Therefore a norm is legally valid (i.e. authoritative) only if its validity does not derive from moral or other evaluative considerations about that which it is there to settle.

There is, of course, much more to be said about these two arguments for the sources thesis. For now, however, it suffices to see how both Raz's argument from the authoritative nature of law and the conventional foundation of law at least initially support the sources thesis. It is now time to consider the alternative view, namely, the idea of inclusive positivism.

INCLUSIVE LEGAL POSITIVISM

Inclusive legal positivism is not one doctrine but several, closely related ones, and I will distinguish them shortly. There are two main points, however, which are characteristic of inclusive positivism. First, unlike Dworkin's theory, inclusive positivism adheres to the basic idea that law is recognized as such on the basis of social conventions. In other words, inclusive positivism subscribes to the thesis about the conventional foundation of law.[8] Secondly, and this is what distinguishes the inclusive from the exclusive version of positivism, the former seems to share a conviction that at least some of Dworkin's arguments against the sources thesis are sound. Inclusive positivists agree with Dworkin that there must be more to law than that which derives from the conventionally identified sources of law. Some moral or political principles are valid law, just in virtue of being sound moral principles. Before I turn to distinguish between the various doctrines that have emerged from this general conviction, however, I would like to provide a brief sketch of the main motivations which underlie it, and the reasons for the uneasiness many positivists feel with respect to the strong interpretation of the sources thesis. Roughly, I think that there are two such reasons: first, because judges say so; secondly, because it seems that the law itself prescribes it. Let me try to explain both of these points.

Much of the plausibility of the criticism of the sources thesis derives from judicial rhetoric. In the Anglo-American legal systems (and many others) one often finds judicial rhetoric which seems to support the view that there is more to law than that which derives from its conventionally established sources. There are moral and political principles judges claim to rely on, and apply to their decisions, whose validity cannot be traced back to the conventional

[8] See, for example, Coleman, 'Second Thoughts and Other First Impressions'; Hart, Postscript.

sources of law. True, some of those principles have become part of the law by incorporation through precedent, which is a conventional source of law. But at least judicial rhetoric seems to suggest that often it is not in virtue of their sources that judges regard certain principles as legally binding, but in virtue of their content.

The argument does not end, however, with pointing to judicial rhetoric. It is more sophisticated than this. It claims that it is on positivism's own terms that such rhetoric ought to be taken seriously. After all, it is the conventionalists—as opposed to the Natural lawyers—who claim that the law simply is what judges and lawyers think that it is.[9] Since it is a fact that the judges themselves think that there is more to law than that which derives from conventionally established sources, the sources thesis would seem to be undermined on conventionalism's own grounds.

A similar line of reasoning is suggested by the second argument. Instead of relying on judicial rhetoric, it relies on the content of the law itself. Many critics of the sources thesis think that we simply cannot do away with the vast number of occasions where the law itself renders the legal validity of norms dependent on moral and political considerations, particularly, though not exclusively, in the realm of constitutional law. After all, it is a remarkable feature of modern constitutional documents that they prescribe moral and political reasoning for the purposes of determining the legal validity of norms. And it is a common practice of constitutional adjudication to turn this into reality, namely, by validating or invalidating norms on the grounds of moral and political principles.[10] Isn't all this too familiar and too central to the functioning of modern legal systems to be swept away by a dogmatic adherence to the sources thesis? It is in a way, then, the desire to bring theory in line with the practice which motivates inclusive positivism. Legal practice strikes many conventionalists to be much more affected by moral reasoning than the sources thesis would seem to allow. The essential question is, however, whether we can make sense of this inclusive positivist theory. As I have already indicated, it is not one doctrine, but several, and it is now time to distinguish between them.

There are, basically, three versions of inclusive positivism that I will take up in turn. The first maintains that the rules of recognition need not exclusively consist of source constraints on legal validity; they may also incorporate, in addition to the sources of law, moral principles as criteria of legality. The second and third versions do concede that such source constraints are inevitable, but they attempt to incorporate morality either by maintaining

[9] This is not quite accurate: conventionalism is committed to the view that the content of law is what judges and lawyers think that it is. It is not committed to the view that judges' views on the nature of their activity is conclusive of anything. As I have argued in Chapter 1, people can follow conventions even if they are not aware of the conventional nature of the rules they follow.

[10] See, for example, Waluchow, *Inclusive Legal Positivism*, 113–17.

that entailed law is also law or, as the more popular version has it, that the law itself can explicitly incorporate morality as a validity condition.

The first and strongest version of inclusive positivism maintains that the rules of recognition need not turn the validity of legal norms to depend exclusively on conventionally identified sources (though they would typically do that as well).[11] A rule of recognition, on this view, can take the following form: the law is whatever follows from sources Si . . . n, *and* whatever follows from the correct moral reasons—or some specific subset of such reasons—that apply to the circumstances.[12]

We have already seen what the initial motivation for holding such a view would be, namely, that it would seem to be more in accord with contemporary judicial rhetoric and perhaps even more so, with (the rhetoric of) contemporary constitutional law, particularly in the major Western democracies. But the question is whether there are any arguments which could support such a view and still remain faithful to the conventional foundation of law that inclusive positivism adheres to. As a matter of fact, we have already noted one main reason why the answer must be negative. The source constraint which is embodied in the rules of recognition is not a peculiarity of particular legal systems, or even of law, as such. It stems from the constitutive nature of the conventions of recognition: conventions can not constitute a practice which partly consists in the expectation that people do what they have reasons to do regardless of the practice.

As a possible rejoinder to this line of reasoning consider the following argument. The rules of recognition are conventional rules. Like other rules, their *application* to particular cases can be controversial, morally, politically, or otherwise. Therefore, the argument concludes, it may well be a matter of moral or political argument determining what a rule of recognition actually prescribes in particular cases, and therefore it is at least sometimes the case that determining what the law *is* depends on moral considerations about what it ought to be.[13]

This argument is almost persuasive. After all, rules and conventions can always be controversial, and some of those controversies are bound to rely on moral considerations. But the main flaw in the argument under consideration

[11] Hart, Postscript, 250; Jules Coleman, see for example, 'Second Thoughts and other First Impressions'.

[12] Coleman has made it very clear, though, that he does not think that inclusive positivism is a necessary feature of law: it is possible, he claims, for a legal system to exist, whose rules of recognition prescribe source-based law as the exclusive conditions of legality. The thesis which acknowledges this possibility he dubbed 'Negative Positivism'. He is less clear, however, about the question whether source constraints are necessary or not. Namely, whether he thinks that it could be the case that the rules of recognition do not embody any source constraints whatsoever. Could the rule of recognition only prescribe that law is whatever is morally the right thing to do, or something like this?

[13] If I understand it correctly, this is at least part of Coleman's argument, and one which seems to be endorsed by Hart as well (at least in the Postscript).

is that it assumes that there is a potential gap between the convention, which is a rule, and its application, a gap that can be bridged by moral or political arguments. The main reply to this is, that there is no such gap. A convention is constituted by the practice of its application to particular cases. It is not the case that we first have a rule formulation, say that convention 'R' prescribes so and so, and then we try to make up our minds how to apply R to particular cases (and then, as this story goes, sometimes we know the answer, and sometimes we argue about it). Conventions are what they are, because there is a practice of applying the rule to certain cases; it is the application of the rule which constitutes its very existence. Once it is not clear to the norm subjects whether the convention applies to a certain case or not, then there is no conventional solution to that matter, and at least as far as the convention is concerned, this is the end of it. People can have different views about the convention they would want to have in those circumstances (or how, otherwise, they would like to solve the problem they face) but they cannot have an intelligent argument about what the convention *really* requires in those controversial cases. The only reality there is to a convention is the actual practice of its application; a social practice. In the case of conventional rules, there is no gap between the rule and its application, a gap which could be bridged by an interpretative reasoning preferring one application to another. Once the application of a convention is not clear there is no convention on that matter.

To illustrate this by a simple example, consider the conventions of a natural language. It is a convention of the English language that the time of day at 9 a.m. is appropriately called 'morning' and it is not clear, from that convention's perspective, whether one can apply the notion of 'morning' to 11.30 a.m., or not. Does it make any sense to ask what it is that the notational convention of 'morning' really requires in the latter case? Hardly. The only thing we could say is that people would not be making a mistake either way, and that if it is important for some reason or other whether 11.30 is 'morning' or not (and one can easily imagine situations where it would be, e.g. in some legal context), then one must decide either way according to the appropriate considerations which would apply to the circumstances, given the fact that as far as the notational convention goes, it could go either way.[14]

Similar examples are abundant in law. Take, for instance, the rules of recognition concerning the doctrine of precedent. In all the jurisdictions which have such conventions, they would normally include some notion about the life expectancy of precedents; how far back in history one could go

[14] Morning may be a vague concept. The so-called epistemic theories of vagueness maintain that there is a truth of the matter about borderline cases, only that it is not knowable. (See, for example, Williamson, *Vagueness*.) I do not find epistemic theories of vagueness persuasive, but it is not part of my argument here. The borderline cases of conventional rules need not stem from vagueness, and the argument here need not take sides on any of the philosophical debates about the nature of vague concepts. The argument relies on the nature of conventions.

in search of a binding precedent. Different jurisdictions have different conventions about these matters. But of course, no such convention can be very accurate. Once we face a borderline case, the only thing to say about it is that it is a borderline case, namely, that there is no convention about that matter and that the question must be answered on its merits.

Perhaps there is a better argument to make here. Suppose the conventions of recognition somehow *presuppose* some general constraints on legal validity which consists in adherence to some shared communal values, or certain conceptions of fairness, or the like. Could it not then be controversial what those, for example, conceptions of fairness really require? And if so, would it not be a case where the appropriate *application* of the rule of recognition turns on moral reasons?

Conventions can, of course, determine their application conditional upon other, non-conventional considerations. It is a widely shared convention, for instance, that one should greet (in a conventionally recognized manner) one's friends and acquaintances when meeting with them. The application of this greeting convention depends, of course, on our ability to determine who is, and who is not, an acquaintance. This is partly a matter of convention too, but not entirely. People may have different views on what is considered sufficient acquaintance for the purposes of the greeting convention, and they may form such views on the basis of, *inter alia*, evaluative considerations. So now suppose that two people disagree about the application of the greeting convention, and that such a disagreement stems from different views they have about what 'sufficient acquaintance' consists in. One party claims that a one-time casual previous acquaintance is sufficient (as it ought to be so), and the other denies it. Of course in one sense it is not a mistake to say that they disagree about the application of the greeting convention. As a matter of fact, they would apply it differently under certain circumstances. But essentially the situation here is not different from the notational convention we have encountered earlier. As far as the greeting convention goes neither party would make a mistake. None of them could claim that his or her view is *the conventional* one. The content of a convention is exhausted by the social practice which consists in the application of the convention. We can never say that 'it is a convention that P' *because* it ought to be that P. Hence it is not really the greeting convention's application which is controversial here, although it may well be the case that people would apply the convention differently under certain circumstances. To the extent that there is a genuine disagreement about such differences in application it is a disagreement about what the convention ought to be, and not about what it is; it is a disagreement about how to apply the convention to novel or unsettled cases, which is, basically, a disagreement about how to change, or extend, the convention.

But can it not be the case that people understand a convention differently, and that one understanding is better than the other? Of course this can happen. People can have a genuine and significant disagreement, for example, over the question of what the point of the convention is, and there may well be better and worse answers to such questions. A better grasp of the point of something is also a better grasp of the nature of that thing. Similar considerations apply to the formulation of a convention, its history, its functions, rationale, and a great many other aspects. In other words, I am not denying that the nature of a convention can be controversial. Anything which is meaningful can be controversial. It is not the possibility of controversy that I object to. The only wrong assumption of the argument under consideration is that there is a potential gap between the convention and its application, a gap which can be bridged by the correct, or true, moral considerations. A convention consists in what people do, as a matter of following a rule. This leaves open the possibility that we would have different interpretations of what people do, and what this doing really amounts to. Hence the room for controversy. But it makes no sense to say that there *is* a convention about doing A, even if people substantially disagree on the question whether doing A is prescribed by the convention or not. [15]

So the idea that judges and lawyers can have genuine arguments about what the rules of recognition *really require* in controversial cases, and that such a phenomenon shows how morality can determine what the law is, involves a misunderstanding of the concept of a convention. It is incompatible with the conventional foundation of law that inclusive positivism adheres to.[16]

The search for a middle ground between Dworkin's legal theory and exclusive positivism has engendered two further versions of inclusive positivism. Let me concentrate first on the more popular version of it. This version concedes that legal validity is basically source based, but it also insists that the conventional sources themselves often include a specific reference to moral considerations which bear on the legal validity of norms. Source-based law often incorporates morality on its own terms, as it were.[17] Here is a simple

[15] There is an obvious distinction between disagreement and misunderstanding. People can, of course, misunderstand a convention. Note, however, that it cannot be the case that nearly everybody misunderstands a convention. Conventions are, essentially, what people take them to be.

[16] What actually may have happened here is that inclusive positivists have tried to turn one of Dworkin's most important arguments against the conventional foundation of law on its head. It was Dworkin who insisted that there is law in such controversial cases, and hence it makes no sense to assume that legal norms derive their validity from conventional rules of recognition. When the convention's application is controversial, there is no convention on the matter. Since judges and lawyers assume that there is, nevertheless, law in such cases, it follows that the law cannot derive its validity from conventions. If my argument is correct, it shows that the inclusive-positivist argument under consideration is not a coherent reply to Dworkin. Either Dworkin is right, namely, that there is law in such controversial cases, in which case, conventionalism is false, or else strong positivism is right, in which case, the appropriate conclusion is that there is no law in controversial cases, judges' rhetoric notwithstanding. There is no middle ground here, at least as far as this argument is concerned.

[17] See, for example, Waluchow, *Inclusive Legal Positivism*.

model of this line of thought: suppose the conventions of recognition in a legal system Si prescribe that law is whatever Rex tells you to do. Suppose, further, that Rex had actually decreed that in cases of type X people should do the right thing, or that they should behave in a fair and just manner. Or else, suppose that Rex had prescribed that none of his own laws should be valid unless they met certain moral constraints, like fairness or equality. In both cases, such incorporatists would maintain, the conditions of legal validity are clearly affected by moral considerations. It is at least sometimes true in Si that the validity of a legal norm depends on its moral merit, and therefore strong positivism must be false.

This version of inclusive positivism embodies two advantages. First, if true, it would seem to constitute a very good answer to some of Dworkin's objections to legal positivism, that is, without giving in to his rejection of legal positivism as such. All we would have to show is that in those legal systems we are familiar with and that Dworkin focuses on, explicit source-based reference to morality is not a rare phenomenon. If this is true, as it certainly seems to be in the case of American law, Dworkin's counter-examples to legal positivism, based on judicial rhetoric and the law itself, are easily explicable on positivist grounds. True, we would say, morality does bear on legal validity pretty much in the way Dworkin depicts, but this follows from the sources thesis itself, it does not necessarily go against it. Second, this version of inclusive positivism, unlike its stronger relative, does seem to be consistent with the conventional foundation of law as it does not make the problematic claim that conventions can establish practices which are there regardless of conventions. The conventions are there to establish the sources of law, and in this they have fulfilled their constitutive rationale. This does not seem to preclude the possibility that the sources of law make it, as a matter of fact, either mandatory or permissible that the validity of other legal norms depend on morality.

THE ARGUMENT FROM AUTHORITY

There are two main ways in which inclusive positivism can claim that morality bears on what the law is. One type of phenomenon can be called 'conditional validity': this is the type of cases where the law imposes certain moral or political constraints, like equality, or fairness, etc., on the legal validity of norms in general, that is, either with respect to all the norms of the system, or some specific subtype of norms (e.g. like state, as opposed to federal legislation, or administrative norms as opposed to private law, etc.). In this type of cases the law seems to make the validity of otherwise source-based law *conditional* upon meeting certain moral constraints. This is, allegedly, the typical case of the familiar constitutional provisions conditioning the validity of all legislation on meeting certain prescribed moral and political constraints. The second type of situation, which for want of a better idea I will call 'content validity', consists of those cases where the law is supposed to be simply what morality, or justice, or some other relevant values dictate. The legislature may decree, for instance, that in cases of type X, the law is whatever morality requires. Suppose, for instance, that the law only prescribes that in cases of type X, one party should pay 'just compensation' to another party, 'just' meaning whatever *is just* according to the relevant moral considerations. Allegedly, then, in such a case the answer to the question what kind of compensation a party should pay to another is simply determined by the appropriate moral reasons.

Both phenomena of conditional and content validity are familiar aspects of modern legal systems. There is, after all, nothing there to stop legislatures or judges from using the language of moral and political values in their prescriptions of what the law requires. And they often do that. The question is how to interpret these phenomena. Inclusive positivism asks us to take them at face value: what the law says is what it does, namely, it requires us to decide what the law is on the basis of moral or political considerations. Hence the law is what those moral and political considerations really require. But this cannot be quite right, even at face value. At the same time that the law incorporates morality into itself, as it were, it also assigns somebody the role of determining, officially and authoritatively, what the moral considerations require, typically judges. After all, it is never simply up to us, as the subjects of law, to decide for ourselves what just compensation really is, or whether to abide by a given law if it seems to infringe a constitutional requirement of fairness, or whatever. It is always the judges (or other officials) who decide these matters, and it is only their decision which could carry any authoritative weight.

This last point was not meant to be a conclusive argument against inclusive positivism. It was only meant to show that the issues are rather complicated, and that there is very little that we can draw from face-value interpretations of the situation, not to speak of conclusions. Eventually, and I think most legal philosophers admit as much, the argument turns on the sense we can make of the authoritative nature of law: can it be the case that a norm is authoritative if it requires the norm subjects to decide what the norm is, on the basis of those considerations which the norm is there to settle. At least on the basis of Raz's theory of authority, the answer is clearly 'no'.

Brian Leiter correctly identifies three main arguments which have been offered as rejoinders to Raz's argument from authority.[18] First, it has been claimed that Raz conflates two possible ways in which an authority's subjects may be required to rely on moral reasoning in order to determine what the

[18] Leiter, 'Realism, Hard Positivism, and Conceptual Analysis'.

authority has prescribed, and only one of them undermines the rationale of authority itself. Coleman writes, for example, that 'not every morality condition of legality directs us to the law's underlying or justifying conditions. Thus, on the assumption that authority precludes identification by appealing to its justifying or dependent reasons, not every Incorporationist rule of recognition will be incompatible with the possibility of legal authority.'[19] A rule prescribing, for example, a general condition of fairness for the validity of all other rules, requires the authority's subjects to rely on moral considerations in determining what the law is, but it 'does not direct us to the dependent reasons that would justify any particular legal rule'.[20]

Important as this distinction may be, however, it is far from clear that it undermines the Razian argument. Undoubtedly, legal authorities can be limited. Judges, officials, and even the legislature are typically limited authorities. They may exercise their authority only within specified areas, or on specified grounds, or according to some specified procedures. The argument under consideration seems to add that such limits on the exercise of a legal authority may also consist of moral constraints, established and recognized as such by the conventional sources of law of the pertinent legal system, and it contends that such moral limits do not undermine the authoritative nature of law. But how does any of this show that a norm can be a legal norm just in virtue of its moral content? Raz's argument from authority does not aim to exclude any type of evaluative or moral consideration from legal discourse. It only aims to prove that morality cannot determine what the law is.[21]

According to exclusive legal positivism, legal norms are products of authoritative resolutions; every legal norm consists of an authoritative directive. This does not entail that everything a legal authority decrees is law; authorities may transgress their legal powers. Now, the argument under consideration claims that such powers can sometimes be specified in evaluative, moral terms. The legal power of authorities can be constrained by moral considerations, if (but only if?) such considerations derive from the rules of recognition. This is true: legal powers can be constrained by moral criteria. But for law to emerge, the power must be exercised. This is what the sources thesis amounts to: law can only derive from authoritative sources. Constraints, of the moral or any other kind, by themselves do not determine the law; they only prescribe ways in which the law can be changed. Thus, even if it is true that some of the constraints which determine the legal powers of authorities are evaluative or moral in kind, it does not undermine the sources thesis, since

[19] See Coleman, 'Incorporationism, Conventionality, and the Practical Difference Thesis', at 414. A similar argument was presented by Waluchow, *Inclusive Legal Positivism*, at 129–40.

[20] Coleman, ibid.

[21] Raz was actually quite explicit on this point; he has long maintained that judges and other legal officials can be bound by moral and evaluative considerations; applying the law is not the only function of judges. See *Ethics in the Public Domain*, at 312n.

it does not entail that a norm can be a legal norm just in virtue of its moral content.

Perhaps we can restrict the argument to the negation of legal validity, saying that although moral considerations cannot, by themselves, establish the legal validity of a norm, they can, nevertheless, establish that a norm is legally not valid as it transgresses a moral constraint. The main problem with this view is, however, that it would require the introduction of a notion of *prima facie* validity. The negation of legal validity on moral grounds would only make sense if we thought that the pertinent norm is at least *prima facie* valid. Furthermore, since most, if not all, legal norms can be defeated, allegedly, by such moral constraints, it would mean that most norms in a legal system are only *prima facie* valid. Such a view, however, would beg many more questions than it can hope to answer. To begin with, it would render the idea of legal validity far less certain than it actually is, since it would always make the conclusion about the legal validity of a norm depend on truths about morality.[22] More importantly, however, such a view is inconsistent with the authoritative nature of law, and for those same reasons we have observed above: legal authority is there to make a practical difference, and it could not purport to make such a difference if authoritative directives are only *prima facie* valid, more often than not awaiting, as it were, the confirmation of their validity on grounds which the putative subjects of the authority should figure out for themselves. It is as if the authority said: 'do what I say, unless what I say goes against moral reasons'. Legal validity is not a *prima facie* construct. Legal authority is needed precisely because it is there to render conclusive, that is, at least from a legal point of view, *prima facie* reasons which apply to the putative subjects.

To illustrate the problem, consider a standard case where the legal validity of a norm is questioned on moral grounds along the lines suggested by the argument under consideration. Suppose that an authoritative resolution has been rendered, say, by the Supreme Court, deciding that the norm is legally valid. Now suppose that the moral reasoning of the Supreme Court was at fault and that the relevant moral reasons would actually call for the invalidation of the norm. Let us assume, for the sake of the illustration, that this is what has happened with the constitutional challenge to capital punishment in the USA; that is, let us assume that from a moral point of view, capital punishment is really cruel and therefore it should not be valid. Nevertheless, unfortunately the Supreme Court decided otherwise. Would we have to maintain that laws prescribing capital punishment in the USA today are actually not legally valid? And if so, what is the practical significance of the authority of the Supreme Court, which has decided otherwise? Natural Law mythology

[22] This problem is all too familiar and I will not try to develop it further here. For a recent discussion, see for example Himma, 'Incorporationism and the Objectivity of Moral Norms'.

is too high a price to pay for such an argument. It is much more natural to say that in such cases, the Supreme Court has been given the legal power to change the law according to moral considerations, and that the change it introduced into the law was not a morally desirable one. On this idea of morally directed power I will expound later.

Coleman offers another argument against Raz's argument from authority, based on a distinction he draws between two possible roles that we can assign to the rules of recognition. One role is basically epistemic and the other is concerned with the notion of legal validity. The epistemic role consists in enabling the citizens and the judiciary to identify the relevant legal norms that apply to them. This, Coleman claims, is at best of secondary importance. Few people know the rules of recognition of their country anyway, and even if they do, it is hardly of great importance. The philosophical significance of the rules of recognition, the role that they are there to fulfil, is not a matter of epistemology, but of validity. The rules of recognition determine which norms are legally valid and not how people would come to realize this. The argument from authority, Coleman claims, 'imposes essentially epistemic constraints. It has to do with the ways in which people figure out what the law is and what it demands of them. The argument from authority isn't about what can count as law.'[23] But these epistemic constraints, Coleman claims, are beside the point. The rules of recognition need not be concerned with the question of how ordinary citizens identify what the law requires of them, it is not a tool that serves them this purpose. Since Raz's argument concerns only this last, epistemic issue, it does not impose an analytic-conceptual constraint on the legal validity of norms, and hence it fails as an argument against inclusive positivism.[24]

What actually fails here, however, is this argument, since it fails to notice that epistemic arguments can have non-epistemic, conceptual, conclusions. Raz's argument from authority is such a case. What matters for our purposes is that the law be able to make a practical difference, and this is a conceptual point. More precisely, it is something that follows from the essentially authoritative nature of the law. The fact that nothing can make such a difference unless certain epistemic constraints are assumed, namely, that the authoritative directive must be such that people *can* identify it without having to rely on those same reasons which the authoritative directive is there to settle, does

[23] See Coleman, 'Second Thoughts and Other First Impressions'.

[24] Scott Shapiro has argued that in the case of judges, the two potential functions of the rules of recognition actually coincide, and hence the argument fails on its own terms. See Shapiro, 'The Difference that Rules Make', at 60. I am not entirely convinced by this argument, however. As I have argued above, the function of the constitutive rules of recognition is not epistemic, and I do not think that this changes where judges are concerned. The constitutive rules of chess, for example, serve the same functions for the players, as for the umpire in the game: they constitute what the game is. The constitutive conventions, whether in chess or in the law, simply define the rules of the game. Needless to say, in order to participate in the game one must first learn the rules.

not entail that the conclusion of this argument is epistemic. The conclusion is a conceptual one. It imposes a conceptual constraint on the kinds of things that can count as authoritative prescriptions.

There is nothing philosophically puzzling, or unique, about such arguments. In fact, a very similar line of reasoning applies to constitutive conventions as well. It is true about constitutive conventions too, that they must be recognizable as such. Consider, for example, the conventions constituting a structured game, like chess, or soccer. Part of what it means to play such structured games is that the players *follow* certain rules. This requires that the rules and conventions be recognizable as such. People can only follow conventional rules which they can recognize as such, namely, as rules to be followed. This is not only a point about how people go about in learning to play the game, or in identifying its rules. It is also a point about what games essentially are.[25]

Finally, the third type of argument which is suggested as a rejoinder to Raz's argument from authority is based on the rejection of Raz's thesis that authoritative directives engender *exclusionary reasons* for action. If authoritative directives are not exclusionary reasons, so this argument continues, then the fact that law is essentially authoritative does not entail that we must be able to identify the law without having to rely on those same considerations which the law is there to settle.[26]

Elsewhere I have already argued that this argument misses its target.[27] Raz's conclusion that it does not make sense to identify the law on the basis of those same considerations which the law is there to settle follows from the fact that the rationale of practical authorities must take into account the ways in which authorities create partly content-independent reasons for action.[28] For the putative subjects of an authority it must be practically significant that the directive has been actually issued by an authority, and their reasons for action must take this fact into account. This entails that the putative subjects of an authority must be able to recognize the authoritative directive as such, namely, as an authoritative directive, regardless of the particular merits of the directive itself. True, Raz believes that the best explanation of this feature of authorities is given by his account of exclusionary reasons. But even if he is wrong about this particular aspect of the explanation, the conclusion remains, namely, that authoritative directives must be recognizable as such without having to rely on the dependent reasons, since this conclusion derives from the fact that authoritative directives must be taken to entail partly content-independent reasons for action. Whether this content independence of

[25] Cf. Wittgenstein, *Philosophical Investigations*, No. 200.

[26] For example, see Dworkin, *Law's Empire*, at 429; Waluchow, *Inclusive Legal Positivism*, at 136.

[27] *Interpretation and Legal Theory*, 118.

[28] For a detailed account of the content independence of authoritative reasons, see Chapter 5.

reasons is best explained as a species of exclusionary reasons, or not, bears on a different question—what *kind* of obligations authoritative directives engender?—but this is presently beside the point.

Even if we reject, as we should, the criticisms of Raz's argument from authority it still remains an open question how best to interpret those phenomena inclusive positivists point at, namely, the pervasive reference to morality in the law. It is, after all, quite unlikely that all this talk of moral and political constraints on legal validity, prevalent in legal practice, is sheer nonsense. I want to suggest that it is meaningful indeed, but not in the way inclusive positivists have envisaged. I will mainly concentrate on what I have called 'conditional validity', but I take it that with the appropriate modifications, this account will apply to content validity as well.

Legal rules which prescribe that the validity of other legal rules depend on certain moral or political considerations actually function as power-conferring rules, granting to the judiciary *limited* and *guided* legislative power. In effect, such power-conferring provisions prescribe to judges that they should legislate new legal standards, sometimes in addition to the existing ones, but often to the effect of modifying or nullifying existing norms. Now, the main function of the moral precepts embodied in such power-conferring rules is to limit either the *kind of purposes* judges should take into consideration in their legislative function, or *the kind of reasons* they should rely upon when justifying it or, typically, both. Consider, for example, the 8th Amendment of the US Constitution forbidding 'cruel and unusual punishment'. Presumably, the question of what kinds of punishment are cruel is a moral one. The purpose of this constitutional provision is to require judges to invalidate legal institutions which amount to cruel forms of punishment. But the judges' power to modify, change, or invalidate existing legal norms is guided by certain aims and by certain types of permissible justifications. They are not given the power to modify existing practices of punishment on grounds of economic efficiency, for example, even if those considerations are sound. The judges' power is thus limited and guided by prescribing a certain type of considerations they may rely upon.

Such guided and limited power-conferring rules Raz called 'directed power'.[29] Power is directed here in two respects: first, it is circumscribed by its legally prescribed aims and reasons. Second, it is a kind of power which the norm subjects (i.e. judges or other officials) have a legal duty to exercise. Unlike the typical case of a power-conferring rule which leaves it entirely to the norm subjects' will whether to exercise the power or not, such a directed power makes it obligatory to exercise it. As Raz pointed out in detail, such directed power-conferring rules are ubiquitous in the law, and they often apply to legislators as well as to numerous officials, and not only to judges.

[29] Raz, *Ethics in the Public Domain*, ch. 10.

The essential point, however, is this: even when power-conferring rules are directed in both ways we mentioned, their exercise *changes* the law. Whenever one makes use of a legal power one introduces a change in the law in the form of creating new rights and duties which have not been hitherto part of the law. This simply follows from the logic of the concept of a legal power, and it is true of the exercise of power both in the private and the public law. The whole idea of a power-conferring norm is to provide the norm subjects and legal officials with a tool to introduce a change in the law. And this, of course, is true of judicial power as well. When judges are granted a directed power to interpret the law according to certain moral considerations, they are given the power to change the law in a limited and guided manner.

An obvious difficulty seems to present itself here: if this is so simple, why is it not generally recognized as such? Why the smoke-screen? The answer is not difficult to surmise: for reasons which have to do with institutional convenience, and perhaps with historical contingencies, it is typically the case that judges' legislative powers must be exercised retrospectively: not only with respect to the particular parties in front of them, but often with respect to many other parties who may have relied on the nullified or modified norm long before any litigation commenced. It is typically the case, as a matter of legal doctrine, that when judges declare a certain legislative act unconstitutional, for example, their decision renders the act *void ab initio*. As a kind of legislative power, such retroactive legislation is problematic indeed. First, because it creates the impression that we must have been wrong about the way in which we had previously understood the law. Mainly, however, it is a moral-political issue: it is, politically, extremely inconvenient to admit that judicial authorities have such a tremendous legislative power which is retroactive in its effect. Hence the smoke-screen.

The power-conferring function of moral concepts embodied in the law is not their only function, although it is the most important one, particularly in the context of conditional validity. Another typical use of moral terminology in the law concerns the reference it aims to make to certain conventions of a community's morality. In other words, legal reference to moral terms often embodies no more than a reference to positive morality. Thus, when a law refers to such notions as 'indecency', or 'obscenity', and the like, it may well do no more than prescribe a reference to certain values which happen to prevail in the community, assumed to be widely shared and recognized as such. In such cases the legal reference to positive morality is not different in essence from other numerous references the law makes to social conventions, assuming (sometimes wrongly) that its subjects know perfectly well what those conventions are.[30] Interestingly, however, such a technique of legislative ref-

[30] The references to matters of sexual morality, which, until quite recently, have been pervasively used in criminal codes, is a good example of such a reliance on conventions of communal morality.

erence to moral conventions is rather precarious. It always faces the 'danger' that judges will actually interpret the reference to moral concepts in the former way I have suggested, namely, as a power-conferring rule, enabling them to change the law in accordance with what they deem the correct moral values which apply to the case. And this often happens.

ENTAILED LAW?

There is, finally, another version of inclusive positivism we should briefly consider. This version maintains that law is fundamentally source based, but it also incorporates those norms which are *entailed* by source-based law. I am not quite sure whether this version of inclusive positivism is actually maintained by inclusive positivists, or whether it was only invented (and repudiated) by Joseph Raz.[31] In any case, since it does seem to carry some plausibility, we should dwell on it for a moment. The basic idea is rather simple, and it may seem to be in accord with the conventional foundation of law: suppose a legal system, say, Si, contains the norms Ni . . . n. Suppose further, that norms Ni . . . n, entail the truth of a further norm, say, Nx. May we not conclude, then, that Nx is also legally valid in Si? But what would it mean to say that Nx is entailed by Ni . . . n? There are several possibilities here. On the most restricted notion of entailment, one would think of it only in terms of logical entailment. (Coupled, I presume, with certain truths about facts.) On the least restricted notion, one could also think of it as moral-evaluative entailment. If it is the case, for instance, that the norms Ni . . . n embody, or manifest, a moral principle M, and M morally requires Nx, then Nx is also part of Si. This latter view brings us much closer, of course, both to Dworkin's views and to the kind of inclusive positivism we have earlier considered.

Despite the considerable differences between these two views of entailment, and perhaps other possible views in between these two extremes, they share a crucial assumption: namely, that the law is necessarily coherent. It is imperative to note that it is not the value of coherence that is the issue here; for establishing the conclusion that entailed law is also law, it is not enough to assume that coherence is an important (even overriding) value that legal interpretation must be guided by. The assumption under consideration here is much stronger than that. It is the assumption that the law is, as a matter of necessity, coherent; it cannot be anything else. Otherwise, if it only maintains that coherence is a heuristic value, then the fact that a norm is entailed by other legal norms could not lead to the conclusion that it *is* a legal norm in virtue of such an entailment; only that it should be.

[31] See his *Ethics in the Public Domain,* at 210–14.

Therefore, the only question we should ask now is whether it makes any sense to assume that the law is necessarily coherent, logically or otherwise. A negative answer to this question is hardly deniable. Coherence might be a necessary requirement that we ascribe to theories, as such. The incoherence of a theory normally indicates that part of it is false. But the law is not a theoretical domain. It is a practical one, where the numerous complexities of our lives are regulated by norms, decisions, and force. It may well be desirable (to some extent!), that these regulations be shaped in a coherent fashion, but it certainly cannot be assumed to be so, by necessity. A priori, the law need not be coherent at all.

Well, this is not quite accurate. Some measure of coherence is a practical necessity. If the law commonly and pervasively prescribed conflicting norms and decisions, it would have created so much confusion that it would make it practically impossible to abide by its rules. This, of course, is a matter of degree. Neither perfect harmony, nor total confusion, are feasible options. There is always *some level* of compliance without which law would not be possible, and there is *some level* of coherence without which such compliance would not be possible. But the question where the line is, is not one for philosophers to answer. Determining law's actual level of tolerance of non-compliance and confusion is a matter for sociologists to indulge in. For our purposes it suffices to realize that there is some such level of tolerance, and that there is no necessity in law's being logically, or otherwise, coherent. If this is true, it immediately follows that there is no reason to assume that entailed law is law, just in virtue of such an entailment relation, whatever its precise nature was meant to be.

As a closing remark for this chapter, let me say what it is that can be concluded from our discussion so far, and what would be premature to conclude. I have tried to present here at least the initial plausibility of a certain version of legal positivism which is best captured by the idea of the sources thesis. This version of positivism, I have tried to show, derives from two main considerations: first and foremost, it derives from the conventional foundation of the law and the nature of social conventions. Second, it is reinforced by the Razian insight that the law is essentially an authoritative social practice, and it must be held to be able to make a practical difference in that respect. These two considerations, I have argued, suffice to show that the inclusive version of legal positivism, which was meant to form a middle ground between exclusive legal positivism and Dworkin's anti-positivist doctrine, is untenable. There is no such middle ground. Dworkin's anti-positivist stance, however, has not been answered. I have shown that at least some objections to the sources thesis, deriving from Dworkin's insights, are ill-founded. But there are, of course, many other arguments which still await to be discussed, and I shall consider some of those arguments in the next chapter.

4
The Separation Thesis and the Limits of Interpretation

THERE are many versions of legal positivism but all of them subscribe to the so-called separation thesis. This thesis basically maintains that determining what the law is does not necessarily, or conceptually, depend on moral or other evaluative considerations about what the law ought to be in the relevant circumstances. As we have seen in the previous chapter, legal positivists differ, however, and quite substantially, over the appropriate interpretation of this thesis. The exclusive version of legal positivism maintains that moral considerations never affect the legal validity of norms. Inclusive positivism, on the other hand, does maintain that there is a close relation between legal validity and morality, but it holds that this relation is a contingent matter; it does not derive from the nature of law or legal reasoning as such. Inclusive positivism claims that moral considerations affect legal validity only in certain cases, namely, in those which follow from the rules of recognition which happen to prevail in a given legal system.

Even this minimalist interpretation of the separation thesis, however, has been rejected by some legal philosophers, most notably, by Ronald Dworkin. Dworkin's criticisms of the separation thesis are numerous and diverse. In this chapter, however, I will only concentrate on one such argument, which is based on the interpretative nature of law.

The essence of Dworkin's argument from interpretation can be summarized in a surprisingly simple form. The argument consists of two main premisses.[1] The first thesis maintains that determining what the law requires in each and every particular case necessarily involves an interpretative reasoning. Any statement of the form 'According to the law in S, X has a right/duty etc., to Y' is a *conclusion* of some interpretation or other. Now, according to the second premiss, interpretation always involves evaluative considerations. More precisely, perhaps, interpretation is neither purely a matter of determining facts, nor is it a matter of evaluative judgement *per se*, but an inextricable mixture of both. Clearly enough, one who accepts both these theses must conclude that the separation thesis is fundamentally flawed. If Dworkin is correct about both theses, it surely follows that determining what the law requires *always* involves evaluative considerations.

This chapter is a revised version of my article in the *Canadian Journal of Law and Jurisprudence*, 12 (1999), 135. I am grateful to David Enoch, Alon Harel, and Wil Waluchow for helpful comments.

[1] Dworkin, *Law's Empire*, mainly chs. 2 and 3.

As simple as this argument is, it actually involves a great many complex issues, many of which have already been brought to daylight both by Dworkin himself and his critics. But the essence of the argument remains basically quite simple: if it is true that law is always a result of an interpretation, and if it is also true that interpretation always involves evaluative considerations, then it follows that determining what the law is always involves considerations about what it ought to be. Note that this conclusion is at odds with the appropriate construal of the separation thesis as maintained both by the exclusive and the inclusive versions of legal positivism. Furthermore, this line of thought has had a great appeal to many anti-positivists of the so-called post-modernist brand, like Stanley Fish, for example, who do not share Dworkin's optimistic views about legal and political interpretation. They would happily endorse both these tenets, about the ubiquity of interpretation and its essentially evaluative nature, but they simply reject Dworkin's optimistic views about the evaluative aspect of interpretation: they think that such interpretations do not admit of genuine integrity, coherence, and objectivity, as Dworkin would have it, and hence they view the law as essentially interpretative, but always up for grabs, so to speak.[2]

The main problem with this argument from interpretation, however, concerns its first premiss. Basically, there is nothing wrong with the second premiss, namely, that interpretation is essentially evaluative.[3] The first premiss, however, is false, or at least, so I shall argue here. It cannot be the case that our understanding of what the law requires is always mediated by interpretation. In order to show this I would like to consider three main lines of thought which seem to underline the pervasive assumption that the understanding of law is always mediated by interpretation. One is a semantic argument, relying on the profound context dependence of meaning. The second is an epistemic argument, drawing on the general defeasibility of legal norms. Finally, I will consider the possibility that Dworkin's conception of legal principles grounds the idea that law is thoroughly interpretative. I do not intend to suggest, however, that these arguments are to be found in Dworkin's writings, or in any other particular legal theory. My main concern here is with a certain type of reasoning which has attracted many legal scholars, rather than with the details of any particular theory. I will consider the semantic argument first.

[2] See Fish, *Is there a Text in this Class*, and 'Working in a Chain Gang: Interpretation in Law and Literature'.

[3] As a matter of fact, this statement is not quite accurate. Certain forms of interpretation are not evaluative, at least not in any substantial manner. But for the sake of the argument, I will not insist on this point. After all, standard and familiar forms of legal interpretation do involve evaluative considerations.

THE SEMANTIC ARGUMENT

Let us begin with the familiar claim that meaning is never quite certain. So suppose that you go out to dine in an expensive French restaurant. You read the menu and pick up your choice, but since you are quite particular about your food, you decide to give the waiter very precise orders, making it absolutely sure that you get the entrée the way you like it. So you cite your choice of entrée to the waiter and add as many instructions and clarifications as you can think of. Your obnoxious waiter, however, brings you the entree precisely as you had asked for it, just that it is all covered with a greasy, disgusting yellow sauce! Well, you tell him, this is not exactly what I had in mind. So now you repeat your order, but you add a specific instruction to the waiter 'make sure that absolutely nothing is added to this'. The next you get is precisely what you had ordered, but in a minuscule scale: the whole dish is just a tiny little thing, like a chestnut. By this time you are really hungry, but also terribly frustrated. You realize that whatever you say can be obeyed literally, without ever finishing up with the meal you wanted. Interpretation, you realize, can turn everything on its head.

This last revelation, however, is premature. Stanley Fish, for instance, would advise you not to despair: the obnoxious waiter, he would assure you, will not last five minutes longer in his job. Interpretative convergence is maintained by social pressure. True, there is nothing the waiter did wrong, as a matter of interpretation. He simply interpreted your orders in a way which is not socially, or institutionally, maintainable. This may be bad for him (unless he is planning a revolution), but it is not a serious worry for our interpretative practices. Under normal circumstances, such interpretative practices are sufficiently convergent to make our lives manageable, since this convergence is imposed on us by institutional needs and social pressure.[4]

There is, I believe, a grain of truth in this Fishy position. It is probably true that a great deal of interpretative convergence is maintained by social pressure and tacit conventions, and not, as it were, by some correspondence with the Truth. But all this should come in later. First, we must consider whether interpretation is needed here at all. That is, we should consider the distinction between understanding the meaning of an expression and interpreting it.

There is something very common and familiar that we call 'understanding the meaning of an expression', and then there are, of course, misunderstandings as well. In our example, however, we could hardly say that there is something that the obnoxious waiter had actually misunderstood! He understood your orders perfectly well, and he only wanted to show you that even if your expression is understood, and *literally obeyed*, interpretation can turn it on its

[4] See Fish, 'Working in the Chain Gang: Interpretation in Law and Literature'.

head. But this is precisely where the argument from interpretation starts to go wrong: from the fact that interpretation *can* turn any expression on its head, it does not follow that *understanding* the meaning of an expression is necessarily, or even typically, an instance of a correct interpretation.

Interpretivists like Dworkin and Fish, who think that all understanding is a matter of interpretation, assume that the understanding of the meaning of an expression is supposed to be a matter of knowing that such and such is the case. Then they claim that there is nothing 'out there' to which the meaning of an expression corresponds, and hence it becomes puzzling what it is that we are supposed to know. Is it, for example, the communication intention of the speaker? This cannot be the case, for a host of familiar reasons. For one, we can understand the meaning of an expression even if we have no idea who the speaker is, or what it is that she intended to convey, quite apart from what she had said. Furthermore, people can actually misunderstand what they themselves have said.[5]

More plausibly, many philosophers have thought that knowing the meaning of an expression consists of the knowledge of those conditions which make it true (or false). Truth conditional semantics, as this brand in philosophy of language is called, maintains that the meaning of a proposition consists in its truth conditions (and it further assumes that expressions which do not convey a proposition can be analysed in terms of variations on the illocutionary force of the expression, as opposed to its constant sense, which is truth-conditional).[6] Interpretivists could still claim, however, that even truth conditional semantics is profoundly context dependent: the truth conditions of sentences are variable according to the context in which they are uttered. Hence the need for interpretation, they would claim, is unavoidable.

It is certainly true that meaning is context dependent. Philosophers of language tend to distinguish between (at least) two senses in which this is so: one concerns utterance meaning, and the other concerns sentence meaning. In one familiar sense, the meaning of an utterance is variable according to the context in which it has been uttered. Consider, for example, a teacher telling her students in class that 'The window is open'. Now, in one context, this could be a simple description of a situation; in another context, it could be an example of a proposition in an introduction to logic class; and yet in another context, it could mean a request from one of the students to shut the window. Note, however, that in all these contexts the sentence meaning (semantics) of 'the window is open' remains the same. Context, in such cases, affects the so-called 'pragmatic' aspect of the communication. It is what we do with sen-

[5] Intention-based semantics, drawing on Grice's analysis of communication intentions, has never been thought to form an adequate account of 'meaning'. See, for example, Schiffer, *Remnants of Meaning*.

[6] Davidson, *Inquiries into Truth and Interpretation.*

tences, what we communicate with them, that depends on context here, not the meaning of the words and phrases themselves.

As philosophers of language have long shown, however, even the semantic aspect of language is profoundly context dependent. Sentence meaning is also variable according to different assumptions about the context of the utterance. The proposition 'This is a glass of water' would have different truth conditions on Earth, where water is composed of H_2O, and say, on Putnam's famous Twin Earth, where water is composed of XYZ. Needless to say, there are complex and controversial explanations of this context dependence of semantics, and their alleged effect on the plausibility of truth-conditional semantics.[7] We need not go into this here, since I do not intend to deny any of this.

Nor do I want to argue that there is something wrong with truth-conditional semantics. The only thing that would be wrong with it is to assume that the use of language as a whole can be reduced to the knowledge of truth conditions of propositions. A very important and fundamental aspect of language, as Wittgenstein famously argued, does not consist in knowledge *that* such and such is the case, but in knowledge *how*; that is, when we use language correctly, we know how to go about doing something. The use of language is a move within a social practice. Furthermore, the idea of 'use' cannot be reduced to some form of knowledge that such and such is the case, which would not in itself involve knowledge of the meaning of the expressions of that language.[8] (We can translate expressions in Hungarian to English, but we cannot translate them to something else which is not a language.)

In other words, it is the way we do things which determines the meaning of expressions in a given language. When we learn how to speak our native language, we learn how to go about doing something; we learn how to engage in a very complex social practice. All this we learn within a given context, of course, set against the specific backgrounds of our lives. In different worlds we would probably have different linguistic practices (and maybe, to some extent, incommensurable ones). The fact that we could always envisage a different way of doing things, however, which would constitute different meanings, does not entail that there is something inherently indeterminate in the way we do things as we do. Context dependence does not *entail* indeterminacy. As long as we are familiar with the context the meaning of the sentences we use is determinate enough. Interpretation is required only when there is something, either in the context or in the expression itself, which is not familiar, or otherwise not clear. Unclarity makes sense, however, only against the background of a great deal of clarity and shared assumptions.[9]

[7] See, for example, Searle, 'Literal Meaning'.

[8] Wittgenstein, *Philosophical Investigations*. See also Putnam's Dewey Lectures, 'Sense, Nonsense, And the Senses: An Inquiry into the Powers of the Human Mind', at 458.

[9] This last insight is not uniquely Wittgensteinian; see, for example, Davidson, *Inquiries into Truth and Interpretation*, at 153.

In other words, it cannot be the case that it is interpretation that we learn when we learn how to go about using language. Interpretation is a kind of clarifying or translating activity: it strives to explain one expression in terms of another. Interpretation need not remain within one and the same language game, of course; we can interpret a piece of music by performing it in a certain way, or by explaining it in English words. But interpretation always explains or clarifies one expression in terms of another. Therefore, interpretation must be based on prior knowledge of how to go about using language. Only once we know the meaning of expressions in a given language can we go about explaining one meaning in terms of another. Suggesting that interpretation always mediates between an expression and our understanding of the expression is simply incoherent. It is like assuming that we can learn Japanese from scratch by merely consulting a Japanese–Japanese dictionary. We must have understanding of expressions first. Interpretation can clarify what, for some particular reason, is unclear. But again, a great deal of clarity is required for unclarity to make any sense at all.

It may be objected that my use of the term 'interpretation' is too restrictive. Some philosophers simply use it to describe the 'mental process' that takes place in our minds when we grasp the meaning of an expression (or, perhaps, when we grasp anything). According to this stipulative definition it is of course true by definition that every understanding of the meaning of an expression involves interpretation. There is nothing wrong with stipulative definitions. On this broad definition of 'interpretation', however, Dworkin's second premiss of the argument loses its grip; it is no longer true that every interpretation, understood as such a mental process, necessarily involves evaluative considerations.

The fact that our linguistic practices are profoundly context dependent does not render meaning profoundly indeterminate. Our ability to use language (or to do anything else with a social meaning, for that matter) is based on a shared context. Only because we do share that context can we learn how to go about using language. If the context was different, in a profound way, we would probably have a different language. As Wittgenstein put it, 'The more abnormal the case, the more doubtful it becomes what we are to say. And if things were quite different from what they are . . . this would make our normal language games lose their point. The procedure of putting a lump of cheese on a balance and fixing the price by the turn of the scale would lose its point if it frequently happened for such lumps to suddenly grow or shrink for no obvious reason.'[10]

But then, does it not follow that unless we can be absolutely sure that the lump of cheese will never grow or shrink, our practice of fixing its price by the scale is in some profound doubt? To such worries Wittgenstein replied: 'It

[10] Wittgenstein, *Philosophical Investigations*, No. 142

may easily look as if every doubt merely *revealed* an existing gap in the foundations; so that secure understanding is only possible if we first doubt everything that *can* be doubted, and then remove all these doubts. The sign-post is in order—if, under normal circumstances, it fulfills it purpose.'[11] And, as we have earlier indicated, one can only learn how to follow the signpost by learning how to engage in a social practice; ' a person goes by a sign-post only in so far as there exists a regular use of sign-posts, a custom.'[12]

But now it may seem as if another type of doubt creeps in. If the acquisition of the concepts of natural language depends on the existence of a practice, then it may well be the case that this contextual background is disturbingly parochial. 'Our' context, as 'our' social practices, may be quite different from 'others' ', and then it becomes doubtful that we really speak the same language. To some extent, this worry is not deniable. Some of us are all too familiar with the difficulties of translation to deny that there are concepts one cannot understand without also being familiar with their particular background which happens to exist in one culture, and is perhaps totally absent in the other. (Try to explain what 'chutzpa' means to someone who has never met an Israeli!) But for our present purposes, this particular worry is beside the point. It is not the problem of transcultural translation that would seem to call for pervasive interpretation in the law.[13] The kind of worry which is relevant to the arguments under consideration is a much more radical one. Proponents of the argument would have to hold that even within one and the same culture, context is radically parochial, and hence every understanding of a linguistic expression is a kind of translation (viz. interpretation). But could it be the case that each and every individual is situated in an individual-specific context? Is there a serious worry about solipsism here? That is extremely unlikely, because language is a *social* practice. Meaning, whatever else it may be, is at the very least *public* and *learnable*. Nor do I think that post-modernists, or interpretivists, of the kind under consideration here would want to hang their argument on the possibility of private language.

So the question is this: if it is neither solipsism (because it is not a serious worry), nor, on the other hand, transcultural translation (since it is an irrelevant worry), which forms our present concern, what is there in between? One may think that it all depends on how broadly we define 'culture'. If we allow for a lenient definition, this argument would maintain, then 'cultures', or

[11] Ibid. No. 87

[12] Ibid. No. 198. See also No. 201: 'What this shows is that there is a way of grasping a rule which is *not* an *interpretation,* but which is exhibited in what we call "obeying the rule" and "going against it" in actual cases.' I have offered a detailed explanation of this Wittgensteinian argument in my *Interpretation and Legal Theory,* ch. 7.

[13] The problem of transcultural translation does pose a difficulty for legal *theory*: it calls into question the possibility of a general, universal, account of the nature of law. I agree with Raz, however, that the problem is generally exaggerated. See Raz, *Engaging Reason*, ch. 6. See also Chapter 8 below.

'subcultures', are abundant even within one and the same legal system, or legal culture, and problems of interpretation would surface anywhere we care to look.

Is this a serious worry? Yes and no. It is certainly true that there are numerous subcultures within any legal community, and it is also true that such cultural divisions may affect the ways in which people understand the law. But none of this can show that understanding the law, or any other form of linguistic expression, is *always* mediated by interpretation. Once it is admitted that solipsism is not a serious worry, and that language is essentially communal, it must be the case that there is a way of understanding the meaning of expressions without interpretation, even if, as we have seen, such an understanding is context dependent. Only people who share the context can learn how to use language. This sharing of context may be relatively narrow, or wide, but sharing it must be, otherwise the meaning of expressions in a natural language would not be learnable.

Furthermore, it should be remembered that in modern legal systems, the law is addressed, first and foremost, to the legal community itself, that is, to lawyers and judges. The legal community is relatively small, and, at least from a linguistic perspective, tightly knit. Lawyers and judges share a very considerable amount of cultural background which is specific to law, due to their uniform legal education. Hence the possibilities of subcultural gaps, and consequently, problems of translation, are not as copious as they would seem to be.

The conclusion that follows is simple enough: the law, like any other form of linguistic expression, can simply be understood, without the mediation of interpretation. Interpretation is an explanation of one thing in terms of another. Such an explanation is called for only if something is not clear within a given context. But a great deal must be clear for a particular unclearness to make any sense at all. The pervasive context dependence of meaning, true as it is, does not entail the conclusion that interpretivists like Dworkin and Fish would like to draw.

THE EPISTEMIC ARGUMENT

It is possible, however, that the first premiss of the argument from interpretation was meant to be understood as an epistemic argument, not as a semantic one. On this reading of Dworkin's premiss, the pervasive need for interpretation does not arise from some inherent indeterminacy of meaning, at the semantic level, but from some deficiency of knowledge, allegedly characteristic of law. Let me try to explore such an epistemic version of the argument. The basic idea would be as follows: even if it is true that we can grasp (that is, without interpretation) the meaning of sentences conveyed in the law at the semantic level, their legal, practical meaning, so to speak, remains uncertain, and we would always need interpretation to remove such uncertainties.

The question is, of course, what is special about such a practice as law that renders it pervasively uncertain. Where is this alleged gap between semantic meaning and practical-legal consequence? The answer, I suppose, consists in the following phenomenon: any given legal norm, precise and explicit as it may be, can be defeated, in the practice of its application by adjudication, by other legal norms which would be held to override or otherwise change the content of the initial norm. Suppose, for example, that a statute of New York State, say, N, prescribes that in all cases of type X, a legal consequence, say C, must follow. Suppose further, that we understand perfectly well what cases of type X consist of, and that there is no doubt that a particular instance, say X_1 falls within its ambit. According to this line of thought, we could still not be certain that N really prescribes that 'if X_1 then C'. Why is that? Because it is always possible to envisage a situation whereby judges would refer to another legal norm, according to which 'if X_1 then C' is invalidated, or otherwise rendered not applicable to the relevant circumstances. In other words, N can always be defeated by other legal standards, and hence if we want to know what the law on cases of types X really prescribes, or whether it is really the case that 'if X_1 then C', we cannot rely on our understanding of N. Only a comprehensive interpretation could yield a reliable conclusion about the law regarding cases of type X, regardless of the clarity or explicitness of N. Hence the alleged gap between the meaning of legal norms, and their practical consequences in concrete cases, which is supposed to be bridged by interpretation.

Once again, we find the claim that interpretation always mediates between the understanding of the law and its application to concrete cases. Note, however, that if the argument is understood as a general epistemic one, it begs the question: if we assume that the law can never be known with adequate certainty, how can interpretation make it more certain? Interpretation is, after all, interpretation *of the law*. If there is *nothing* one can *know* there, then it simply becomes mysterious what epistemic certainty interpretation could add. Therefore, I will not assume that the argument under consideration was meant to be understood as a general epistemic thesis about the possibility of *knowledge* in the domain of law.

Quite apart from this general epistemic point, however, the argument from defeasibility is not convincing. The apparent plausibility of this argument stems from a confusion between *revisability* and *uncertainty*. It is true that from the practitioners' perspective, the law can be uncertain, even where it is clear what the law requires. But this is a peculiarity of law indeed, and it stems from the fact that judges typically have the legal power to *change* the law, and revise it in countless ways.[14] Therefore, if we are interested in the prediction

[14] See our discussion of 'directed powers' in Chapter 3.

of what courts will do in fact, such a prediction is often problematic, since the courts may not follow the law even when the law is quite clear and explicit. But we should be very careful not to confuse the question 'What is the law?', with the question, 'What will the courts decide in particular cases?' As the American Legal Realists were right to point out, the answer to the latter question cannot be derived simply from knowing what the legal rules prescribe. But this truism does not entail that we cannot know what the law is. More often than not, we know what the law is, we just don't know whether the courts will enforce that law, or change it in one way or another. This simple point is often missed, because judges' decisions which change the law typically affect the change retrospectively, and this retrospective change may give the impression that we must have been wrong about the law when we had thought that we know what it is. Furthermore, since the retrospective aspect of changes in the law has a bad taste, as it seems to go against the ideal of the Rule of Law, judges have a particularly strong incentive to conceal the real nature of such decisions by presenting their decision in a law-application rhetoric. This pervasive tendency to speak the language of application when it is really a change that is being done is understandable and perhaps even politically justified; but we should not let ourselves to be confused by it. The revisability of law is indeed what it is, namely, revisability, and not inherent uncertainty. Pervasive uncertainty faces only those who are interested in the possibility of prediction of what the courts will decide (in problematic cases), but this is not necessarily tantamount to uncertainty about what the law is.[15]

Perhaps we can think of a better version of this argument. The pervasive defeasibility of legal norms could be substantiated, if we rely on Dworkin's conception of legal principles. If there are legal principles of the kind Dworkin envisaged, the epistemic argument against the separation thesis would gain considerable strength. Such principles could explain how the application of all legal norms is endemically defeasible. Legal norms, on this view, come in a double layer: on one level, we have legal rules, which, if they apply, determine a particular outcome. On the second level, we have legal principles, which may always apply, though they never determine a particular outcome. Principles only provide a certain reason, legal reason, to decide the case one way rather than the other, reasons which may, or may not, prevail over legal rules. Hence, according to this double-layered picture of legal norms, the application of each and every legal rule must be filtered, as it were, through the relevant principles, and this filtering process is, undoubtedly, a matter of interpretation. Hence interpretation, that is, determining whether

[15] I do tend to agree with Coleman and Leiter, however, that lawyers' general ability to predict legal outcomes is much better than usually assumed by theorists. We can often predict quite accurately what the courts will do in fact, due to our ability to rely on general information about politics, psychology, and similar considerations. Folk psychology has its limits, of course, but it often works well enough. See Coleman and Leiter, 'Determinacy, Objectivity, and Authority'.

the application of the relevant rule to the particular circumstances meets the constraints embodied in the pertinent legal principles, always mediates between the understanding of the law and its application to particular cases.

All this could make sense, of course, only if it is true that there are legal principles of the kind suggested by Dworkin. But there are very good reasons to doubt that there are such principles, and for the rest of this chapter I would like to substantiate those doubts.

LEGAL PRINCIPLES

Let us begin by reminding ourselves what the distinction between rules and principles was meant to be. According to Dworkin's original suggestion, the distinction between rules and principles is basically a logical one.[16] Rules, Dworkin tells us, apply in an 'all or nothing fashion'. If the rule applies to the circumstances, it determines a particular legal outcome. If it does not apply, it is simply irrelevant to the outcome. On the other hand, principles do not determine an outcome even if they clearly apply to the pertinent circumstances. Principles basically provide the judges with a reason to decide the case one way or the other, and hence they only have a dimension of weight. That is, the reasons provided by the principle may be relatively strong, or weak, but they are never 'absolute'. Such reasons, by themselves, cannot determine an outcome, as rules do. Rules, on the other hand, possess no such dimension of weight; or one may say, alternatively, that their weight is always infinite, or absolute.[17]

The most interesting, and from a positivist perspective, most problematic aspect of legal principles, however, consists in their moral dimension. According to Dworkin's theory, unlike legal rules, which may or may not have something to do with morality, principles are essentially moral in their content. It is, in fact, partly a moral consideration which determines whether a legal principle exists or not. Why is that? Because a legal principle exists, according to Dworkin, if the principle follows from the best moral and political interpretation of past judicial and legislative decisions in the relevant domain. In other words, legal principles occupy an intermediary space

[16] Dworkin, *Taking Rights Seriously*, ch. 2.

[17] Dworkin has also been held to maintain that legal principles, as opposed to rules, do not have a canonical formulation. This is probably wrong even as a rough generalization. There is nothing in the logic of principles to entail that they cannot have a canonical formulation. Principles may well acquire a canonical formulation, either by judicial custom or by the enactment of a legislative body. Most standard examples of legal principles do have, in fact, a canonical formulation. Many principles are embodied in constitutional documents, and many others have gained canonical formulation in important precedents (e.g. the famous Learned Hand formulation of the principle of negligence liability). This mistake about canonical formulations should not be confused, however, with the separate question, concerning the *source of validity* of principles, which I discuss in the text below.

between legal rules and moral principles. Legal rules are posited by recognized institutions and their validity derives from their enacted source. Moral principles are what they are due to their content, and their validity is purely content dependent.[18] Legal principles, on the other hand, gain their validity from *a combination* of source-based and content-based considerations.[19] As Dworkin put it in the most general terms: 'According to law as integrity, propositions of law are true if they figure in or follow from the principles of justice, fairness, and procedural due process that provide the best constructive interpretation of the community's legal practice.'[20] The validity of a legal principle, then, derives from a combination of facts and moral considerations. The facts concern the past legal decisions which have taken place in the relevant domain, and the considerations of morals and politics concern the ways in which those past decisions can best be accounted for by the correct moral principles.

Needless to say, if such an account of legal principles is correct, the separation thesis can no longer be maintained. But I will try to argue that this idea of legal principles is seriously misguided. There are no such principles. Neither the logical distinction between rules and principles nor the content-based validity of the latter can be substantiated. Let me explore the logical point first.

Dworkin, as we have seen, envisaged the distinction between rules and principles as a categorical one. Rules apply in 'an all or nothing' fashion. If a rule applies, it determines the outcome. Principles, on the other hand, only have a dimension of weight. As Dworkin himself pointed out, one way to see this logical difference is by noting the difference in the potential relevance of counter-examples to rules and principles. In the case of rules, counter-examples necessarily refute the rule (or, at least, its original formulation) whereas a counter-example to a principle does not necessarily require any revision in the formulation of the principle. Principles, as we have noted, only provide a reason for decision, but the reason is always finite in its weight, and it can be overridden by other reasons which may apply to the particular circumstances. Thus, for example, the often cited principle prohibiting wrongful gains can be defeated by other considerations, allowing certain parties to gain from their own wrongful action as, for example, in the case of adverse

[18] Well, this is actually not quite accurate. It is possible that even morality is partly, though in a very limited way, dependent on social conventions.

[19] Wil Waluchow tells me that it is not so accurate to speak of Dworkinian principles as valid at all, since Dworkin sees validity and weight as logically incompatible properties. This, of course, hinges on Dworkin's claim that legal principles cannot satisfy the criteria of validity embodied in the rules of recognition. I agree that this is how Dworkin sees the point, but I doubt that we have any good reasons to follow such a stipulative definition. We will see later in the text that Dworkin has very good reasons to distinguish between moral principles and legal principles, that is, principles which form part of the law. Forming part of the law is what I call legal validity here. I don't think that Dworkin can object to that.

[20] *Law's Empire*, 225.

possession. Thus, although the existence of adverse possession is a counter-example to the principle that 'no man should be allowed to gain from his own wrong', this does not undermine the validity of the principle itself. The principle only provides a general reason against wrongful gains, but it does not preclude such wrongful gains in an 'all or nothing fashion'. On the other hand, since rules are supposed to have absolute weight, any counter-example to a rule necessarily refutes it. There can be no conflicting legal rules in one and the same legal system.

Even on first impression, however, such a categorical, logical, difference between rules and principles is highly suspect. After all, it is often difficult to tell whether a given legal norm is a rule or a principle. Borderline cases are abundant. Consider, for example, the norms defining the formation of a valid contract, the norms determining the legal responsibility for negligence, the norms determining the right to private property, the general defences in criminal law, and countless such examples. Are these rules or principles? How could we tell? I see no substantial difference between saying that they are principles, which need not necessarily determine a particular outcome even if they apply to a given set of circumstances or, alternatively, that they are a set of rules determining particular outcomes and a set of further rules determining exceptions to the rules. Since both classifications are coextensive in their legal consequences, it may well be impossible to determine the superiority of one description to the other. Either way, we simply know that there is a general norm, and countless more or less recognized exceptions to the general norm.

We should acknowledge, of course, that just pointing to borderline cases is rarely a good argument against a suggested classification. Most classifications have borderline cases. The problem with the rules—principles distinction, however, consists in the ubiquity of such borderline cases. If it is the case that more often than not the decision whether we face a rule or a principle is far from self-evident, then the idea that these two types of norms differ categorically is, to say the least, highly suspect. It simply comes more naturally to think of such a distinction in terms of degree, and not as a dichotomy. As Raz pointed out a long time ago,[21] the relevant difference here concerns the level of generality, or vagueness, of the norm act. Legal rules can be more or less general, or vague, in their definition of the norm act prescribed by the rule, and the more general or vague they are, the more they tend to have those quasi-logical features Dworkin attributes to principles.[22] And vice versa, of course: the more the definition of the norm act prescribed by the rule is

[21] Raz, 'Legal Principles and the Limits of Law'.

[22] There is, of course, a distinction between generality and vagueness of the norm act's definition. Not every norm act defined in general terms is necessarily vague, and vice versa. Often the definition of a norm act, however, is both general and vague (e.g. 'act with reasonable care'). For a more comprehensive account of these distinctions, see Schauer, 'Prescriptions in Three Dimensions'.

specific, the more it would apply in an 'all or nothing fashion', namely, the fewer exceptions to the rule would be recognized. And there is little wonder about that. The more a rule is generally formulated, in terms of the generality of the norm act it prescribes, the more exceptions to its application are to be expected.

Furthermore, the very idea that rules, as opposed to principles, apply in an 'all or nothing' fashion is dubious. It simply means that the reasons for action prescribed by a legal rule must always be assumed to have an absolute weight. If the rule applies to the circumstances, it determines a particular outcome. But this is extremely unlikely. To begin with, and Dworkin basically admits as much,[23] it would entail that rules cannot really conflict. Any apparent conflict between two legal rules must be construed as an appearance of a conflict, which must be assumed to be resolved by another legal rule, determining which one of the two seemingly conflicting rules prevails. But this solution is suspiciously artificial. It is true, of course, that often conflicts between legal rules are actually resolved by a third rule, determining which one prevails. But why should we be so optimistic as to assume that this is always the case? After all, there is no limit to the variety of legal cases potentially falling under different and possibly conflicting rules. Expecting that all such potential conflicts are somehow resolved by the existing rules (or principles, for that matter) seems to be quite groundless.[24] Furthermore, it is doubtful that it makes sense to say that rules have an absolute weight. Weight is a dimension of relative importance that we attribute to reasons or values. Some reasons or values are more important than others, and they weigh more in a potential conflict. But it seems extremely unlikely that there should be reasons or values which are so important as to be of some 'absolute' or 'infinite' weight, even from the limited vantage point of the law.

My argument so far is rather limited. All I have tried to show so far is, that it is more natural to think of the distinction between rules and principles in terms of a continuous scale concerning the level of generality of the norm act prescribed by the rule, than in terms of a dichotomy between two logically distinct types of legal norms. Perhaps no such argument can be conclusive. Nor is this the crucial issue here. The main question is whether it makes sense to suggest, as Dworkin clearly does, that there is a logical space between legal rules and moral principles, occupied by legal principles. Are there, in other words, legal norms which gain their legal validity from a combination of source-based and content-based considerations? If it can be shown that there

[23] *Taking Rights Seriously*, at 72–3.

[24] Here is a typical case of conflict of rules: it often happens that one and the same action in tort potentially falls under two different torts, so that one of the torts comprises a defence denied by the other. In such cases, often the question which tort prevails must be decided by a straightforward comparison of the relative reasons supported by each tort rule. How could such conflicts be resolved if we assume that rules have no dimension of weight?

are such norms, the logical distinction that we have discussed so far is of secondary importance.

In a recent article published by Larry Alexander and Kenn Kress,[25] the authors argue that even if such hybrid norms are 'metaphysically' possible, they would be very unattractive from a normative-moral point of view. Essentially, their main argument is the following. Suppose we face a legal decision which is not determined by the recognized legal rules available in the relevant legal system. How should the judge decide such a case? According to one option, the judge should apply the best *moral* principles available, and reach the best decision, all things considered. Dworkin, on the other hand, would urge the judge to consider whether there is a relevant legal principle. How could the judge decide that there is such a principle? Well, the judge is expected to interpret the relevant past legal decisions in the best possible light. However, the only difference between these two options consists in the requirement of fit. According to Dworkin's option, the judge is constrained by the requirement to fit the interpretation with past legal decisions. Hence there is no assurance that the decision required by this interpretative method would be the best moral decision, all things considered. In other words, if the requirement of fit is not just lip-service, but a meaningful constraint on the available interpretations, then the best interpretation may not be the best moral decision. It would only be a second best, given the constraint imposed by the requirement of fit. Now the following dilemma emerges: either the judge has a conclusive moral reason to prefer this second best solution, or she may have no such reason. If the latter applies, then Dworkin's insistence on the second best is simply groundless, that is, at least from a moral point of view. If, on the other hand, we can show that there are conclusive *moral* reasons to opt for the second best, namely, that there are good moral reasons to opt for the decision which accords past legal decisions a constraining effect, then there is simply no need for legal, as opposed to moral, principles. Morality provides all that is needed for reaching the interpretative decision Dworkin is anxious to assert. Thus, either legal principles are morally unattractive, or else they are simply redundant.

Basically, I think that this is a very good argument against the idea that legal principles should be accorded the role Dworkin assigns them in legal reasoning. But it is doubtful that such a normative argument can show more than this, namely, why adjudication based on legal principles is either morally unattractive, or else, superfluous. Such an argument cannot show, however, that there is something conceptually problematic about the idea of legal principles.

I think that it would be a mistake, however, to leave it at that. Quite apart from being morally incredulous, the idea of legal principles is also untenable

[25] Alexander and Kress, 'Against Legal Principles'. (A symposium was held on this article, see *Iowa Law Review*, vol. 82, Mar. 1997.)

from a conceptual point of view. In order to see this, we should first pull some of the strings together. We can now distinguish between two different conceptions of 'legal principles'. According to one conception, legal principles are simply general rules. That is, they are legal rules which prescribe norm acts in relatively vague or general terms. As a consequence, such rules should be expected to have a relatively large number of exceptions and modifications in further rules and decisions. According to this conception, however, the distinction between rules and principles is not a dichotomous one. Rules and principles are on a continuous scale: the more specific the norm-act definition of the rule, the more 'rule-like' the norm is, and vice versa.[26] It is important to note that the existence of legal principles in this sense, namely, as general rules, poses no particular difficulty for legal positivism. It does not threaten the separation thesis. But of course, Dworkin's conception of legal principles is different. According to Dworkin, legal principles are unique in their source of validity. Their legal validity derives from a combination of source-based and content-based considerations. Is this plausible?

I think that the crucial question is this: can legal principles, of the Dworkinian kind, be distinguished from moral principles? Note that it is Dworkin who must insist on such a distinction between legal and moral principles. After all, he would certainly like to avoid the suggestion that just about everything which is required by morality is, *ipso facto*, part of the law of the community. Only legal, as opposed to moral principles, form part of the law. Hence the crucial question: what is it that distinguishes the two? Now, at least according to Dworkin's recent interpretative theory of law, the answer, as we have seen, is readily available: the requirement of fit. Only those principles which figure in the best interpretation of past legal decisions are legal principles. So it is the constraint of fit with past legal decisions which distinguishes the legal from the non-legal material.

The constraint of fit, however, cannot carry this conceptual burden, and for one main reason: the constraint of fit is far too flexible to yield any reasonable distinction between the legal and the extra-legal material. It is simply indeterminate as regards the potential trade-offs between fit and moral attractiveness. Any interpretation of a piece of legal history can yield countless dilemmas between more fit and less moral attractiveness, or less fit and better morality, and the different results can easily turn out to be *inconsistent*. To this objection Dworkin has actually provided two, almost contradictory, replies. On the one hand, he indicated that he cares little about the distinction between the legal and the extra-legal domains.[27] On the other hand, he insisted that there must be some threshold of fit, below which interpretation becomes invention.[28] Either way, however, the answers are unsatisfactory. As we have earlier indi-

[26] This conception of legal principles is often referred to as the 'standard–rule' distinction.
[27] See his reply to critics, in *Ronald Dworkin and Contemporary Jurisprudence*, at 263.
[28] *Law's Empire*, at 66–7.

cated, Dworkin cannot disregard the distinction between law and morality altogether. After all, the whole interpretative enterprise Dworkin constructed relies on the distinction between interpreting the law and inventing it (in 'hard cases'). Hence the distinction between the legal and the extra-legal cannot be ignored. But the idea that there is a threshold of fit, even if we assume that it makes sense (which is far from clear), would not solve the problem under consideration here. It still leaves open the problem of trade-offs above the threshold. How should judges choose between countless possible equilibria, each one comprising different amounts of fit *v.* morality? After all, both fit and morality admit of degrees, and the higher one scores on both, the better.

To exemplify the problem, consider this, very simplified, case. Suppose Judge Hercules considers the suggestion that there is a legal principle of 'good faith' in pre-contractual negotiations. Assume further, that this alleged legal principle passes the threshold of fit. That is, the interpretation of the relevant legal history would not score very high on the dimension of fit, but it would somehow fit enough to be within the bounds of an acceptable interpretation. Let us further assume that this principle of 'good faith' is highly desirable from a moral point of view. But there is this drawback: a relatively large number of rules and decisions in the country's contract law would have to be interpreted as a mistake; they simply do not fit with this principle of 'good faith'.

Now, it seems to me that according to Dworkin's theory Hercules simply faces an irresolvable dilemma: both assumptions, that the principle of 'good faith' is part of the law, and that it is not, are equally acceptable. Could Dworkin reply to this that *any* principle which passes the threshold of fit is a legal principle, even if this entails that contradictory principles would be part of the same legal system? There is a strong temptation to consider this option seriously. After all, legal principles, according to Dworkin, are only meant to provide reasons of a certain kind; they do not determine, by themselves, legal outcomes. Hence it may seem as if the possibility of contradictory principles is not terribly threatening. But this would be a serious mistake. There is a logical difference between conflicting and contradictory principles. The principle that people are not allowed to commit an assault, and the conflicting principle, that self-defence is permissible, are not in any real contradiction with each other. The principle of self-defence is an exception to the principle forbidding assault, and both principles can be subsumed under one and the same coherent moral conception. But this is not always the case. Some principles are simply contradictory, and mutually exclusive. Either we think, for example, that people should be under an obligation of good faith in their pre-contractual negotiations, or not. Those who suggest that no such obligations should be imposed at the pre-contractual stage do not think of this as an exception to the relevant principle, but as its denial.

Thus, to sum up the argument: we were looking for a possible distinction between moral and legal principles. The only available option Dworkin's theory offers is the criterion of fit. This criterion, however, cannot provide the goods, since it allows for the possibility of contradictory, mutually exclusive, principles.

I realize that the rules–principles distinction has become so much inveterate in contemporary jurisprudence that there is little hope of uprooting it. But there is no need to. As long as it is acknowledged that there is nothing more to principles than the generality, or vagueness, of the norm acts they prescribe, the separation thesis remains intact.[29] Legal principles of the kind suggested by Dworkin, however, are neither morally attractive nor conceptually feasible. Relying on legal principles, then, would not salvage the argument from interpretation. More often than not, the law can simply be understood, and applied, without the mediation of interpretation.

[29] In a recent article on legal principles Stephen Perry has suggested an alternative account of legal principles which may seem to avoid some of these objections to Dworkin's original thesis. See Perry, 'Two Models of Legal Principles'. I cannot go into the necessary details of Perry's arguments here. Suffice it to say, however, that the role Perry assigns to legal principles does not seem to be at odds with the essentials of the separation thesis. What both his arguments and detailed examples seem to show is only the way in which moral considerations are combined with constraints of fit, deference to precedents, etc., in the formation of acceptable legal solutions to *hard cases*. No legal positivist is bound to object to such an account.

5
Authority and Authorship

In this chapter I want to support a certain conception of legal authority. The question I want to address is this: Is it possible to attribute legal authority to a given norm if its authority does not derive from the authority of someone who has issued that norm? Basically, I will try to defend here a negative answer to this question, espousing a personal conception of authority.

In his recent book, *Law and Disagreement*,[1] Jeremy Waldron has put forward a series of arguments purporting to show that the personal conception of legal authority is seriously misguided, at least as applied to the modern conditions of legislation. In this misapprehension of the nature of authority he finds the main flaw in my thesis that legislative intentions could play certain roles in the interpretation of statutes.[2] My intentionalist thesis, he argues, rests on a 'primitive picture of legislation', one which is all too close to John Austin' s notorious command theory of law. The authority of law, Waldron argues, does not necessarily derive from the authority of the legislators.

Now this is a very old topic. At least since Austin formulated the command theory of law[3] the personal conception of authority has been the target of repeated and powerful criticisms, most notably by H. L. A. Hart.[4] In his criticism of intentionalism Jeremy Waldron adds weighty arguments to Hart's stance in this debate and thus presents us with a challenging opportunity to reconsider this important aspect of the nature of legal authority.

Attempting to defend Austin's command theory of law, however, is the surest way nowadays to commit something like intellectual suicide. I shall try to refrain from that. It is certainly not the analogy of law with commands that I want to salvage from Austin, nor is it Austin's conception of legal authority in terms of political sovereignty. On the contrary: part of my argument is meant to show that Hart's most powerful, and indeed convincing, criticisms of Austin's personal conception of authority gain their plausibility from Austin's confusion between the concepts of legal authority and political sovereignty, and from his crude definition of the latter. Austin's superiority over

This chapter is a revised version of my article 'Authorities and Persons', 1 *Legal Theory* (1995), 337. I am indebted to Meir Dan-Cohen, Chaim Gans, Stephen Perry, Joseph Raz, and Martin Stone, for their helpful comments of drafts of this essay.

1 Waldron, *Law and Disagreement*, ch. 6. In the footnotes of this chapter page numbers without further indication will hereinafter refer to ch. 6 of *Law and Disagreement*.

2 Marmor, *Interpretation and Legal Theory*, ch. 8.

3 See Austin, *The Province of Jurisprudence Determined.* I use 'formulated' advisedly: the basic intuitions of Austin's personal conception of authority, and the resemblance of law to a command issued by one person to another, has been well known and espoused by many philosophers before him, most famously, perhaps, by Hobbes.

4 See Hart, *The Concept of Law*, mainly chs. 2–4.

his critics, however, consists in his insight that the law is a product of communication. It is on this basis, namely of the communication model of law, that I will strive to defend the conceptual ties between authorities and persons.

LEGISLATIVE INTENT

The contemporary version of the debate stems from yet another age-old jurisprudential question concerning the role of legislative intent in the interpretation of statutes. My 'attempt to revive the view that reference to legislators' intentions should play a role in the interpretation of statutes whose texts leave issues of meaning, purpose, or application unclear or controversial'[5] forms the immediate target of Jeremy Waldron's criticism. To repeat my argument very briefly: I have claimed that the reasons for deferring to the intentions of legislators can only be derived from the reasons for complying with legal authorities in the first place. Drawing on Joseph Raz's analysis of authority[6] (with which Waldron basically agrees), I have argued that there are two kinds of such reason, both deriving from Raz's 'normal justification thesis'. Roughly, Raz's conception of practical authority maintains that the justification for compliance with an authority must rest on the likelihood that the person subject to the authority will do better by following its provisions than by attempting to rely on his or her own judgement. Now this justification thesis allows for two kinds of reason for the legitimacy of an authoritative directive, which I have called the coordination and the expertise theses. Moreover, the two kinds of reason yield different results with respect to the relevance of the authority's intentions. Very often the relative superiority of the authority over its alleged subjects rests only on its role, or function, in solving coordination problems.[7] In such cases, I have argued, the intentions of the authority are no longer relevant when questions of interpretation arise about the directives it has issued. On the other hand, when the relative superiority of the authority rests on what I have called the expertise thesis, namely, on the fact that the authority 'knows better what ought to be done' in the circumstances, as it were, it does make sense to consult the authority's intentions when questions of interpretation arise. My thesis about the potential relevance of legislative intent to the interpretation of statutes, however, is strictly conditional: if, but only if, it is plausible to ground the authority of certain statutes on the expertise thesis (and if certain other conditions obtain), then it would also be plausible to defer to the

[5] See Waldron, 119.

[6] See Raz, *The Morality of Freedom*, chs. 2–4. See also Raz, 'Authority, Law and Morality'.

[7] That is, very broadly understood to include Prisoner's Dilemma situations, and other collective action problems.

intentions of the legislature in trying to solve interpretative questions that the application of the statute may raise.

Waldron does not challenge any of this. In fact, he seems to be perfectly content to allow the argument to apply under certain conditions, namely, when a 'single author jurisprudence' is appropriate. But such a single author jurisprudence, he claims, is a rare phenomenon in our modern society. 'The modern situation . . . is not that of a person's having authority, but (at most) a group having authority, and of its having authority only by virtue of the way in which it combines the interests and knowledge of its members in the act of legislating.'[8] Thus, the problem, according to Waldron, stems from the multiplicity of legislators, from the fact that statutes are normally the product not of a single legislator who may or may not have expertise relative to his or her subjects, but of legislative bodies, often comprising hundreds of people with a great diversity of views and interests they represent.

It is important not to be tempted to underestimate the force of this argument by thinking that Waldron is worried by the very possibility of attributing intentions to groups of people, as such. By emphasizing the multiplicity of legislators, Waldron does not mean to doubt the conceptual possibility of attributing intentions to the legislative body. His point is much more profound: the multiplicity of legislators in a modern democracy, he argues, is a crucial factor determining the authority of law. The moral and political aspects of this 'multiplicity' point to important reasons for the need to separate the authority of law from the authority of its legislators. Waldron realizes, of course, that one cannot have moral reasons for separating the two if it does not make sense to do so. Hence his argument against intentionalism rests on two limbs. First, he purports to show that there is no conceptual necessity in the connection between the authority of a piece of legislation and the authority of its legislator. Secondly, he advances a series of arguments purporting to show that, at least in modern democracies, the authority of the law should not be derived from the authority of its legislators. I will henceforth call these the conceptual argument and the argument from democracy, respectively. My main concern in this chapter is with the conceptual argument. Let me begin, however, with a few comments on Waldron's argument from democracy.

THE ARGUMENT FROM DEMOCRACY

Waldron presents us with three different models of democracy, each viewing the legitimacy of the democratic legislative procedure from a different perspective. According to the first, the utilitarian model, the democratic procedure is meant to 'aggregate individual preferences in the way required by the applicable social

[8] Waldron, 121.

welfare function.'[9] According to this model, legislators' votes are taken to represent the preferences of their constituents, and the voting procedure is hoped to yield the result which would maximally satisfy those preferences. The second model draws on the Condorcet theorem: it rests on the probabilistic calculation that if (1) voters are more likely to get a given choice right than not, and (2) votes are cast independently of each other, then the probability of getting a correct answer rises as the size of the voters increases. Finally, the third model Waldron presents is the one drawn from Aristotle's claim that the multitude of persons, by a process of deliberative synthesis, may forge a better view than even the wisest of them could come up with on his own.[10]

Waldron is of course well aware of the difficulties these models give rise to, and one gets the impression that he himself would subscribe only to the last, Aristotelian synthesis model.[11] Be this as it may, the main problem with these models is not so much their plausibility as the fact that it is far from clear what it is that they actually show. One may easily get the impression that these models (or one of them) can explain how it is that a decision reached by majority vote can yield results which are better than the reasons for action each agent can figure out for himself. With this I should be the first to agree: it would seem to show just how it is possible for the democratic legislature to have relative expertise precisely in the sense required by the intentionalist thesis. Surely, then, Waldron must mean something else here. I take it that Waldron intends to show how expertise is possible, without the assumption that anyone in particular is an expert; it is only in this aggregative sense, inherent to the majority vote, that 'the legislature' is an expert. Therefore, Waldron concludes, it is pointless to seek further interpretative advice from the intentions of any particular legislator, or group of legislators, as none of them, individually considered, is rightly considered an expert.

But this line of thought is either too strong or too weak. It is too strong if one is to understand the models presented by Waldron in terms of an 'invisible-hand mechanism' (as he at one point suggests[12]). An invisible-hand mechanism may be said to be in place when there is a pattern of behaviour which looks as if it is driven by a certain purpose or *telos*, whereas in fact it is not a purpose that anyone in particular actually had. As Nozick aptly put it, 'An invisible-hand explanation explains what looks to be the product of someone's intentional design, as not being brought about by anyone's intentions.'[13] None of the models presented by Waldron can show that anything like this normally takes place in the process of legislation.[14] At most, the mod-

[9] Waldron, 133. [10] Ibid. 137. [11] See also his *Dignity of Legislation*, ch. 5.
[12] Waldron, 138. [13] Nozick, *Anarchy, State, and Utopia*, 19.
[14] The Utilitarian model might be an exception: if numbers are sufficiently large, and votes are cast independently of each other, representing only self-interested considerations, something like an invisible-hand mechanism might be said to be in place. Waldron, however, does not rely on this particular model.

els can show that *occasionally* a legislative act may not represent the actual purpose or intention of any one of the legislators, in which case, there may not be a legislative intention to consult.[15] To suggest, however, that each and every act of legislation is the product of an invisible-hand mechanism would amount to rendering the act of legislation far more mysterious than it actually is. Legislators, after all, often have well-defined intentions and purposes, and they frequently manage to realize those intentions in enacting the statute they want to enact. There is nothing invisible or mysterious about that.

Furthermore, it is worth noting that the Aristotelian synthesis model is incompatible with invisible-hand mechanisms. As Waldron himself recognizes, the model only works on the assumption that the participants share a common, *bona fide* purpose: differing in their views and personal knowledge as they may, no synthesis will ever emerge if the participants do not share the common purpose of reaching the best possible decision on a particular issue. In other words, the Aristotelian synthesis model is a model which is only applicable to a group-decision procedure, and the invisible-hand mechanism is not. The latter assumes that something like a group decision will emerge under certain conditions, precisely where no decision had been intended.

If Waldron concedes as much, as I believe he does, his argument remains too weak. Suppose it can be shown that in a democratic regime the legislators' expertise is conceivable only in the aggregative sense suggested by Waldron's models. Once we abandon the invisible-hand-mechanism explanation of this, it remains unclear why we should refrain from deferring to the combined, albeit perhaps complex, intention of the group as a whole. Moreover, it is Waldron himself who provides one of the best examples of how such a group intention/expertise is possible, namely, by the Aristotelian synthesis or the 'wisdom of the multitude'.

Waldron is aware of this, and his reply is, to my mind, the crux of his argument: 'The point here is that a particular legislator's intentions may reveal only a partial view of the synthesis embodied in the legislation.'[16] And later he writes, 'For if a judge appeals beyond the text of a statute to the intentions of particular legislators, he will be appealing to things said or done *during* the course of the bill's passage. At that stage, the decisive synthesis may not have emerged or crystallized in individual minds . . .'[17]

Now look how thin the argument has become: we have come a long way only to see that it is not a normative conception of democracy that undermines intentionalism, but the fact that judges are normally bound to see only part of the real legislative intention, because they can only learn about those intentions by appealing to things said or done at too early a stage in the process of legislation. In effect, Waldron claims, judges cannot rely on the

[15] This is a conclusion that I have initially accepted, and I gave an example of how this may come about; see *Interpretation and Legal Theory*, at 163–4.

[16] Waldron, 141.

[17] Ibid.

advantages of the Aristotelian synthesis simply because they have no knowledge of it. Judges have no access to the emergent synthesis, he claims, because it only crystallizes at the very last moment. If one waits for the final synthesis to emerge, Waldron says, 'one will be waiting in effect for the text of the final statute.'[18]

I can certainly concede that legislation sometimes works that way: namely, that it is sometimes the case that only at the very end of the process of legislation the best synthesis underlying the statute crystallizes, as it were. I find it very difficult to understand, however, why this is bound to be the case in each and every act of legislation. The ultimate synthesis may well emerge earlier than the final vote. Furthermore, Waldron's assumption that judges are somehow bound to see only part of the picture seems to me unwarranted as well. When judges look at those things which were said and done during the course of the bill's passage, it is their purpose to gather evidence about the group's intention, that is, if there is one. Nowhere have I claimed that those things which were said and done during the course of the bill's passage are to be equated with the legislature's intention. Such particular intentions, or manifestations of intentions, purposes, and motives, are only of evidential merit. The judge must use such evidence in order to form his or her best judgement about the ultimate synthesis underlying the intention behind the statute, as a whole. The difficulties involved with the reliability of such evidence are well known, of course, and it is certainly not my intention to underestimate them (nor has it escaped my mind in the original essay subject to Waldron's criticism). But I find it difficult to see how these practical difficulties cast a doubt on the conceptual and normative aspects of the intentionalist thesis I have presented.

The impatient reader may well conclude that the disagreement between Waldron and myself at this stage concerns only the frequency of deference to legislative intent, rather than its conceptual possibility or general desirability; I have been trying to suggest that this may well be the case, and perhaps much more so than Waldron concedes.

Quite apart from these models, Waldron seems to suggest another argument based on democratic principles, one which I find politically appealing. Deference to legislative intent, he claims, would entrench a misconception about the morality of the principle of majority rule. 'A statute passed in Parliament', he says, 'is an Act of Parliament, not an act of the majority party.'[19] The moral legitimacy of democratic procedures, Waldron rightly emphasizes, should be based on a non-partisan characterization of such a process, thus disavowing too tight a connection between the authority of the legislature and the authority of the majority. No doubt this is an important ideal, one which should be respected by judges interpreting statutes. But I find

[18] Waldron, 142. [19] Ibid. 144.

it very difficult to see how this political ideal is at odds with the intentionalist thesis I have espoused. Waldron seems to forget at this stage that my argument in favour of deference to legislative intent is strictly confined to the expertise branch of the normal justification thesis. Deference to legislative intent is warranted, I have argued, only if, and to the extent that, the legislature is rightly held to be an expert about the particular issue it had enacted, as compared with its alleged subjects and the courts. If this ever happens, surely it is precisely in those cases where the grounds of legislation are not to be found in partisan politics or in ideologically controversial matters.

Perhaps there is a broader issue here. Waldron believes that a deep tension pervades the 'circumstances of politics', namely, the tension between deep and widespread disagreement over the just and the good, and our social need for concerted public action. The point of legislation, Waldron argues, is to achieve the concerted action we need in spite of the deep disagreements we have over what is just and good.[20] The fact that legislative assemblies typically comprise hundreds of people, representing different world-views, different conceptions of what is right and just, is a key factor in determining the authority of law. It accounts for the fact that acts of legislation deserve our respect precisely because they result from a delicate compromise of radically differing views about justice. Waldron believes, as we have seen, that the same fact also entails that it is only the final result of such a compromise, namely, the canonical text of legislation, that we should treat as the law of the land and respect as such.

This view about the 'circumstances of politics' raises, however, two difficulties. First, once Waldron insists, as he does, on the depth and pervasiveness of disagreement in pluralistic societies, and on the fact that legislative assemblies reflect such a radical pluralism, the Aristotelian synthesis model of legislation becomes highly suspect. If disagreements are so deep and unavoidable, how can we seriously hope that Aristotle's 'wisdom of the multitude' would be applicable to legislative assemblies? How can a coherent synthesis emerge from such a divided legislature?

One plausible answer is that Waldron has initially exaggerated the background of disagreement in politics, and this is the second, and more significant, problem here. Sure, we disagree about justice and rights as we disagree about the good. Waldron is probably right to maintain that even under ideal modes of deliberation rational people may still end up with reasonable disagreements about justice. His mistake lies, however, in the assumption that most of the functions of law in our society concern such deeply disputed matters of principle. In fact they do not. As we have seen in Chapter 2, a great many functions of law in a modern society, perhaps most, concern such issues as the solution of coordination problems, resolution of collective action

[20] See Waldron, *Law and Disagreement*, ch. 5.

problems like Prisoners' Dilemma situations, and what Thomas Aquinas famously called 'determinatio', that is, rendering concrete abstract principles which need to be applied to specific situations. Law is often required to achieve all this, and much more, despite the fact that there is no disagreement of principle lurking in the background of such collective action problems.[21]

THE CONCEPTUAL ARGUMENT

These brief comments on Waldron's argument from Democracy cannot be conclusive either way. The plausibility of Waldron's thesis mainly depends on his conceptual argument, and it is to his conceptual point that we must turn now. The main fallacy in my thesis, he argues, 'lies in forging too tight a connection between authority and authorship. On the Raz/Marmor account authority cannot be systemic: it must be attributable to an author.'[22] In order to show that this is indeed a fallacy, Waldron suggests a reformulation of Raz's normal justification thesis, which reads as follows:

> [J]: A statute (or any text) S has authority over a person Y only if person Y is likely better to comply with reasons which apply to him by following the provisions of S, than if he tries to follow those reasons directly.[23]

In order to satisfy thesis [J], Waldron argues, there is no need to assume that S has an author. The actual authorship of S, he claims, is at most a special case. S can be conceived as authoritative in the sense required by [J] even if there is no person who has ever issued S.[24]

Waldron is certainly correct to contend that his impersonal conception of authority is at odds with my own. In my arguments concerning legislative intent, I have assumed, following Joseph Raz,[25] that (1) law is intelligible only if it claims to possess legitimate authority; (2) for something to be able to claim legitimate authority, it must be of the kind of thing which is capable of possessing it; and (3) only persons who can communicate with others are capable of possessing authority.[26] Now it seems clear that Waldron is challenging only my last premiss. For something to be capable of possessing authority, he argues, it need not be a person.

Waldron provides us with two examples of how this may come about. The first is the 'Wollheim machine': suppose we envisage a certain machine, say a computer, which is fed with various choices of individual citizens. The machine then aggregates these choices according to a pre-established method

[21] A great many disagreements in the legislature about policy and the enactment of statutes concern matters of fact and assessments of efficiency and cost–benefit calculations. Interestingly, the Condorcet theorem might explain why large legislative assemblies are likely to get such factual matters right due to the large number of voters.

[22] Waldron, 130. [23] Ibid. 131. [24] Ibid.

[25] Raz, 'Authority, Law, and Morality'.

[26] For a more detailed argument see Chapter 3.

and so comes up with 'what may be called a "choice" of its own'.[27] The citizens of this Wollheim democracy, then, will regard the machine's outputs as authoritative. The point of this thought experiment (which, of course, is not the same as Wollheim's), Waldron claims, 'is that it enables us to envisage a piece of legislation that cannot be conceived as . . . something produced "by an intentional being . . . situated in some enterprise in relation to which he has a purpose or point of view".'[28]

The second example is yet another machine, but one which we are more familiar with: for those who are bad at keeping track of their financial transactions, the bank may provide an easy solution. Call a certain telephone number, and an automatic voice machine will let you know your balance within seconds. The output of this automatic voice machine, Waldron claims, 'is authoritative for me in terms of thesis [J]: I do better by relying on this text for information about the outstanding balance on my credit card than I would by relying on my own forgetful computations.'[29]

To this we may add a third example, one suggested by Michael Moore: 'Suppose it were the case that clouds, like dreams, were in fact devices for generating self-knowledge. . . . The value of self-knowledge in such a case makes clouds and dreams a text even though there need be no author of them.' [30]

What these examples are meant to show, then, is that we can regard certain texts as authoritative, even if those texts have no author and thus do not express the views of anyone concerning how others ought to behave. I find these examples, however, unconvincing, mainly because they fail to distinguish reasons for action (or belief) that texts can generate from reasons that are distinctively authoritative. No one need deny the former. Surely, people can regard certain texts, machine outputs, clouds, or whatever, as reasons for action or belief, regardless of authorship. But such reasons cannot be authoritative. The reasons for action that emerge from an authoritative directive must have certain features, and those features are absent in these examples.

First and foremost, authoritative directives are taken to yield (partly) content-independent reasons for action.[31] Admittedly, the concept of content independence in this context is notoriously difficult to define, but I hope that it will become clearer as we go along. For the moment, it suffices to say that one's reasons for complying with an authority's directive, as such, cannot be based solely on the content of the directive. They must he based, *inter alia*, on the fact that the directive has been issued by an authority. The authority, as such, must make a practical difference. After all, there is an indefinite number and variety of texts that can yield reasons for action which are not authoritative in any meaningful sense. A text is authoritative only if there is no direct connection between the reasons for complying with it and its content. Now, I

[27] Waldron, 126; see Wolleheim, 'A Paradox in the Theory of Democracy', 75.

[28] Waldron, 127. [29] Ibid. 132. [30] Moore, 'Interpreting Interpretation', 13.

[31] See, for example, Hart, *Essays on Bentham*, ch. 10.

take it that Waldron would agree with this. His mistake lies, however, in a misconception of what content independence consists of: having a reason for believing that a certain text contains the truth, so to speak, does not render the reason content independent, as Waldron's examples seem to imply.

Consider this example: suppose I am travelling in a foreign country. Naturally, I have very good reasons for believing that I am more likely to get from A to B by consulting my roadmap. The roadmap, however, is not an authoritative text. My reasons for consulting the map are exclusively content dependent. Even the slightest suspicion that the map I happen to possess is inaccurate would cast a doubt on my reasons for following it, and in a way which is directly related to the objective correctness of the map. Suppose that I observe a path which is not depicted in the map. The only conclusion I may draw is that the map is not up to date, and that I had better be cautious. The inaccuracy of the map is bound to have a direct bearing on my reasons for following it, because the map is not an authority, even if it is still true that I am more likely to get from A to B by consulting the map than by trying to figure out the way for myself.

Waldron's conception of authority however, renders it impossible to distinguish content-independent reasons from content-dependent ones. According to thesis [J], a roadmap is an authoritative text, and so is every text one would have reasons to believe is useful or indicative of truth in some other way. But not every useful text is authoritative. Waldron's conception of authority in terms of thesis [J] disregards the most distinctive feature of an authority in yielding content-independent reasons for action.[32]

This, I take it, suffices to show the inadequacy of two of the three examples mentioned, namely the automatic voice machine and the self-knowledge-generating clouds.[33] The Wollheim machine might be different. There it seems that the subjects do have something like a content-independent reason for following the machine's output in a way akin to authoritative directives. But it should be realized that there are two possible interpretations of the situation here, depending on how the citizens of this imaginary Wollheim democracy regard this unique process. It is not impossible to attribute to them the belief that the machine is the author of its directives as this is required by the personal conception of authority. Note the interesting formulation Waldron cites from Wollheim here: 'the machine then . . . comes up with what might be called a "choice" of its own.' We all know, of course, that machines do not make choices. But some of us atheists know that of God too. Yet for those who believe in divine commands, God is the author and the

[32] Note that it is not the particular formulation of thesis [J] that I find wanting, nor do I claim that it is an implausible interpretation of Raz's normal justification thesis. Waldron's mistake lies in the fact that he ignores other, important elements in our conception of authority, some of which I will indicate more clearly in the sequel.

[33] As Martin Stone pointed out to me, it is hard to see how the voice machine's output is based on reasons at all, in which case Raz's dependence thesis is out of place here too.

authoritative source of His directives. And so may be the Wollheim machine. Whether the procedure can be taken as a reasonable model of legislation is, of course, a separate question (and in the previous section I have already indicated my reasons for believing why it could not be so viewed). To the extent, however, that people have reasons to follow the machine's outputs, this unique process must be made intelligible to them, and one way of doing this is by regarding the machine as if it comes up with a 'choice' of its own.

The more serious option, however, is that the citizens of the Wollheim democracy do not regard the machine's output as anything beyond the product of a calculus. Say, the machine simply adds up the individual preferences according to some agreed method, and that nobody regards the process as representing anything like a choice of the machine. The question then arises: in what sense is the machine's output authoritative, over and beyond the authority of the pre-agreed method which is bound to be (as Waldron readily concedes) the product of someone's authorship? The answer is simple: in no sense whatsoever. To see this, suppose that there is a great mathematician in the Wollheim democracy who carries out precisely the same calculations concomitantly with the machine and, let us assume, with exactly the same accuracy. Surely there would be no difference whatsoever between the authority of the machine's output and that of the mathematician's. Both would be conceived of only as 'tools' for discovering the authoritative resolution; none of them is the authority.

Perhaps another way to summarize the point I have been trying to make is this: Waldron's conception of authority is, at best, an account of theoretical authorities; thesis [J] provides the essence of theoretical authorities. It does not capture, however, the unique features of a practical authority. Only practical authorities can be regarded as yielding content-independent reasons for action. As opposed to this, if a certain text is conceived as a theoretical authority, the reasons for action or belief it generates cannot be regarded as content independent along the lines I have suggested. A person or a text may be regarded as a theoretical authority if indeed the conditions of thesis [J] are fulfilled. As long as I have reason to believe that I will get things right if I rely on S, better than I would if I had been trying to figure out the reasons for myself, S is a theoretical authority for me, be it the product of authorship or not.

The distinctions between practical and theoretical authorities are notoriously controversial, but I think they may be worth exploring here further, as they may facilitate our understanding of content independence, which I claim to be of unique relevance to practical authorities. Theoretical authority is often distinguished from practical authority in terms of the distinction between reasons for belief as opposed to reasons for action. A theoretical authority, it is often suggested, is the source of reasons for belief, as opposed to a practical authority, which is taken to generate reasons for action. It doesn't take much to realize that this distinction, as it stands, is rather dubious. When I consult a physician, and she advises me to undergo a certain treatment, obviously I have reasons for believing that she is more likely to be right than I am, and this in itself is also a reason for me to undergo the treatment. The same more or less applies to just about every authority I can think of. And no wonder; after all, reasons for action are necessarily entangled with a whole range of beliefs about facts, values, and what not. Having a reason for action must involve reasons for believing that this action, and not some other action, ought to be done, and this normally involves a wide range of beliefs about numerous things. And vice versa, of course: reasons for belief often give rise to reasons for action. We must have some other grounds for distinguishing a theoretical authority from a practical one.

We often speak about theoretical authorities while referring to some special expertise a given person or text is held to possess. Thus, one might say, for example, 'Jones is an authority in the history of seventeenth-century England.' What one means by this is simply that Jones is an expert in his field and therefore he is probably much more likely to get things right in his field than most others. (The same, perhaps, might be said of a text, even if we know nothing about its author. We may have established in the course of time and experience, for instance, that this text 'gets things right' for us in its field, even if we do not quite understand why and how.) Now one may wonder, what is it that distinguishes such theoretical authorities from practical, and I would want to say, genuine authorities? Why should there be a difference at all?

Joseph Raz suggested that the answer lies in the fact that the directives of a practical authority are taken to impose obligations, whereas the reasons engendered by so-called theoretical authorities are not conceived as obligatory.[34] Thus, one who accepts the practical authority of S must believe that he has an obligation to obey S's authoritative directives. Theoretical authorities, on the other hand, do not impose obligations. Raz's distinction is, in fact, more sophisticated than this: The nature of the obligations created by practical authorities is of a special kind, explained by his pre-emption thesis.[35] The details of this pre-emption thesis, however, should not concern us here. Instead, I would like to dwell on some of the implications of Raz's main insight here, namely, the idea that there is a special practical significance of practical authorities, which is absent in so-called theoretical authorities. Whether this practical difference is best captured by the idea of an obligation or pre-emptive reasons is a difficult question I will not try to resolve here.

We cannot begin to understand the concept of a practical authority, however, unless we first clarify the idea that an authority must make a practical difference. One important way in which an authority makes such a difference consists in the fact that the reasons for action generated by the authority are

[34] Raz, *The Morality of Freedom*, ch. 2. [35] Ibid. 57–62.

not directly and exclusively affected by their objective correctness. If S is an authoritative text, prescribing an action A, it must be conceivable for the alleged subjects of S to have a reason for doing A (which is not necessarily conclusive of course), even if S is objectively mistaken and there is no reason for doing A, that is, apart from the fact that A has been prescribed by an authority. This is an element, of course, which is completely absent in the case of theoretical authorities. To revert to our example: if Jones states a certain observation concerning seventeenth-century England, say T, which I happen to *know* to be false, then the fact that Jones is an authority in his field provides no independent grounds for my believing T. Of course, Jones's authority may make me suspicious of my grounds for disbelieving T, and it may drive me to double-check my evidence; but none of this adds an independent reason for believing T. Once I know that T is false, Jones's authority becomes irrelevant. This is not the case, however, with practical authorities. The fact that S is an authority for me and that it prescribes doing A may well give me a reason for doing A, even if I know that S is mistaken in prescribing it. The reasons created by authoritative resolutions can be overridden, of course, but they are never rendered practically irrelevant.

PRACTICAL AUTHORITY AND THE PROBLEM OF MISTAKE

The conclusion that authorities must make a practical difference even if they are known to be objectively mistaken is doubly problematic. First, it requires an explanation: why should people have reasons to follow an authoritative directive if they know that the directive is mistaken? Second, and more specifically, the thesis may seem to be at odds with the expertise branch of the normal justification thesis I have relied on. I have argued that deference to legislative intent is sometimes warranted on the grounds that the authority knows better what ought to be done, as it were. If the authority's legitimacy rests on its relative expertise, however, it would seem to rule out the irrelevance of mistake. The knowledge that the authority is mistaken, so this argument would run, undermines the entire basis of its legitimacy.

These two questions are related, of course, but not in a straightforward way. The irrelevance of mistake is easily accountable on the grounds of the coordination branch of the normal justification thesis. If it is the case that the legitimacy of an authoritative resolution rests on its function in solving a coordination problem, the fact that its resolution is not optimal, or partly mistaken, does not necessarily undermine the subjects' reasons for obeying it. After all, even a partial or imperfect solution of a coordination problem is often better than no solution at all. Suppose, for example, that my faculty is considering the purchase of new personal computers, deliberating whether to buy IBM or Macintosh. Now it may well be the case that it is more important to insist on the uniformity of the computers purchased than the particular choice between the two kinds. Suppose, then, that the faculty decides on the Macintosh and that the decision was objectively wrong: the IBM would have served us better. Nevertheless, given the greater importance of uniformity we have good reasons to obey the faculty's decision, even if it is partly mistaken.

The situation is more complicated when we consider authoritative resolutions which are based on the expertise thesis. In order to account for the irrelevance of mistake in this case, we must point out that there is a distinction between the legitimacy of an authoritative directive and the subjects' reasons for following it. In other words, the normal justification thesis points only to the primary reasons for following an authority's directive, but the alleged subjects of the authority typically have other, secondary and auxiliary reasons as well. It is these auxiliary reasons which provide one important explanation for the fact that people should follow an authority's directive which is objectively mistaken, even if it purports to be based on the expertise thesis.[36]

Auxiliary reasons for obeying an authority are of various kinds. First and foremost are those which consist of the subjects' reasons for maintaining and upholding the authority's general ability to carry out its tasks.[37] These reasons may comprise both personal and institutional aspects. Consider this trivial example: my dean happens to be a fairly good dean; his decisions are mostly sensible and warranted. However, in some cases, he reaches decisions which are far from optimal. Sometimes he is simply mistaken. I believe, however, that I have good reasons for obeying his mistaken decisions, partly because my doing so helps to maintain his personal authority among our staff and, more importantly, because it helps in upholding the authority of the dean's office. These are auxiliary reasons, of course, as they do not form part of the normal justification thesis. But they are quite common and often provide powerful reasons for obedience, even if the authority happens to be mistaken.

Needless to say, auxiliary reasons of this kind would normally prevail only if certain conditions obtain. For one, the authority must be presumed to be by and large legitimate, along the lines required by the normal justification thesis. Second, the auxiliary reasons must weigh against the objective primary reasons for disobeying the authority's directive when the latter is mistaken. Finally, if the reasons for obedience are auxiliary, the act of obedience must

[36] Note that Raz was careful to formulate his justification thesis in terms of 'the normal' justification, thus indicating, I believe, his own view that a distinction may exist between the legitimacy of an authoritative directive and its alleged subjects' reasons for following it. On the other hand, his explanation for the need to follow, occasionally, mistaken directives, partly based on his interesting distinction between 'clear' and 'great mistakes', is, I believe, not entirely persuasive. A detailed analysis of Raz's views on these issues, however, exceeds the scope of this chapter. Basically, my point is that Raz has underestimated the importance of auxiliary reasons in this context.

[37] See, for example, Gans, *Philosophical Anarchism and Political Disobedience*, 71.

be public. After all, if the only reason for following an authority consists of the need to support and uphold its ability to function effectively, this objective would not be achieved unless people are aware of the act of obedience and it is publicly recognized as such.

There is a second important kind of auxiliary reasons for following authoritative directives, one which is more closely tied to the primary reasons for obedience. Very often, the authority purports to decide a practical issue on expertise grounds (or so it should be expected to do), but the subjects' reasons for obeying such a directive consist mainly of coordination considerations; this is a prevalent category of mixed justification. Sometimes, even in matters requiring expertise, it may be practically more important to have an authoritative resolution than having the details of the resolution right. Determining the levels of income tax, for instance, requires a great deal of expertise in economics, social welfare policy, morality, etc. An authority purporting to decide on these matters must be presumed to rely on the expertise branch of the normal justification thesis. Nevertheless, it may well be more important for us to have an authoritative resolution on these matters than to have the details right. Even if the authority has made a mistake, its alleged subjects may have reasons to follow its directive, reasons which are based on considerations of coordination. Once again, there are numerous conditions which must obtain for these auxiliary reasons to prevail, but we need not go into the details here.

To sum up the argument so far: it is typical of practical authorities that the reasons for following their directives are a combination of primary and auxiliary considerations. The auxiliary reasons explain why the putative subjects of an authority may have good reasons for following its directives, even if the authority's directive is known to be objectively mistaken. This, I have argued, is one important sense in which an authority is rightly held to generate content-independent reasons for action. Now if this is correct, it would also show why the so-called theoretical authorities are very different from practical authorities: the reasons for belief (or action) they engender lack these features of content independence. Nor do we have auxiliary reasons for following theoretical authorities. Finally, to revert to Waldron's arguments, we may conclude that he has failed to demonstrate how the examples of authority without author he relies on are practical authorities: none of them can be taken to engender content-independent reasons for action.

Admittedly, all this only leaves us with a partial reply to Waldron. The conclusion that his arguments in support of an impersonal conception of authority are not convincing does not prove that he is basically wrong. We need some positive arguments showing why authorship is a conceptual prerequisite of practical authority. We also need, as Waldron rightly claims, a convincing reply to H. L. A. Hart's famous arguments against Austin's personal conception of authority.

HART *V.* AUSTIN

One of John Austin's greatest mistakes in his description of legal authority consists in his failure to recognize that an authority, as opposed to a gunman, must *claim* to be legitimate. It may well fail to satisfy its claim to legitimacy, of course, but it must be presumed to claim it. In other words, an authoritative directive is either binding on its subjects, or else it fails to be binding. But it must claim to be binding in order to count as an authoritative directive. This, I thought, following Joseph Raz, should be sufficient to show that only those things which can claim legitimacy can be authorities. In order to claim legitimacy one must be able to communicate with others; only those who can express a view about how others ought to behave, I have concluded, can count as authorities, hence the conclusion that authority requires authorship. But perhaps the conclusion is not so evident, and for reasons which lurk behind some of Hart's main arguments against Austin's conception of legal authority. The problem is this: even if one concedes that—as a matter of fact—the authority of law needs some authorship, the authority of the law may not derive from the authority of its factual author. Not, as Waldron suggested, because there need not be an author, but because the author may lose its authoritative significance over time or if certain conditions obtain.

Assessing Hart's arguments, however, it is important not to be misled by specific flaws in his target; Austin's characterization of legal authority is seriously misguided, even from the vantage point of the personal conception of authority. Much has been said against his crude definition of sovereignty in terms of habitual obedience, and we need not repeat those obvious points here. More importantly, however, Austin has made a grave mistake in identifying the concept of legal authority with that of political sovereignty. Hart was right to observe that from a legalistic point of view, the identity of the sovereign thoroughly depends on the rules of law, not vice versa.[38] Only on the basis of the rules and conventions constituting the rules of recognition can we identify certain people as the (legal) sovereigns. Moreover, the fact that we can have non-legal definitions of political sovereignty would not save Austin's view either, simply because the concept of political sovereignty is not necessarily tied to that of legal authority. From a political or sociological vantage point, the two institutions are not necessarily (and often not even practically) identical. Hence, either Austin's identification of legal authority with political sovereignty is legalistic, in which case it involves a vicious circle (as Hart observed), or else it is sociological, in which case it is an empirical generalization, and a dubious one at that.

[38] Hart, *The Concept of Law*, 75; and compare Austin, *The Province of Jurisprudence Determined*, 11.

What remains as a genuine target, however, is Austin's insight that the authority of law derives from the authority of its author. Furthermore, Austin's definition of law in terms of commands, flawed as it is, involves an insight that is basically correct, namely that the law is a product of an act of communication.

Bearing these clarifications in mind, let us turn to the assessment of Hart's argument. Our aim, then, is to see whether his arguments have a bearing on a personal conception of authority, even if we no longer subscribe to Austin's definitions of legal authority in terms of political sovereignty and the latter in terms of habitual obedience.

Apart from his argument concerning the circularity of Austin's definition, mentioned earlier, Hart has advanced three main arguments against Austin's personal conception of authority. The first is the argument concerning the continuity of law: 'How can law made by an earlier legislator, long dead, still be law for a society that cannot be said habitually to obey him?'[39] In every legal system, Hart claimed, we have 'rules which bridge the transition from one law giver to another,'[40] and the authority of these rules, *ex hypothesi*, cannot derive from the authority of the habitually obeyed lawgiver, that is, even if at one point or another, it has originated in a law-creating act.

Hart's second argument, one which is also mentioned by Waldron, concerns the ideal of the rule of law. As Austin himself readily admitted, his definition of legal authority entails that the sovereign cannot be subject to law; there cannot be any legal limitations on legislative power. But this conclusion, Hart rightly observed, is at odds both with legal practice and the moral ideal of the rule of law.[41]

Finally, Hart has argued at length that Austin's definitions make it utterly problematic to account for custom as a source of law. Custom cannot be viewed as the expression of an authority about how its alleged subjects ought to behave. Austin's device of a 'tacit order' to account for customary law has been Hart's main target of criticism here.[42] Let us now take up these points one by one.

The continuity of law

The problem of the continuity of law should be divided into two separate questions. Hart's main worry here is best summarized by the question: how is it possible, on Austin's account, to explain the legal authority of transition rules? But it is easy to see that this particular worry stems exclusively from Austin's definition of legal authority in terms of habitual obedience. As Hart aptly put it, '[the question is] how, on the basis of the simple scheme of habits of obedience, it could be said that the first law made by a successor to the

[39] Hart, *The Concept of Law*, 60–1. [40] Ibid. 53. [41] Ibid. 42. [42] Ibid. 46–8.

office of legislator is already law before he personally received habitual obedience.'[43] Thus, once we jettison Austin's theory of habitual obedience as the basis of the identification of authority, the question about the continuity of law can no longer be seen as the question about the authority of transition rules. According to Raz's account of legal authority, transition rules are no more mysterious or question-begging than any other legal rule that is held to be in force after its legislator is personally not the legal authority any more.

But now it seems that Hart's worries about the continuity of law can be reformulated, and this is the second, more relevant question that arises here: how, based on the personal conception of authority, do we account for the legal authority of old laws? (By the term 'old laws' I mean those legal rules which are taken to be authoritative, despite the fact that their author is no longer the legal authority). To account for the authority of old laws, it seems that the authority of law must be presumed to extend beyond the authority of its author. In democratic regimes it is a frequent phenomenon that the laws of one legislature are held to be binding even after it has been replaced by another legislature several years later. How should we account, then, for the authority of old laws?

It may well strike the reader at this point that the puzzle is itself somewhat puzzling. After all, it is one of the most entrenched conventions of each and every legal system that the laws enacted by an authority are held to be valid until they are repealed by a subsequent authority (or until they lose their validity on some other established grounds). Thus, it seems that we have an easy answer to the question about old laws: their authority derives from the rules or conventions determining the continuing validity of norms in the legal system. These continuity rules or conventions may well be regarded as part of the rules of recognition of the legal system.

It seems to me that the only reason for seeing a mystery where there is none stems from a misconception of the personal nature of the personal conception of authority. The latter requires that the law, like any other authoritative directive, be the product of an act of communication, as it must reflect the view of someone in an authoritative capacity about how others ought to behave. It is not the personal attributes of the author, however, which render him or her an authority. We defer to certain people as authorities not because they have certain personal attributes, but because they act in an authoritative capacity or role. It is their role identity and not their personal identity that matters. Of course, it normally matters who occupies the particular role. We are never indifferent to the personal identity of the authority; it always matters who the legislators are. But the reasons for deferring to an authority are basically role-dependent reasons: we defer to the authority of X, because X is an authority and not because he is X.

[43] Hart, *The Concept of Law*, 46–8.

The importance of role identity is not confined to authorities. It plays a similar role in numerous other contexts where reasons for action or belief are partly content independent. Consider Sarah's reason for deferring to her friend's requests. Jim is Sarah's best friend. Sarah believes that she would have reasons for acting on Jim's requests, because she believes that it is part of her conception of friendship to defer to requests of her friends. Her reasons, then, are partly content independent. But they are also, and for the same reasons, role dependent. If Jim asks her, say, to make some inquiries for him, she would feel that she has a good reason to do so, partly (or perhaps even mainly) because Jim happens to be her best friend. It is his role as a friend which matters here. The fact that she does not regard it as accidental that Jim and not somebody else is her best friend is beside the point now. Given that the role of best friend is occupied by Jim, so to speak, and given her convictions that one should defer to one's best friend's requests, Sarah has a reason to defer to Jim's request.[44]

The same holds true, and more obviously so, with the role identity of legal authorities. Thus, once we see that there is nothing really personal about the personal conception of authority, the mystery about the authority of old laws should dissipate. The rules of recognition define the sources of legal validity, and these must comprise the role identity of the legislators and, *inter alia*, the rules about the continuity of law. The only assumption of the personal conception of authority is that somebody in an authoritative capacity must have issued the law. This is a conceptual point about the sources of law. It should not be taken to entail that the requirement of authorship is exhaustive of the conditions of the validity of law. Old laws are valid because they are held to be valid according to the rules of recognition; but they must be made law first.

The rule of law

The concept of role identity may also help in the discussion of Hart's argument concerning the rule of law. Hart was certainly right to observe that Austin's definition of legal authority renders it difficult to account for the fact that legislators see themselves, as they should, subject to the laws they enact. In other words, it seems that the personal conception of authority is incapable of explaining the self-binding force of legislation. A similar point is raised by Waldron: 'It is an important part of our normative concept of legal authority that the legislators themselves should be bound by the laws they enact. On the

[44] Note, however, that I do not intend to claim that role dependence is a necessary condition for content independence of reasons. It is possible that one's reasons for action would be partly content independent even in the absence of a structured role, such as friendship. Sarah may simply be in love with Jim, and consequently she may act on the basis of his requests, in a manner which is partly content independent. This is intelligible even if we are reluctant to define the object of 'being in love with . . .' in terms of a role. I am indebted to Meir Dan-Cohen for bringing this to my attention.

Raz/Marmor approach, it is impossible that the law could have authority *vis-à-vis* a legislator, for it makes no sense to say that X has better reason to trust the directives of X than he has to trust his own reasoning on the matter that X is addressing.'[45]

Hart, however, was well aware of a possible solution: Austin could rely on the distinction between the personal and the official capacity of the sovereign. He could then claim that the sovereign in his personal capacity is bound by those laws which he has enacted in his official capacity. Hart's objection to this model is twofold: first, he claims, even if we can distinguish between the two capacities of the legislator, it is a distinction we can only draw on the basis of pre-existing laws—i.e. those power-conferring rules which define the legislative power. Secondly, Hart argues, the device is superfluous. Once we understand that legislative power, as such, presupposes the existence of rules, the self-binding force of legislation is explicable on the same grounds as the self-binding force of promise (or indeed, Hart could have claimed, like the self-binding force of a move in a game). Thus, he concludes, 'The legislator is not necessarily like the giver of orders to another: someone by definition outside the reach of what he does. Like the giver of a promise he exercises powers conferred by rules: very often he may, like the giver of a promise must, fall within their ambit.'[46]

Both these points, however, are only partly correct. As regards the first, it is certainly true that the concept of an official capacity, or as I would prefer to call it, role identity, requires the background of a practice. There must be a practice of friendship, for example, for someone to be able to count as a friend. But as the example of friendship shows, the practice need not be constituted by power-conferring rules (though perhaps it happens to be so constituted in the case of legislators). In their everyday transactions, people normally act in different roles and capacities, some more structured than others, and these roles are defined by practices with which people identify, to various degrees. Most of these roles, however, have little, if anything to do with power-conferring rules. The actor on a stage, the secretary of a commercial firm, a scholar, a spouse, and so on, are acting in their roles, and they are easily identifiable as such, regardless of power-conferring rules.[47] Thus, the fact that people feel bound by the conventions of the roles they play is far more prevalent, and often much less structured, than Hart seems to have noticed.

All this shows, however, that it is only Hart's second argument which is potentially addressed against the personal conception of authority. It is not the dual capacity that explains the self-binding nature of legislation, he claims, but the analogy of lawmaking with the making of a promise. In both cases, it is not necessarily 'other-regarding'. Lawmaking, in other words, is more like a move in a game; the consequences of the move are defined and

[45] Waldron, 138–9. [46] Hart, *The Concept of Law*, 43.
[47] See Dan-Cohen, 'Law, Community and Communication'.

constituted by the rules, and those may either be other-regarding, self-regarding, or both.

At this point, however, one becomes somewhat bewildered. What is the difference between a promise and an order, then? Is it not clear that, just like a promise, an order is also intelligible only on the background of 'certain rules which govern the process'? If the making of a promise is like a move in a game, so is the issuing of an order. The fact that promises are self-regarding and orders are other-regarding is simply beside the point in this respect. Both are possible only against the background of a practice constituted by rules and conventions which give the action its particular significance. One difference is that the practice of promises is not tied to any specific role the promisor is held to occupy, whereas the practices which lie behind orders are normally closely tied to certain roles the giver of the order must be held to occupy. But, surely, legislation is much more like giving orders than like making a promise in this respect.

The conclusion of all this is that we have two valid explanations for the self-binding nature of legislation. One explanation consists in the dual capacity of legislators: there is no reason, or at least none has been offered by Hart, to reject the simple point that legislators, in their personal capacity, are held to be bound by those laws they enact in their official capacity. Moreover, even from the vantage point of their official capacity, legislation can be self-binding, like a promise or a move in a game. The fact that this is a feature of legislation which is only explicable on the grounds of a pre-existing practice, constituted by rules or conventions, may pose some difficulties for Austin's definition of sovereignty, perhaps, but not for a personal conception of authority as such.

Waldron may concede as much. But, he seems to suggest, there is a special problem here concerning the expertise branch of the normal justification thesis. How can we understand the self-regarding nature of expertise, he asks? How can a legislator, even from the vantage point of his dual capacity, be thought to be an expert compared to his own reasoning? If the authority of the legislator consists in his or her expertise, we cannot make any sense, he claims, of the self-binding nature of authority. The reply to this is actually twofold: first, there is no reason to assume that the self-binding nature of legislation (i.e. in terms of its underlying legitimacy) rests on the same grounds as its other-regarding authority. The legislator's reasons for respecting the laws they have enacted need not always be the same as the reasons applying to their alleged subjects. The former consists of those values served by certain well-known aspects of the rule of law. They simply need not derive from the normal justification thesis. Secondly, it is not so absurd, as Waldron implies, to think of someone as bound by his or her own expertise. A physician, for example, who becomes ill, may consult herself, as it were, about the best way to treat herself. If she's an expert in the relevant field she may follow her own expertise, just as she would have followed one of her colleagues' advice. Reasons deriving from expertise can be self-binding.

Custom as a source of law

Austin was at pains to show how custom can be a source of valid legal rules, because it can hardly be said that custom is the expression of the sovereign's wishes about how others ought to behave. It seems that a similar point can be raised against any personal conception of authority, including mine. Customary law seems to be law without an author.

I do not intend to deny that there is a valid point here. Nor do I believe that Austin's device of 'tacit orders' can be salvaged from Hart's criticisms.[48] As a first step, we must admit that the personal conception of authority does not quite fit pure cases of customary law. When people regard a certain norm as authoritative only because it has been regarded as such by the previous generations, it is difficult to say that the norm expresses the explicit view of any particular person, or group of persons, about how the alleged norm subjects ought to behave. But, and this is the crucially important point, customs do reflect the view of the bulk of the community about how they themselves ought to behave; in other words, custom is not simply a regularity of behaviour recognized by the community as such. It is a regularity of behaviour which is considered by the community as binding, as a norm which they themselves ought to adhere to. In other words, it seems to me that custom may well be regarded as an informal structure of a collective expression that is, in certain important respects, equivalent to the formal structures of collective decision-making, such as majority vote. Once we realize that the self-binding nature of legislation is not at odds with the personal conception of authority, much of the difficulty with custom is mitigated too.

To sum up: we have seen that Hart's arguments against Austin's conception of legal authority, though basically valid, have no bearing on the personal conception of authority as such. None of Hart's arguments can be taken to repudiate the idea that the law is basically a product of communication; it must be the product of an authority that expresses its views on the desirable behaviour of its alleged subjects (including, typically, the authority itself).

As a final remark, a brief comment on Waldron's politically motivated worries: I have already indicated that I share Waldron's aspiration to refrain from forging too tight a connection between the authority of law and the authority of the ruling majority. I don't think that the personal conception of authority is at odds with this ideal. On the other hand, I do believe that there is a real danger in the opposite view, espoused by Waldron, that the author-

48 See Hart, *The Concept of Law*, at 43–8.

ity of law can be abstracted, as it were, from the authority of the legislators. This impersonal conception of authority, quite apart from being mistaken, carries the danger of political mystification. The farther one takes the abstractions of authority from real persons, the easier it becomes to present the law as something divine and sublime. The will of particular people easily becomes the myth of the 'will of the people', or even worse, the 'real will' of the people. I am sure that this romanticism is just as unattractive to Jeremy Waldron as it is to me.

6
Three Concepts of Objectivity

THIS chapter is about the concept of objectivity and its possible roles in the interpretation of works of art. 'Objectivity', however, is one of those notions philosophy students are well advised to avoid in their essays. There is very little agreement on what it means, and there is a great deal of confusion about its different and often conflicting uses. This may sound puzzling, and perhaps it is; however, unlike philosophical concepts such as 'realism' and 'cognitivism', which have received extensive philosophical attention in the last two or three decades, the concept(s) of objectivity has been left pretty much in the lurch. Consequently, any discussion of the objectivity or subjectivity of a certain realm must begin with a clarification of what one means by these terms. I shall begin with an outline of the distinction between three different concepts of objectivity which, I will suggest, are philosophically useful. Once the boundaries between these different uses of objectivity are clearly drawn, we shall be able to see that there are several aspects of interpretation which can be characterized as 'objective' or 'subjective' in a rather non-controversial manner; that is, depending on the kind of 'objectivity' ascribed. Other aspects of the objectivity of interpretation, however, remain genuinely controversial, and I will try to add a few drops of my own to this ocean of philosophical literature. I will have nothing directly to say, however, about legal interpretation; my main concern will be with interpretation in the realm of the arts. The objectivity of law will be discussed in the next chapter.

PART I. SOME BASIC DISTINCTIONS

The objective–subjective dichotomy is a philosophical invention and one, in fact, with a rather peculiar history.[1] There is very little to gain, then, from an ordinary-language analysis of these concepts. The definitions of the objective–subjective dichotomy must be based on theoretical considerations, and their usefulness must be tested against theoretical objectives. This much, at least, I will take for granted.

This chapter is a substantially revised version of the article published in Marmor (ed.), *Law and Interpretation* (Oxford, 1995), 177. I am indebted to Meir Dan-Cohen, Chaim Gans, Ruth Gavison, Alon Harel, David Heyd, Dori Kimel, Brian Leiter, Ariel Porat, Joseph Raz, Jeremy Waldron, and Timothy Williamson for their invaluable comments on drafts of this essay.

[1] The philosophical discourse about the objective–subjective dichotomy probably stems from seventeenth century Rationalism. Interestingly, however, the Cartesian use of these notions was almost the opposite of their current one. For Descartes the idea of objectivity carried skeptical connotations with it, whereas the subjective realm was associated with truth and certainty. See, for example, his *Meditations on First Philosophy*.

I will also assume that the objectivity–subjectivity pair, like that of realism and anti-realism, is a distinction usefully applied to classes of statement. It is only about certain kinds of statement, as a kind, that we normally want to know whether they are objective or subjective. Those who assert, for example, the objectivity of statements about mid-sized physical objects, make a claim about the objective standing of each and every statement in this particular class only as an instance of its belonging to the class of statements about mid-sized physical objects. It is the objectivity (or subjectivity) of the class of statements as such that is normally the subject of philosophical controversy, not the standing of a particular statements in isolation.

There are (at least) three different and, as I shall argue, basically independent concepts of objectivity. First, there is objectivity or subjectivity in what I shall call the semantic sense. In this sense statements (or, perhaps more precisely, speech acts) are either semantically objective or subjective, regardless of their validity or truth. In the second sense, the objective–subjective dichotomy is a matter of metaphysical truth. The question of objectivity in this metaphysical sense is a question about the world, and not about the meaning of the statements. Finally, there is what I shall call discourse objectivity: a certain class of statements is objective in this sense if it makes sense to ascribe truth values to statements of that class.[2]

Before we proceed to the elaboration of these three concepts of objectivity, however, a clarification is called for: it should not be assumed that these three concepts exhaust all the prevalent uses of objectivity in ordinary language. As we shall see in the next chapter, for instance, 'objectivity' is often used as a synonym or a quasi-synonym for 'impartiality'. It is often in this sense that judges and arbitrators are required to be objective, or that we seek the objectivity of scientists, namely, as a quest for impartiality in the rendering of judgements.[3] This, and perhaps some other prevalent uses of objectivity, will not be part of the analysis offered below.

Semantic objectivity

The semantic sense of the objectivity–subjectivity dichotomy is basically a characterization of a given type of speech. Roughly, a statement is semantically objective if and only if it is a statement about an object; and it is a subjective statement if and only if it is about an aspect of one's self, that is, about some mental state of the subject making the statement. Thus, a statement is subjective in this semantic sense if it is (or if it is equivalent in meaning to) the expression of the speaker's tastes, desires, perceptions, and so on. And a

[2] In the previous publication of this essay I have called it 'logical objectivity'. Admittedly both labels are unfortunate, but 'logical' is even worse.

[3] This sense of objectivity is particularly relevant for law; for a detailed discussion see Chapter 7.

statement is objective if it has as its grammatical subject an object in the world, other than the speaker's state of mind, as it were.[4] This, I take it, is the most simple (but not useless) sense of the objective–subjective dichotomy. The most important feature of this sense of objectivity is that it is purely a matter of the meaning of the speech act in question, independent of the statement's truth or falsehood. More precisely, a given class of statements can be objective in the semantic sense even if there is no truth of the matter about the objects described by those statements (for example, because they do not exist at all). And vice versa, a class of statements can be subjective in the semantic sense even if there is a truth of the matter about the meaning of those statements. As an example of the former, consider the discourse about God; people can talk about Him (or Her, as the case may be) even if there is no such entity. And vice versa: many kinds of subjective statement can easily be conceived as determinedly true or false. For instance, 'I love Sarah' is a semantically subjective statement, but of course, it can be true (or false) in a fairly standard manner.

Is it the case, then, that all statements are either semantically objective or subjective? Not necessarily: first, there may be types of mixed statement, which involve subjective and objective elements inextricably.[5] Second, there may be statements which are neither objective nor subjective in the semantic sense, simply because such statements do not appear in a propositional discourse, or context (for example, like a move in a game, or as part of a greeting, and so on). Be this as it may, the important point is that there is a sense of objectivity and subjectivity which only pertains to the characterization of the given speech, independently of its objectivity or subjectivity in any other sense.

One might wonder why this semantic distinction between objective and subjective statements would be of any philosophical interest, particularly as it is alleged that the objectivity of a statement in this sense is no indication of its truth. The answer lies in the distinction between the superficial and the deeper layers of grammar. It is quite common for philosophers to claim in various contexts that the superficial appearance of grammar is misleading; sentences that appear semantically objective can turn out to be semantically subjective (or vice versa) on closer scrutiny. To take one familiar example, consider the meta-ethical theory Richard Hare called 'old-fashioned subjectivity'.[6] This

[4] Two notes of caution: first, the semantic sense of subjectivity is not meant to capture all those philosophical positions labelled subjectivist in current literature. Secondly, semantic subjectivity is not committed to any particular metaphysics of the 'self'. The latter may be relevant for an adequate account of the truth conditions of semantically subjective statements, but this is a different story.

[5] One such case occurs when the statement is basically about the subject asserting it, but it involves certain objective presuppositions rendering the statement complete or intelligible. Other examples could be statements expressing a relation between the subject and external objects, like, for example, the statement 'I am Sarah's best friend'.

[6] Hare, *Moral Thinking*, 76

view suggests that moral judgements, despite appearances to the contrary, are actually equivalent in meaning to reports of the subject about his or her psychological state (for example, of disapproval of the act being judged). Thus, the judgement 'act X is cruel', which appears to be semantically objective, namely, a statement about the properties of an act X, becomes according to the analysis of 'old-fashioned subjectivity' semantically subjective: it is a statement about a certain kind of reaction experienced and reported by the subject asserting it. Whether this is a plausible meta-ethical stance (or indeed, whether any philosopher has ever held such a view) does not matter for our purposes. What does matter, however, is the philosophical relevance of this semantic sense of the objectivity–subjectivity dichotomy. 'Old-fashioned subjectivity' as a semantically subjectivist stance on the appropriate analysis of the meaning of ethical judgements is anything but trivial. If true (and again, I certainly don't claim that it is), it would render our understanding of ethical discourse radically different from what we normally take it to be. Indeed, so radically different as to render it highly implausible; as Hare rightly points out, 'old-fashioned subjectivity' cannot make any sense of ethical disputes and arguments.[7] (More on this later, however.)

Furthermore, although I wish to reiterate that semantic objectivity is never an indication of the truth of a statement, it does have, nevertheless, a bearing on the kind of truth conditions appropriate for the statements in question. According to 'old-fashioned subjectivity', for example, the truth conditions of an ethical judgement must always refer to the mental state of the subject asserting it. If, on the other hand, ethical judgements are semantically objective (as they appear to be according to their superficial grammar), the mental state of the subject asserting the statement in question would not be a constituent of the statement's truth conditions.

Semantic objectivity then, is basically a matter of grammar, but not necessarily of the superficial grammar. Statements that look like objective ones, can turn out to be subjective, and vice versa.[8] The importance of this sense of objectivity, however, lies mainly in what it does not imply namely, truth or validity. There is no contradiction involved in asserting that a given class of statements is objective in the semantic sense, while maintaining that there are no objects of the kind purportedly described by the class of statements in question.

Furthermore, people often tend to talk in semantically objective terms even if they are perfectly aware of the fact that the discourse is not objective in any

[7] Ibid. 77.

[8] As an example of statements which look subjective but are in fact semantically objective, consider the statement 'I have to visit Jones'. This is not really a statement about the subject asserting it but about the application of a reason for action. Statements about reasons for action are semantically objective.

other sense. Certain elements of aesthetic discourse may be precisely of this kind. Many people talk about beauty, for example, as if it were a property of objects in the world, despite the fact that they do not really believe this to be the case. Aesthetic discourse, in other words, is regarded by many people like the atheist's discourse about God. Now, this 'as if' kind of discourse, namely, one which is cast in objective terms despite the common assumption that there are no objects in the world of the kind purportedly described by it, is not so bewildering as it may seem on first impression. Many types of discourse have a social or a psychological rationale, and serve social and cultural functions, in ways which have very little to do with truth or falsehood.

Metaphysical objectivity

Objectivity in the metaphysical sense does imply truth, and in a rather special manner. Roughly, it implies that there is a truth of the matter consisting in the fact that there is an object with properties corresponding to its description by the statement in question. It would be safe to assume that most philosophers (and laymen) interested in the objectivity or subjectivity of a certain type of statements have the metaphysical sense of objectivity in mind. Two kinds of confusion regarding metaphysical objectivity are prevalent, however. Objectivity in this sense is all too often conflated with realism (and subjectivity with anti-realism). Although there is a close link between these two pairs of philosophical concepts, they are not identical. Secondly, metaphysical objectivity is often confused with the third, discourse, sense of objectivity. Both confusions, I will argue, are prone to engender superfluous controversies.

The metaphysical objectivity–subjectivity dichotomy must be defined in terms of the relations between types of statement and the existence of the appropriate categories of objects. A given type of statements is objective in the metaphysical sense if, and only if, there exist objects of the kind purportedly described by that type of statements; and a class of statements is subjective if no such objects exist in the world. Thus, a given statement is objectively true in the metaphysical sense if, and only if, there exists an object in the world with the properties attributed to it by the statement in question; and it is objectively false if the object it purports to describe does not have the properties attributed to it by the statement. A statement cannot be objectively either true or false, however, if there are no objects of the kind purportedly described by the type of statements in question. Thus, the typical subjectivist or sceptical stance on the objectivity of a given type of statements consists in the contention that those statements which are semantically objective turn out to be subjective in the metaphysical sense.

It may be worth noting, perhaps, that the objective–subjective pair is not always symmetrical; subjectivity in the metaphysical sense is simply the denial of objectivity, and hence, it is merely a negative view. In the semantic sense, on the other hand, subjectivity is a kind of opposite to objectivity, and not its denial.

The definition of metaphysical objectivity seems to imply two presuppositions: first, that the kind of statements which can be metaphysically objective are only of the descriptive kind. They must be statements which purport to describe objects in the world, and they are objective if and only if there are objects of the kind referred to by the description. Second, as indicated by the latter sentence, metaphysical objectivity seems to assume something like a correspondence theory of truth (at least with respect to the kind of statements about which one is objectivist). Both assumptions are basically correct. Beginning with the latter, it is easy to see that metaphysical objectivity assumes that statements are rendered true or false by how things are in the world. For example, the proposition 'this chair is black' would be objectively true in this metaphysical sense if and only if there is an object, namely, the chair referred to, and it *is* black. Does this imply that the truth of the statement consists in this relation of 'correspondence'? Basically, yes. Whatever the flaws of the correspondence theory of truth might be, something like it must be assumed for sentences to be metaphysically objective. Even if we take the notion of 'truth' as simple or primitive, not analysable in terms of other notions like 'correspondence', it must be assumed, at some intuitive level, that a statement is rendered objectively true or false by the constitution of reality, by how things are, anyway. If it does not make sense to say that truth somehow consists in the relation between sentences and the world, metaphysical objectivity would not make sense either.

There is a considerable overlap between metaphysical objectivity and realism. Realism, like objectivity, is seen as a position on a metaphysical issue, a view on the way our thoughts and language relate to the world. Since much of the current debate on realism has been initiated by Michael Dummett, it may be useful to base the discussion on his formulation of realism, which runs as follows: 'The primary tenet of realism, as applied to some given class of statements, is that each statement in that class is determined as true or not true, independently of our knowledge, by some objective reality whose existence and constitution is, again, independent of our knowledge.'[9]

One is tempted to say that the difference between realism and objectivity is that realism is even 'more metaphysical' than metaphysical objectivity, if I may use this terrible expression. This is so, as realism presumes the existence of an objective reality which is ontologically independent of our knowledge. On the other hand, one can be an objectivist about kinds of object that do not meet this independence condition. Objectivity, in other words, does not entail, as realism does, the possibility of verification-transcendent truths within the realm about which one is objectivist. For example, the existence

[9] Dummett, *The Interpretation of Frege's Philosophy*, 434.

and constitution of many types of object is a matter of social or cultural construction. There is no reason to deny the possibility of objectivity about such cultural objects. There is, in fact, a whole range of concepts and classes of statement about which it would make perfect sense to hold an anti-realist and objectivist stance. Consider, for example, statements describing: the annual rate of inflation in the UK; the rules of chess; the legal speed limit for driving in California; the ordinary perceptions of colours; the ordinary meanings of words in a natural language; and, say, the basic plot of *Pride and Prejudice*. Would it not be pointless to deny the applicability of metaphysical objectivity to all these, and doubtless many other, kinds of statement? Yet it seems equally clear that (Dummettian) realism does not apply here.[10] The reference of concepts like inflation, chess, or the legal speed limit, and so on cannot be conceived as ontologically independent of our knowledge and culture. Moreover, at least with respect to some of these examples, one cannot separate the meaning of the concept from its verification conditions. Our concept of inflation, for instance, is closely tied to the way in which economists think that they can verify the existence and constitution of its reference.

Objectivity about a given class of statements, then, does not necessarily entail realism about that class. On the other hand, it would be safe to assume that realism does entail objectivity. If one is a realist about a given class of statements, one is, *ipso facto*, a metaphysical objectivist about that class of statements.

Finally, the question arises whether one can be an objectivist even with respect to non-existent entities. Would metaphysical objectivity make any sense with respect to, for example, statements about fictional characters, or mythological ones? On first impression, it might all seem to depend on the appropriate definition of the idea of 'objects existing in the world' one is willing to allow. Once we allow objectivity (as opposed to realism) about cultural objects, this argument would run, there is no reason to deny its application to non-existent objects as well. Now perhaps the example of fictional characters is potentially misleading. I do not intend to deny that they can be objects, of course, *qua* fictional characters. The oddity concerns the actual reference of such characters, which, I gather, do not exist in any sensible way. Now, if this were true without further qualifications, it would show that metaphysical objectivity collapses into semantic objectivity; if there is no limitation on the kinds of object about which one can be an objectivist, that is, in the metaphysical sense, then potentially each and every statement which is grammatically about an object could also be objective in the metaphysical sense. Which is to say that the semantic and the metaphysical senses of objectivity can turn out to be equivalent in extension. But this, I think, would be a serious distor-

[10] On Putnam's version of so-called 'internal realism', which is markedly different, see Chapter 7.

tion. The distinctions between the various senses of objectivity are basically a matter of theoretical convenience; I do not believe that there can be an independent truth of the matter about these philosophical classifications. From a theoretical vantage point, however, there is a very good reason for holding on to the distinction between the semantic and the metaphysical senses of objectivity. Generally speaking, the former is a stance on the characterization of the speech whereas the latter is a characterization of the world. In other words, it must be possible to describe various forms of discourse in the semantically objective sense, even if the discourse is such that the pertinent kind of objects does not really exist, and hence, there can be no truth of the matter about the properties of those objects.

All this is just another way of saying that metaphysical objectivity must always be accompanied by a well-defined notion of the kinds of object one is willing to allow and their existence conditions. There is no logical constraint on the kinds of object to which metaphysical objectivity is applicable, as long as the objectivist can make it clear what would distinguish objects of the kind about which he or she is objectivist, and which exist, and those which do not exist. To be sure, the existence of objects need not be, necessarily, spatio-temporal existence; but it must be distinguishable from non-existence. Otherwise, metaphysical objectivity would make very little difference indeed.[11]

Discourse objectivity

Metaphysical objectivity about a given class of statements, as we have seen, is only applicable to statements of the descriptive kind. A statement can be objectively true (or false) in this sense, only if it is, or can be reduced to, a description of an object in the world.[12] Some philosophers believe that only descriptive propositions can be true or false. According to this view, nothing but metaphysical objectivity about a given class of statements admits of truth values for the statements in that class. This need not be the case, however. Equally respectable is the philosophical stance that allows for the validity or truth of statements which are not descriptive (or reducible to descriptive) statements. Kantian constructivism in ethics is one prominent example. R. M. Hare's prescriptivism may be another. According to these, and doubtless many other views, statements which do not purport to describe anything

[11] In a critical comment on this explication of metaphysical objectivity, Joseph Raz raised some doubts about the intelligibility of the idea that statements are *about* objects (see Raz, *Engaging Reason*, 121). I must admit that I am not quite sure that I understand those doubts. In any case, Raz himself introduces pretty much the same idea a few pages later, when he comes to elaborate on his own conception of objectivity. Condition number 5 reads as follows: 'thoughts are objective only if they are *about a reality* which exists independently of them, that is, whose truth is independent of the fact that those thoughts are entertained' (emphasis mine). Ibid. 125. The accompanying n. 13 further clarifies that Raz believes this condition not to entail metaphysical realism.

[12] That may include, as we have noted, the subject's own mental state.

can still be true or false, valid or invalid. This indicates that there is at least a logical space for a third kind of objectivity, one which would not necessarily require descriptivism. Discourse objectivity, as I will call this view, holds that a given class of statements is objective if and only if each and every statement in that class has a determinate truth value.[13] Consequently, discourse subjectivity is the denial of the above, and hence amounts to one of the most common forms of scepticism about the class of statements in question. The discourse subjectivist denies the possibility of ascribing truth values to the statements of the kind about which he or she is subjectivist.

Discourse objectivity has very close affinities to cognitivism (particularly in meta-ethics), and so before we proceed perhaps I should clarify some of the differences (others will become clear, I hope, as we go along). Cognitivism is a complex doctrine, and it normally involves a two-stage position. First and foremost, it is a view about the possibility of attaining knowledge in the realm about which one is cognitivist. If one is a cognitivist about morality, for example, one holds that moral judgements purport to represent moral knowledge, and that this aspiration is at least sometimes attainable and warranted.[14] The second stage involves the notion of truth. The cognitivist is expected to maintain that one can come to know that P, because P is true (or, more precisely, perhaps, one can come to know that P if and only if one can come to believe that P because P is true). Now, it is in this second stage that cognitivism and discourse objectivity more or less converge, that is, as long as the cognitivist's explanation for the possibility of attaining knowledge is based on the availability of truth (which is not necessarily the case[15]). In other words, discourse objectivity is a standard (but again, not necessary) component of cognitivism.

It need not be assumed that the discourse objectivity–subjectivity dichotomy is only applicable to non-descriptive statements (as some of the examples mentioned above may be thought to suggest). This will become apparent once we take a closer look at the relations between the discourse and the metaphysical senses of objectivity. These relations are somewhat complex. Basically, metaphysical objectivity about a given class of statements entails discourse objectivity about that class, but not vice versa. The relation of entailment is pretty clear. One who maintains that a given class of statements can be objectively true or false in the metaphysical sense *ipso facto* must

[13] Whether discourse objectivity presupposes the principle of bivalence and the excluded middle is a difficult question I cannot hope to answer here.

[14] See, for example, Wiggins, 'Moral Cognitivism, Moral Relativism, and Motivating Moral Beliefs', 62.

[15] Intuitionism in mathematics may well be such an exception. But it is difficult to generalize here since intuitionism can be understood as espousing a constructive notion of truth which, according to certain interpretations, may well be compatible with discourse objectivity. See, for example, Putnam, *Realism and Reason*, 20, and Dummett, *The Interpretation of Frege's Philosophy*, 66.

also maintain that statements in that class can be assigned determinate truth values. Note that a parallel relation of entailment holds between discourse subjectivity and metaphysical subjectivity: if one denies the possibility of discourse objectivity about a given class of statements, one must also deny the possibility of metaphysical objectivity about that class, and for the same reason. Now the important point is that the reverse does not hold—discourse objectivity does not entail metaphysical objectivity—even with respect to statements of the descriptive kind. In other words, there are classes of statement about which it is possible to subscribe to the following three theses:

1. Statements of class A are semantically descriptive: they purport to describe objects of type X.
2. Objects of type X, as such, do not exist in the world.
3. Each and every (well-formed) statement in class A has a determinate truth value.

How is it possible, then, to maintain these three theses about a given type of statements? What kind of discourse could fit such a characterization? Admittedly, it would be very difficult to think of non-controversial examples. There is one trivial and perhaps, as such, not very interesting example: it is always possible simply to construct an artificial language game, or as a matter of fact, just a game, that will fit the conditions mentioned above. But again, such examples would not show a great deal.[16] Thus, consider the analysis of our discourse describing mental events according to those who believe in something like central-state materialism. According to such a reductionist conception of the mental to the physical, mental events as such, namely, as forming a separate ontological category, do not really exist. When we describe a mental event or a mental process, our description is of objects (that is, of the mental kind) that do not really exist. Nevertheless, central-state materialism need not deny the possibility of ascribing truth values to statements describing mental events and processes. On the contrary: since each and every statement about the mental sphere is assumed to be reducible to statements about the physical, if one is a discourse objectivist about the physical, one must also admit discourse objectivity about the reduced class, that is, about the mental sphere. This, in fact, is precisely what is meant by the possibility of complete reduction. Thus, far from denying the discourse objectivity of mental statements, central-state materialism reinforces it, despite its outright denial of the metaphysical objectivity of the mental sphere.[17]

To take another example, consider the traditional empiricist analysis of concepts such as causation. Hume, for example, presumably did not intend to

[16] A coherence theory of truth could be another example.

[17] Cf. Dummett's discussion of the distinction between *naive* and *sophisticated* realism in Dummett, *The Interpretation of Frege's Philosophy*, 448. But compare Marmor, *Interpretation and Legal Theory*, 88–9.

deny the possibility of truth and falsehood about statements describing particular causal relations; what he meant to deny is the metaphysical objectivity of such relations. Thus, at least according to a fairly standard interpretation of Hume, we can say that he advocated metaphysical subjectivity—without denying the possibility of discourse objectivity—about the concept of causation. On this interpretation, then, Hume would subscribe to all three conditions mentioned above: (1) statements about causal relations are semantically descriptive; (2) such statements describe objects of a certain type that do not exist, as such, in the world; and (3) statements about casual relations can be assigned determinate truth values.

To be sure, nothing should be understood here as commending a particular theory about the mental or about the Humean analysis of causation. These examples are meant to illustrate a fairly limited point, namely, that there is a philosophically useful notion of discourse objectivity which does not necessarily entail metaphysical objectivity. If I am right about this, it will enable us to see that there are two distinct forms of scepticism one can hold about the objectivity of a given kind of discourse. All too often, moreover, these two forms of scepticism are not properly distinguished by their advocates and foes alike. They consist in the denial of metaphysical and discourse objectivity, respectively. What usually goes unnoticed is the fact that the denial of the former does not entail the repudiation of the latter as well. In the realm of interpretation this confusion is of considerable importance. Before we get to interpretation, however, allow me a small detour.

In his celebrated book *Ethics, Inventing Right and Wrong*[18] John Mackie set out to establish moral subjectivity. His argument in chapter 1, called 'The Error Theory of Meta-Ethics', runs basically as follows. Ethical discourse, Mackie admits, is by and large semantically objective. The ordinary language of morals includes, in a very pervasive manner, a claim to objectivity: the assumption 'that there are objective values', that is, in the metaphysically objective sense. But this claim to objectivity, Mackie argues, is based on a factual/metaphysical mistake. Simply put, there are no objects in the universe of the kind purportedly described by ethical discourse. Hence, he concludes, regardless of the superficial grammar of ethical discourse (or more precisely, despite it), one must adopt outright scepticism about its objective status. Mackie advances two well-known arguments in favour of his crucial claim that ethical discourse is based on a metaphysical mistake: the argument from relativity and the argument from queerness.

Let me begin with the argument from queerness, which is more relevant to our concerns. The upshot of this argument is that 'if there were objective values, then they would be entities or qualities or relations of a very strange sort, utterly different from anything else in the universe.'[19] This queerness of moral

[18] Mackie, *Ethics, Inventing Right and Wrong*, ch. 1. [19] Ibid. 38.

entities, or qualities, Mackie concludes, suffices to cast a serious doubt on the objectivity of moral values. It should be clear by now, however, that Mackie's target of this argument is far from clear. On one possible reading, the argument is addressed to the standard realist stance. It expresses the age-old worry about Platonic realism about values. The idea that there is an ontologically mind-independent moral reality 'out there in the universe' is difficult to maintain indeed. But perhaps this interpretation of Mackie's argument is too restrictive. Mackie seems to suggest that his argument applies to other objective accounts of morality besides realism. But what kind of objectivity? At most, the argument applies to metaphysical objectivity. Discourse objectivity, which is not committed to descriptivism, remains intact. In other words, the argument from queerness seems to cut no ice with those versions of objectivity which have discarded the metaphysical version of objectivity. This raises some doubts about the question of whether, for example, Kant's stance on the objectivity of morality is an appropriate target for the argument from queerness, as Mackie takes it to be. It may be a more plausible reading of Kant to assume that it is only the discourse sense of objectivity he strove to establish.

Be this as it may, the main question is whether the argument from queerness raises serious worries about the metaphysical objectivity of values. Once we realize that the latter is not committed to realism, the contention that moral entities or qualities are metaphysically queer is much less compelling. Why would they be more queer, or mysterious, than say, social constructs in general, relational properties, or mathematical entities? Once we realize that metaphysical objectivity is compatible with anti-realism, the argument from queerness loses much of its intuitive appeal. To be sure, I don't think matters can be left here. As we shall see in Chapter 8, Mackie's argument from queerness is based on a larger context, essentially doubting that objectivity about values can be fit into our scientific world-view. The only point I wanted to make here is, however, that the distinctions between objectivity and realism, and the various senses of the former, make it easier to assess the force of such arguments as Mackie's argument from queerness, and enable us to separate the different types of worries we should try to handle.

The argument from relativity raises different problems and I'll just mention them here very briefly. Mackie invokes the alleged fact about the cultural relativity of moral values to show that any objective stance about morality would require the attribution of large-scale mistakes about morality to entire cultures. Since the moral values held by people in different cultures are substantially at odds with each other, Mackie claims, the objectivist is bound to maintain that a great many people, perhaps most of us, are wrong about the content morality, and this Mackie finds a rather suspect and highly implausible stance. But again, Mackie's version of this argument is utterly incomplete. It is based on two observations which cancel out each other's point, as it were. Mackie grants that moral discourse is pervasively objectivist: peoples' moral assertions typically make a claim to objectivity. The second observation consists in the fact of cultural relativity. Now the problem is that when these two points are granted, both objectivity *and subjectivity* would render it necessary to attribute large-scale mistakes to most people most of the time: if the objectivist is right, whole cultures and communities err in the realm of substantive morality. But if the subjectivist is right, most people err in their meta-ethical stance since their claim to objectivity is groundless. So according to Mackie's argument, we must hold an error theory either way, and it is not clear why should we prefer the attribution of one kind of mistake to another.[20]

Second, and this point is not unique to Mackie's version of the argument from relativity, it is possible to doubt the extent to which relativity is a fact.[21] The appearance of profound moral disagreements between different societies and cultures may well be misleading, and for several reasons. For example, many disagreements which look like moral ones, may turn out, on closer scrutiny, to be, in fact, about other non-moral assumptions and world-views. (If we really believed that there are witches, perhaps we would burn them too). Also, moral disagreements often stem from divergent choices which are based on incommensurable values and value judgements. Finally, it is perhaps not so absurd to maintain that there is progress in morality. After all, we think that we now know better than our medieval ancestors did what it is to have a rational account of Nature surrounding us. Perhaps we also know better what it is to respect human beings as moral agents.

None of this was meant to be conclusive, of course. The argument from relativity may still hold good after it is refined of its crude assumptions.[22] In any event it was not my purpose here to argue for the objectivity of values. My purpose was limited to showing that some of the distinctions we have drawn so far may prove useful. In the next part of this chapter I will try to resolve some of the puzzles concerning objectivity in interpretation drawing on these distinctions.

PART II. OBJECTIVITY IN INTERPRETATION

Objectivity in the realm of the interpretation of works of art is almost universally discredited. In its popular manifestation the subjectivity associated with interpretation is often expressed by people saying 'it is only your interpretation', or something like that, as if the label 'interpretation' is equivalent to

[20] There is no particular reason to suppose that we are generally more willing to accept the possibility of widespread errors in the meta-theoretical realm compared with substantive mistakes. In the realm of science, for example, probably the contrary is true. None of this proves, of course, that Mackie's argument fails, only that it is utterly incomplete and begs the question.

[21] See, for example, Wiggins, 'Moral Cognitivism, Moral Relativism, and Motivating Moral Beliefs'. See also Raz, 'Moral Change and Social Relativism'.

[22] See Chapter 8.

subjectivity. This popular scepticism is largely echoed in the philosophical literature as well. The philosophical origins of this scepticism are not difficult to trace. Most of them are based on sound observations, but the conclusions drawn from them are not always carefully stated. Generally speaking, I will try to show that the interpretation of works of art is typically objective in the semantic sense; rarely, and only in a subordinate manner, objective in the metaphysical sense; and under certain conditions, it is often objective in the discourse sense.

It may be useful, then, to take a closer look at some of the main sources of subjectivity in interpretation, following the three concepts of objectivity distinguished in Part I.

Interpretation and semantic subjectivity

The idea that interpretations of works of art are typically subjective in the semantic sense is widely shared, though, admittedly, more so by laymen than by philosophers and art critics. The first point to notice here is that people are led to the conclusion that interpretative statements are typically subjective in the semantic sense, not because of, but despite the superficial grammar of such statements. Most interpretations of works of art are not presented by the interpreter as a report of his or her state of mind; rarely, if at all, would an interpreter present the interpretation only as a subjective reaction to the object interpreted. Subjective preferences of, and reactions to, aspects of works of art make perfect sense as expressions of personal taste and are indeed quite common as such. Interpretations, however, are rarely presented as expressions of personal taste. Why the common assumption to the contrary, then? Why is it so tempting to suggest that superficial grammar is misleading here?

The puzzle is increased when we recall that the subjectivist account of the interpretative discourse involves a very high price: it renders the phenomenon of a dispute or an argument about the interpretation of a work of art quite irrational. After all, if interpretative statements are semantically subjective, namely, reports of personal impressions, there is no point whatsoever in arguing about them. More precisely, if interpretative discourse is semantically subjective, two people with different views on the appropriate interpretation of a work of art could never be in a real disagreement with each other; each would be simply stating that he or she had a certain attitude, feeling, or whatever, and these statements would always be mutually consistent.

Undoubtedly, the failure to separate between the semantic and the metaphysical senses of objectivity can explain at least part of the tendency to describe interpretative discourse in subjectivist terms. Since most commentators are inclined to deny the possibility of objectivity in the metaphysical sense (and sometimes rightly so), they assume that despite the superficial grammar, interpretative statements are equivalent in meaning to statements about the subject's state of mind. But this move is quite unnecessary, as the previous sections have argued at length.

There is, perhaps, another source for this confusion, one which is based on a sounder point. It is often assumed, and rightly so, I believe, that interpretation involves a rather special notion of epistemic tolerance. One important aspect of this tolerance is captured by the idea that whenever there is one interpretation of a work of art, there must also be others that do not necessarily coincide with it. As Joseph Raz rightly emphasized, the very idea of interpretation imports the possibility of more than one interpretation, of several good or acceptable interpretations.[23] This is a crucially important observation, and we shall have to explain it in some detail. Any account of interpretation must explain this paradoxical feature of it, namely, that interpretations admit, on the one hand, of plurality and inconsistency, and on the other hand, of ascription of good or bad, right and wrong, and the like. I will try to offer at least a partial explanation for this in the last section. For the time being, however, suffice it to say that nothing in this epistemic tolerance requires the characterization of interpretative discourse in semantically subjectivist terms. On the contrary: interpretative statements could not be good or bad, acceptable or unacceptable at all, if the semantic subjectivity attributed to them were true. Interpretations can be commensurable and subject to appraisals and intelligible controversies, only if they are by and large objective (at least) in the semantic sense.

Finally, there is an important distinction between an interpretation of a work of art and its description that might account for the tendency to describe the former in semantically subjectivist terms. Once again, the subjectivist conclusion is unwarranted but the confusion stems from a sound point. Grammatically, by and large, interpretative statements are descriptive; they purport to describe certain aspects of the work interpreted. But in this case we must be very careful not to be misled by the superficial appearance of grammar. A statement describing an aspect of a work of art is never, by itself, an interpretation of the work in question. The latter always involves, explicitly or implicitly, evaluative judgements of various kinds which give the descriptive part of the interpretation its particular significance. When this evaluative significance is absent, or perhaps when it eludes us, the description is not grasped as an interpretation of the work of art. Saying, for example, that 'the American Gothic is a picture of a man and his daughter' is part of an interpretation of the picture, only if it is somehow significant, or important, to know this piece of information. When this significance is absent (like when someone informs us that the length of a novel is 500 pages) the description in question is not grasped as interpretative. Needless to say, often the very same

[23] Raz, 'Interpretation without Retrieval'.

piece of information can be significant within one interpretative framework and insignificant within another. There is no hard and fast line to draw here between descriptions which are part of interpretations, and those which are not. The important point is, however, that descriptive statements about a work of art are always subordinate to a larger framework of the interpretative explanation, and this framework must include evaluative judgements about the significance of the descriptions offered.[24]

We have not equipped subjectivism, however, with the weapon it needs. Semantic subjectivity would follow from the considerations mentioned above if, but only if, it could also be shown that the kind of evaluative judgements pertinent to the interpretation of works of art are, by and large, semantically subjective. But this, of course, does not follow. Those evaluative judgements which provide the significance and relevance of the descriptive parts of a given interpretation need not be semantically subjective. On the contrary, as we have already noted, interpretative discourse would not make much sense if it were based on semantically subjectivist terms. People can only have a genuine and intelligent argument or disagreement if their judgements are not meant to reflect only preferences of taste, as it were; it is not enough that they are talking about one and the same object if the former condition is not met. If I say, for example, that I like this picture and you say that you don't, there is not much left to argue about, as both statements are mutually consistent. We may, of course, attempt to influence each other's personal tastes, but this is not normally achieved effectively by an interpretative argument. Sometimes a change in another's personal taste or preference is an additional (and perhaps welcome) achievement of a good interpretation; but this is hardly the main point of interpretations generally. Interpretations aim to present the work of art in a certain light, they are *about the work*, not about the interpreter.

As a final remark about semantic subjectivity, it should be kept in mind that we are talking about generalizations that do not always hold. My contention is that, by and large, interpretative discourse cannot be presumed to be based on semantically subjectivist terms. This does not rule out the possibility that sometimes it is. Impressionistic interpretations, so to speak, make perfect sense, as such. But again, the point is that they cannot be characteristic of the discourse; they do not present the paradigm of an interpretation of a work of art.

[24] Cf. Dworkin, *Law's Empire*, at 59–61 and Marmor, *Interpretation and Legal Theory*, at 38. Needless to say, evaluations without any descriptive element whatsoever do not amount to interpretations either. Saying something like 'this is a beautiful picture' does not form an interpretation of the picture.

Interpretation and metaphysical subjectivity

There are several lines of thought purporting to repudiate the possibility of metaphysical objectivity in the realm of artistic interpretation. Most of them, I shall argue, are basically sound. Let me begin, however, with one prevalent type of argument which is misconceived, as it confuses subjectivity with anti-realism. The argument under consideration would basically run as follows.

The interpretation of works of art is paradigmatically the interpretation of cultural products. Works of art, as objects existing in the world, exist only as such cultural entities. No interpreter is interested in, for example, Michelangelo's David as a piece of marble *qua* physical object; the object of interpretation is the statue. There is a clear sense, however, in which it is possible to deny the reality of this statue, namely, as an object whose properties are independent of our perceptions, conventions, culture, and so on. As an object which is totally independent of our knowledge and culture, Michelangelo's David exists only as a piece of marble. Now this much can be conceded without much difficulty. The simple point about its significance, however, is that it only shows, at best, the repudiation of realism as applied to the construal of interpretation of works of art. That is, one can hardly be a realist about the interpretation of works of art, as such interpretative statements cannot be assumed to be rendered either true or false by some objective reality whose existence and constitution are independent of our knowledge. But, as we have observed earlier, the denial of realism about a given class of statements does not necessarily amount to the denial of objectivity, even in its metaphysical sense, about that class of statements. Objectivity without realism, as we have seen, makes perfect sense.

This distinction between metaphysical objectivity and realism, however, does not rescue the former; there are other considerations which support metaphysical subjectivity as applied to the interpretation of works of art. Something like Mackie's argument from queerness might be one of them. Note that there is a distinction between a Mackie-like argument concerning the queerness of the existence of objects purportedly described by interpretations of works of art, and the anti-realist argument criticized above. The latter relies on the cultural nature of the objects of art. This, as we have just seen, is not enough to cast a doubt on the possible objectivity of interpretation. The argument from queerness, however, aims to show that the entities, or qualities or characters, and so on, purportedly described by typical interpretations of works of art do not exist at all; they are queer entities, so to speak. In other words, the argument from queerness would deny that features of works of art meet any reasonable conditions of existence. Whether this is a plausible line of thought is rather doubtful, but in any case I shall not try to develop it further. I will offer a different line of thought instead, drawing on the idea that metaphysical objectivity presupposes descriptivism. In other words, I will try to show that metaphysical objectivity about interpretations of works of art is rendered problematic because a descriptivist account of interpretation is misguided.

There are two prevalent accounts of interpretation of works of art which are basically descriptive and hence potentially support the objectivist stance. The more familiar one is the authorial intent doctrine.[25] Roughly, this maintains that an interpretation of a work of art should strive to retrieve the author's intentions with respect to the work he or she has created, and the interpretation is successful—and objective—if and only if it succeeds in doing so. Note that one need not hold this intentionalist doctrine *tout court* for the purposes of our discussion: in order to show the possibility of metaphysical objectivity in interpretation, it is sufficient to show that at least in certain (but a not insignificant number of) cases the intentionalist doctrine holds. After all, no one has to claim that interpretations of works of art are always objective. The second type of interpretation which seems descriptive in the requisite sense is the historic interpretation. An interpretation of a work of art sometimes tells us a story about the way in which the work has been conceived, appreciated, and so on, by the culture in which it has been created, or by later cultures in which it played a certain part. In other words, historic interpretations are descriptions of the cultural significance of the work in question, and hence they are basically descriptive.

Neither of these two accounts, however, suffices to show the possibility of metaphysical objectivity as a significant aspect of the interpretation of works of art. The fallacy of intentionalism is more readily apparent. It is, of course, quite correct to maintain that if an interpretation of a work of art consists in the description of its author's intentions, such an interpretation is objective in the metaphysical sense (that is, of course, as long as it makes sense to hold an objectivist position about the relevant kind of mental states); it will be objectively true if the description fits the intentions the author had, and objectively false if it doesn't. But the point is that an interpretation can never be thoroughly descriptive in this sense, even if it focuses on the author's intentions, and even if it makes perfect sense to do so. In other words, a description of the author's intention does not constitute by itself an interpretation of the work he or she has created. There is always the implicit assumption that the author's intentions are relevant, important, or significant for our understanding of the work in question. Even the most devout intentionalists do not assume that just about any fact about the author's state of mind bears on the interpretation of his or her work. The fact that the author has had a terrible headache, or that she has been bothered by domestic problems, may or may

[25] Notably, Hirsch's famous book *Validity in Interpretation* advocating intentionalism has been explicitly motivated by the point of securing the objectivity of interpretation of works of art.

not have such a bearing on the meaning of her work, depending on numerous, *inter alia* evaluative, considerations. Similarly, the fact that the author has intended her readers to understand the motives of one of the characters in her novel, say, in a sinister manner, may or may not shed light on the meaning of her work. Whether it does or does not, however, cannot be determined by a closer scrutiny of her intentions. Not, primarily, because there simply may not be anything to discover there (which is very often the case), but mainly because it would be absurd to assume that authors are infallible interpreters of their own works of art. I shall not dwell on this point further, as it is well known and rarely disputed. Its significance, however, needs to be stated. The point is that even if there are certain aspects of an interpretation of a work of art which are purely descriptive (for example, the description of the author's state of mind), such aspects are always subordinate to other, essentially evaluative aspects of the interpretation in question. Hence it is simply misleading to say that the interpretation is basically a matter of description: only an aspect of it, and one whose significance is always to be determined on non-descriptive grounds, can be characterized as descriptive.

To be sure, I have not been assuming that evaluative judgements, as such, cannot be objective in the metaphysical sense. Far from that. The argument offered here is limited to showing that the reference to author's intentions, even where plausible, does not render by itself the interpretation objective. The objectivist must also show that the evaluative judgements grounding the significance of the author's intentions are metaphysically objective.

Now, similar, but not identical, considerations apply to historic interpretations. Such interpretations vary a great deal; some are closer to straightforward descriptions, while others are better described as critical interpretations set against a historic background. The plausibility of metaphysical objectivity here depends on its plausibility in the realm of historical explanations generally. The latter involves intricate issues that cannot be discussed here. Suffice it to emphasize one point, namely, that the more an interpretation is descriptive, the less of an interpretation it is. The cultural history of art is what it purports to be, namely, history; and the more it is so, the less it can count as a piece of interpretation of a work of art. The fact that there is no hard and fast line to be drawn between the history of art and its interpretation should not obscure the functional and conceptual differences between the two. There is a clear conceptual distinction between a historic interpretation, which basically attempts to describe how a given work of art has been understood by others, and a critical interpretation which purports to suggest how the work should be understood. It should be readily admitted that, as far as one can be objectivist about the construal of others' understanding of a work of art, objectivity is applicable to historic interpretations. Nothing follows from this about the objective standing of critical interpretations.

Once again, it may not be pointless to emphasize the limited scope of the arguments presented in this section. I have not tried to deny any possible role for metaphysically objective statements in the realm of interpretation of works of art. As we have seen, certain aspects of interpretation can be objective in this sense. What remains very doubtful, however, is the assumption that metaphysical objectivity can be regarded as a paradigm, or as a significant aspect, of interpretation of works of art.

Interpretation and discourse subjectivity

Perhaps I should not complain if the reader has gained the impression that I am oversimplifying the controversies over the objectivity of interpretation in the realm of art. This impression is premature, however. Most of the genuine controversies over the possibility of objectivity in this field should be seen as concerning the possibility of objectivity in the discourse sense. And here I think that we must face a very intriguing puzzle indeed, concerning what I have called the epistemic tolerance of interpretations of works of art. To reiterate, the puzzle is this: on the one hand, we must account for the fact that interpretations admit of plurality: the very idea of an interpretation of a work of art imports the possibility of other interpretations of the same work which are potentially inconsistent with it. On the other hand, we must also account for the fact that interpretations of works of art can be good or bad, interesting or silly, right or wrong, and so on.

Of course, if one espouses discourse subjectivity about appraisals of interpretations in terms of right or wrong, good or bad, there is not much of a puzzle left. Such a sceptical approach to interpretations of works of art would simply reinforce their plurality. If anything goes in interpretation, as it were, no wonder that we should be 'tolerant' with respect to conflicting interpretations of the same work. As a matter of fact, for most sceptics it is precisely this plurality of interpretations which leads them to their subjectivist conclusions. But this move, I shall argue, is unwarranted. In other words, I will try to show that we can account for the epistemic tolerance of interpretations of works of art without eschewing the possibility of them being objective in (at least) the discourse sense. Notably, this is a modest claim; it would not prove the correctness of discourse objectivity as applied to interpretations of works of art, as there might be other reasons for denying it, besides this one (that is, the argument from plurality). But at least it could show that one prevalent source of subjectivity is unsound.

Consider this question: can it be the case that discourse objectivity is consistent with relativism? If the answer is basically yes, as I shall now argue, then we have the key to the solution of our puzzle. In brief, the idea is this: interpretations admit of plurality, of epistemic tolerance, mainly because they are based on different frameworks of reference; they are always relative to a certain scheme (or 'myth', as Margolis has called it),[26] and these different schemes of reference need not be consistent with each other. If it can be shown, however, that this relativism inherent in the interpretation of works of art is consistent with discourse objectivity, the puzzle about the epistemic tolerance would be solved. Let us now take it step by step.

Interpretations of works of art normally work from a certain scheme, whether it is explicit or only implicit. Authorial intent, historical context, Freudian psychology, Catholic religion, Marxist political theory, and feminist critique are but a few, familiar examples of such perspectives or schemes guiding interpretations of works of art. Moreover, as we have seen above, the fact that there is such a perspective underlying the interpretation is essential for distinguishing an interpretation of a work of art from mere description on the one hand, and from expressions of personal tastes and impressions on the other. Now, the plurality of interpretations in the relativist sense is secured not merely by this plurality of possible schemes, but mainly by the fact that none of them can be accorded a privileged status. Or at least, this is what the subjectivist assumes, and we need not argue with this assumption. Furthermore, the acceptability of an interpretation of a work of art is rarely affected by the truth or falsehood of the scheme upon which it is based. An interpretation of Dante's *Commedia*, for example, could hardly be affected by the truth or falsehood of Catholicism.[27] Now these three points, namely, that interpretations are typically guided by a certain scheme, that none of these schemes can be accorded a privileged status, and that the truth or falsehood of these schemes does not normally affect the acceptability of the interpretations based on them, establish a fairly strong relativist position.

The only question we need to ask, however, is whether this relativism characteristic of interpretations of works of art is compatible with discourse objectivity. The answer would seem to be as follows: as long as one can hold an objectivist stance about the scheme of reference, one must also allow objectivity about the interpretations based on it. Thus, for example, as long as one may assume that certain kinds of statement about, for example, Catholicism are objective in (at least) the discourse sense, one would have to admit that the same is true about interpretative statements concerning Dante's *Commedia* which are based on the Catholic scheme. For instance, if there is a truth of the matter about the meaning of a certain symbol according to Catholicism, there can also be a truth of the matter about the meaning of that symbol in Dante's work, if it is interpreted from the perspective of the Catholic scheme. There may not be a truth of the matter about the choice of the appropriate scheme, but that does not undermine the discourse, as opposed to the metaphysical, objectivity of the particular interpretation

[26] J. Margolis, *Art and Philosophy*, ch. 7.

[27] Note that there are possible exceptions to this: psychoanalytic and perhaps even Marxist interpretations may well be affected, to some extent, by the truths of these underlying theories.

offered. From the Catholic perspective, one can easily be mistaken about the meaning of a certain symbol in Dante's work, and there is no reason to deny that this would be a mistake, objectively speaking, even if it is not a mistake to strive to interpret Dante's *Commedia* according to a totally different scheme.

It should be conceded, however, that interpretations admit of plurality and inconsistency even from within one and the same scheme. For example, from the perspective of psychoanalysis it may be controversial whether Hamlet's character is best described in terms of an Oedipus complex, or not. But this internal plurality of interpretations is explicable on the following grounds: very often interpretations of works of art which stem from a certain scheme are concomitantly interpretations of both the work in question and certain aspects of the scheme itself. A psychoanalytic interpretation of Hamlet may be both an interpretation of the play and of certain aspects of psychoanalytic theory. Whether the interpretation of the scheme admits of discourse or metaphysical objectivity would obviously depend of the nature of the particular scheme in question, and the nature of the particular controversy.

Generally speaking, then, discourse objectivity is not typically at odds with relativism.[28] Yet there is one important proviso that must be taken into account here: we must draw a distinction between modest and comprehensive interpretative claims. An interpretative claim is modest if it does not claim truth (that is, in terms of exclusivity, or some other form of privileged status) for the choice of its underlying scheme, but only for the truth of the interpretation from the perspective of the scheme chosen; and an interpretative claim is comprehensive if it does claim truth for the choice of the scheme as well. Relativism might not be compatible with discourse objectivity if the interpretations of works of art are typically of the comprehensive kind. I do not believe that they are, however. Epistemic tolerance is so widely acknowledged in this field, precisely because it is characteristic of interpretations of works of art that they are not comprehensive. After all, art is basically a cultural product, and it is reasonable to suppose that there are as many ways of interpreting works of art as there are imaginative schemes embodied in our cultures.[29] In other words, interpreters and art critics normally assume that there is no truth of the matter about the choice of the appropriate scheme for the interpretation of a work of art. Note that it is the claim for the truth of the choice of the underlying scheme which is being denied here; not its relevance or relative importance from a cultural (or some other theoretical) point of view. We can easily understand, for example, why the Catholic scheme is more

[28] In Chapter 8 I argue that the metaphysical objectivity of values is also compatible with a considerable extent of cultural relativism.

[29] Dworkin's 'constructive model' of interpretation presupposes, I think, that interpretations must be of the comprehensive kind. Otherwise, it is difficult to understand Dworkin's insistence on the general availability of *'the best'* interpretation. See his *Law's Empire*, ch. 2.

appropriate for Dante's work than for Shakespeare's. But this appropriateness, so to speak, is a matter of cultural significance, not of truth and falsehood.

The fact that interpretations of works of art are typically of the modest kind may serve well to illustrate a fairly obvious point, namely, that objectivity is only one aspect of the appraisal of interpretations of works of art, and probably not the most important one. In other realms of interpretation the case may be quite different, of course. In the next chapter I will consider in some detail certain aspects of the objectivity of law.

7
Four Questions about the Objectivity of Law

In this chapter I will consider four main questions concerning the objectivity of law. This list is not meant to be exhaustive. There may be other questions which are relevant and interesting. Let me state from the outset what these questions are, though more precise formulations will be presented as we proceed. First, there is a question about the identification of law: can we have objectively right and wrong answers to the question *what the law is* on particular issues? Secondly, there is a question about the merit of the law: even if we do know what the law is, we can still ask whether it is objectively right or wrong, good or bad. This second question is inextricably linked to yet another question about the relative autonomy of law. We cannot hope to answer the question of whether particular legal standards are objectively right or wrong, without first clarifying whether such standards of 'right' and 'wrong' necessarily reduce to moral worth. Thirdly, there is an important sense of objectivity which pertains to law's major function as an adjudicator of disputes and conflicts of interests. Can the law be expected to resolve disputes in an objective manner? What does objectivity mean here? Finally, for reasons to be explained in due course, I will also consider a question about the possible objectivity of legal theory. Is legal theory such that it can meet an appropriate sense of methodological objectivity? I will take up these four questions in the next four sections.[1]

OBJECTIVE IDENTIFICATION OF LAW

We are very familiar with countless statements of the form—'According to the law in ____ X has a right/duty/ etc. to ____.' Can such statements be objectively true (or false)? In what sense would they be true, if they are? Is the law, particular laws, that is, an objective domain we can describe correctly or incorrectly? Most legal philosophers tend to assume that the question here is actually twofold: on one level, it is a question about the objective standing of *the criteria* for identifying law, as such. Legal positivism, for instance, has traditionally maintained that in each and every legal system there are such criteria, and that those criteria are of a factual nature, therefore, metaphysically objective. Allegedly, however, there is a further question here about the

[1] The first two sections are largely based on part of my article 'An Essay on the Objectivity of Law', in B. Bix (ed.), *Analyzing Law: New Essays in Legal Theory* (Oxford, 1998), 1. Let me confess, however, that I no longer subscribe to some of the conclusions which I expressed there. In particular, I no longer believe that a theory of truth is sufficient to ground objectivity.

application of the criteria of legality. Even if such criteria are objective, metaphysically or otherwise, we would still need to inquire whether the application of those criteria to particular cases admits of objectively correct and incorrect answers.[2]

What kind of objectivity is being disputed here? Let us take up the semantic perspective first. Would it make any sense to claim that the criteria for the identification of law are not objective in the semantic sense? What would such a semantic subjectivism amount to? Well, it would mean that whenever judges and lawyers claim that the law is such and such, what they are really doing is not describing anything, but only expressing a certain subjective preference, as it were. Note that such a semantic subjectivism entails a discourse-error theory. It must hold that the superficial grammar of legal discourse about the identification of law, which is certainly descriptive, assertoric, and semantically objective, is profoundly misleading. As a matter of fact, at some deeper level of analysis, the discourse is semantically subjective: it is not really about anything, out there, so to speak, that one can talk and argue about. Is this a tenable position? Does it make sense to maintain that legal discourse about the identification of law only expresses subjective preferences?

The simple, and hardly disputed answer is, that semantic subjectivism makes sense in some cases, but not as a characterization of the whole discourse. Legal positivists, for instance, have long argued that adjudication sometimes involves a kind of pretence: judges, particularly in higher courts, sometimes claim that they have identified the law on a given issue, and that 'the law is . . . such and such', while they know perfectly well that there was no law to discover, but only to be made afresh. (Notably, Dworkin vigorously denies that such a pretence makes sense; according to his account legal discourse must be seen as semantically objective *tout court*[3].) One need not be a positivist, however, to realize that such pretence cannot characterize the whole discourse. For well-known reasons semantic subjectivism makes it impossible to account for any intelligent disagreement between two parties: if statements about what the law is on any given issue are basically reports of personal preferences, or attitudes, etc., then all such statements are consistent with one another; people could never be in any real disagreement with each other.[4]

The conclusion that legal discourse about the identification of law is by and large semantically objective hardly settles any serious dispute. As we saw in the previous chapter, the semantic sense of objectivity does not necessarily entail any commitment to truth. What we would like to know, however, is

[2] In Chapter 3 I have argued that this distinction is much more limited than usually assumed.

[3] Dworkin, *Law's Empire*, ch. 1. I have explained the rationality of this pretence in *Interpretation and Legal Theory*, 119–21.

[4] See, for example, R. M. Hare, *Moral Thinking*, 77. Perhaps a more sophisticated version of moral subjectivism could escape this predicament. For a more detailed discussion, see Chapter 8.

whether there is a truth of the matter about the identification of the law, and what this truth would consist in. Here we must proceed with great caution. First, it might be helpful to examine the main motivations for subjectivist accounts about the identification of law. Why would people tend to think that there are no objective criteria for the identification of the law? There are, I believe, two prevalent motivations for subjectivism in this area. The first stems from the tendency to equate objectivism with realism. Realism, as it is normally understood in contemporary analytical philosophy, is a very difficult position to maintain about almost any given realm of discourse. If anti-realism entails the denial of metaphysical objectivity, then there are plenty of reasons for denying the metaphysical objectivity of legal discourse as well. The second reason stems from doubts about the objectivity of values in general. For those who maintain that the identification of law is partly a matter of evaluative judgements, any doubts one would have about the metaphysical objectivity of the latter would cast similar doubts on the objectivity of identifying the law. Let me take up these points in turn.

As we observed in the last chapter, in the last three decades or so much of the traditional debate about objectivity has been overshadowed by the realism/anti-realism debate. With few exceptions, most analytical philosophers have assumed that objectivity, is, at best, just another label for the realist stance.[5] There is, of course, no point in arguing about labels. The problem with this predominance of the realism/anti-realism debate is that it does not actually capture all that is important about objectivity and truth. Realism, as defined by the protagonists of this debate (mainly Dummett[6] and Putnam in his earlier writings[7]) entails a commitment to the existence of an objective reality which is ontologically independent of our knowledge, and hence also to the possibility of verification-transcendent truths within the realm one is a realist about. It is worth citing Dummett's formulation again:

> The primary tenet of realism, as applied to some given class of statements, is that each statement in that class is determined as true or not true, independently of our knowledge, by some objective reality whose existence and constitution is, again, independent of our knowledge.[8]

Undoubtedly, such a definition of realism excludes a very large number of realms. That, in itself, would not constitute a problem, of course; perhaps we are simply doomed, as Dummett claims,[9] to an anti-realist position in a very large number of domains. But it immediately turns into a problem once we let

[5] See, for example, Wright, *Truth and Objectivity*; Brink, *Moral Realism and the Foundation of Ethics*; Coleman and Leiter, 'Determinacy, Objectivity, and Authority', The exception I have in mind is Wiggins, 'Moral Cognitivism, Moral Relativism, and Motivating Moral Beliefs'.

[6] Dummett, *The Interpretation of Frege's Philosophy*, particularly ch. 20. See also his *Truth and Other Enigmas*.

[7] Putnam, *Realism and Reason*.

[8] *The Interpretation of Frege's Philosophy*, 434.

[9] Ibid.

ourselves be drawn by the sceptical implications which are traditionally associated with anti-realism: if only the existence of a mind-independent, transcendent reality can assure us truth as correspondence, what is the notion of truth, if any, that the anti-realist is left with?

This line of thought, however, is based on a false premiss. It assumes that any sensible notion of truth as correspondence must presuppose that propositions are only rendered true or false by the existence of an ontologically mind-independent reality. A sensible notion of truth as correspondence, however, need not be committed to metaphysical realism. What we need, then, is simply to disassociate anti-realism from scepticism about truth. In other words, we have to show that anti-realism and objectivism are compatible positions.

As we saw in the previous chapter, this is neither a revisionist nor a very difficult task. It must be observed that there is a wide range of domains where we feel certain about truth (and knowledge), and equally certain that it would not make much sense to be a realist about those realms. One important group of such domains concerns practices which are constituted by social conventions. For example, there is a truth of the matter about the rules of chess, the current conventions of fashion in Paris, and I would certainly add, the legal speed limit in the state of Illinois (as I have painfully experienced several times). In these, and countless other examples, we safely use the notions of truth and falsehood, despite the fact that it would make no sense to hold a realist position about such domains. The truths about the rules of chess are not rendered so by an objective reality which is ontologically independent of human creation and human knowledge. Realism applied to a given type of discourse entails the possibility of attributing comprehensive mistakes (that is, when a whole community of speakers can err) about the truth of any given proposition within the realm one is a realist about.[10] For any concept one is a realist about, it should be possible to envisage a *whole community of speakers* misidentifying its real reference, or extension. With respect to concepts constituted by conventional practices, however, such comprehensive mistakes about their reference is implausible. If a given concept is constituted by social conventions, it is impossible for the pertinent community to misidentify its reference. There is nothing more we can discover about the content of the rules of chess than what we already know.

The above conclusion is modest but important. It is a modest conclusion, since we have only shown that anti-realism does not necessarily entail the denial of objectivity. Hence we have shown that one of the main worries about the possibility of an objectivist stance on the identification of law, namely, the worry stemming from the implausibility of realism in this area, is an idle one. However, at least for legal conventionalism this conclusion is very

[10] For a more detailed account, see Marmor, *Interpretation and Legal Theory*, ch. 5.

important. In fact, legal conventionalism may not need more than this, namely, the plausibility of objectivism about conventional practices to show the plausibility of moderate objectivism with respect to the identification of the law. Law, according to legal conventionalism, is basically identified by the conventional practices (or Rules of Recognition) which constitute the sources of law. If there can be a truth of the matter about such conventional practices, understood along the lines suggested by metaphysical objectivity, then legal positivism would have almost everything that it needs to substantiate an objectivist position. Basically, the picture would be this: in each and every legal system, there are conventionally established practices that are taken to constitute the source of law. These are the conventions establishing the procedures for the creation, modification, and annulment of legal standards. These conventions leave certain gaps. But in most standard instances they also make it possible to say that there is an objectively determinate answer to the question of what the law is on a given issue. The answer is given by the truths about the conventions establishing the sources of law, coupled with the relevant truths about those facts which are taken to yield legal results of various sorts according to the conventions (such as the fact that a certain act of legislation had taken place, or a judicial decision rendered, etc.).

Before we proceed to the next point, however, allow me a small detour. According to Dummett's original definition of the realism/anti-realism debate, one of the main issues in this debate is the question of whether truth is a non-epistemic concept, as the realist would have it, or an epistemic one, as Dummett's own verificationism maintains.[11] Since Dummett's verificationist semantics has not convinced even his more sympathetic readers, many philosophers have sought an alternative, maintaining his basic idea of truth as warranted assertability. Most influential amongst these alternatives is Putnam's version of it in *Reason, Truth and History*, which has been called 'Internal Realism'.[12] Instead of identifying 'being true' with 'being verified', as Dummett suggests, Putnam's internal realism identified truth with *being verified to a sufficient degree to warrant acceptance under sufficiently good epistemic conditions*.

Although Putnam himself no longer subscribes to this position, it still exerts considerable influence in contemporary legal theory. In a series of articles devoted to the issues of objectivity in law, Jules Coleman and Brian Leiter have sought to provide an account of objectivity which draws on Putnam's internal realism and the notion of truth as warranted assertability under ideal epistemic conditions.[13] Let me explain why I think that this is not a promising route.

[11] Dummett, *The Interpretation of Frege's Philosophy*.

[12] Putnam, *Reason, Truth, and History*, at 55–6.

[13] See, for example: Coleman and Leiter, 'Determinacy, Objectivity, and Authority'; Leiter, 'Book Review: Objectivity and the Problems of Jurisprudence'; see also their respective replies to Putnam in the first volume of *Legal Theory*.

It was Richard Rorty's scepticism which lay at the background of Putnam's internal realism. According to Rorty's picture of modern philosophy, the latter is burdened with an irresolvable problem about truth: truth as correspondence requires us to have referential access to things, out there in the world, so to speak, but it will always remain a mystery how such referential access is attainable. Putnam's original idea of truth as warranted assertability under ideal epistemic conditions was meant to resolve this problem by dissolving the need for referential access. Truth, then, would be an epistemic concept, not implicated with the problem of our inability to step out of our own skin. But Putnam himself later realized that the solution is illusory, since 'there is an equal problem as to how we can have referential or other access to "sufficiently good epistemic situations"'.[14] In other words, if the problem is that there is an interface between the 'knower' and the 'world', then this interface is still there, only shifted from the 'world' at large, to the conditions which render a situation epistemically appropriate. This is mainly so because the idea of an ideal epistemic condition must be, as Putnam put it, 'a world involving notion'.[15] If not, then we will be quickly forced to draw the highly implausible conclusion that the totality of human knowledge *determines* the totality of truths. Perhaps another way to put it is this: the Rortian problem was, initially, that the traditional conception of truth is inextricably linked to an epistemology without foundations. Such a problem cannot be solved by turning truth itself into an epistemological concept. The relevant epistemology could either be *indicative* of truth, or *constitutive* of it. If it is the former, we are back to the problem of lack of access (to the extent, of course, that it is indeed a problem). If, on the other hand, the epistemology is constitutive of truth, then Rorty's scepticism, far from being resolved, has actually been reinforced. If human knowledge determines what truth is, then the concept of 'truth', as it has been traditionally conceived, is redundant indeed.

Whatever the realm in which we talk about truth may be, it is crucial that we be able to distinguish between the notions of truth and that of a *justified belief*. Note that this is precisely what Rorty denies; he claims that since these two notions are not distinguishable, truth is superfluous. Having an idea of what it is to hold justified beliefs is the best we can hope for. Now, the problem is not the equation of truth with warranted assertability. In certain kinds of discourse, truth may well be a matter of warranted assertability. The problem lies in the attempt to explicate the conditions which warrant assertability solely in epistemic terms.[16] Once we take that path, we will inevitably end up

[14] Putnam, 'Sense, Nonsense, and the Senses: An Inquiry into the Powers of the Human Mind', at 462.

[15] Ibid.

[16] That is why I don't find Crispin Wright's notion of 'superassertability' a considerable improvement on Putnam's original position. 'Superassertability' is also an epistemic concept. See Wright, *Truth and Objectivity*, 44ff.

with a *reduction* of truth to justified belief. The beliefs we would hold under favourable epistemic conditions are the beliefs we are epistemically justified in holding. But when we come to consider the relation between justified beliefs and truth, we are immediately forced back to Putnam's dilemma. Either the conditions which justify the belief are constitutive of its truth, in which case we must side with Rorty, or else, they are not, in which case we must confront afresh Rorty's scepticism.[17]

The second problem regarding the objectivity of the identification of law concerns the moral-value dependence of legal validity. The standard subjectivist argument comprises two theses. First, it is claimed that the criteria of legality, and even more so, the application of those criteria to particular cases, are profoundly affected by moral and other evaluative considerations. Secondly, it is maintained that those moral or other evaluative considerations are essentially subjective, thus rendering the identification of law subjective throughout.[18]

As it stands, however, such an argument would not be applicable to the *exclusive* version of legal positivism, since exclusive positivism denies the first premiss. Inclusive legal positivism, on the other hand, readily admits the first premiss, namely, that the identification of law may depend on moral considerations. In order to defend the possibility of objectivity about the identification of law, it must, therefore, deny the second premiss. Inclusive legal positivism must claim that those moral and other evaluative considerations which might determine what the law is on particular cases are sufficiently objective, as it were. Notably, Dworkin's legal theory is in a similar position. Both allow for the criteria of legality and the application of those criteria to depend on moral considerations. Therefore, both theories need to have an account of the objectivity of the relevant types of moral consideration to be able to reject the so-called 'critical' charge that determining what the law is depends on subjective assessments or preferences as to what it ought to be. In other words, defending the objectivity of morality is essential both for Dworkin's legal theory, and for the inclusive version of legal positivism: if the identification of law depends on morality, as both these theories maintain, and morality does not admit of objective truths, the identification of law would turn out to be disturbingly subjective.[19]

[17] In a reply to this argument, Jules Coleman claimed that the same argument can be turned against my own position about the nature of truth, expressed in the article mentioned in n. 1 above. See Coleman, 'Second Thoughts and Other First Impressions', 293–4. I think that Coleman is right about this, and therefore I no longer argue for pluralism about truth.

[18] This is the kind of scepticism expressed, for example, by Stanley Fish (see, for example, his 'Working in a Chain Gang: Interpretation in Law and Literature'), and Critical Legal Theorists, such as Mark Tushnet (see, for example, his 'An Essay on Rights'.).

[19] The need to defend the objectivity of morality has not escaped the attention of any of the protagonists of these views. See Dworkin, 'Objectivity and Truth: You'd Better Believe It', and Coleman and Leiter, 'Determinacy, Objectivity and Authority'.

In Chapter 3 I argued at length that the identification of law does not depend on moral considerations. In the next chapter we will have the opportunity to see that moral considerations are rarely as subjective as proponents of the argument under consideration would have it. Generally speaking, then, legal conventionalism is not threatened by this particular brand of scepticism. More often than not, the identification of law is an objective domain. The criteria of legality are determined by social conventions, and these conventions are social facts. As such, they can be described and one can be objectively right or wrong about their content. We have also seen in detail that it rarely makes sense to say that we know what the relevant criteria of legality are, but their application to particular cases depends on moral or other considerations.[20]

Nevertheless, as I indicated earlier, there may be cases in which the criteria of legality are indeterminate. The appropriate conclusion in such cases is that there is no settled law on the relevant issue. Such legal gaps are of various kinds and are due to various causes. Typically, they are divided into those cases for which there is simply no legal standard covering the particular case confronted, and those cases for which there is a putative standard which would apply to the case, but its relevant prescription is indeterminate due to vagueness, ambiguity, or some other form of communication failure.[21]

The crucial point to note is, however, that legal gaps do not render the law subjective in those cases in which such gaps exist. Once we face a legal gap, the appropriate conclusion is that *it is objectively the case that there is no settled law* on the particular issue. Suppose, for example, that the relevant law prescribes that all subjects of type P have a legal duty to do X. Suppose that the category P consists of a vague concept, and that a particular instance, say P_1, is a borderline case of P. Is P_1 legally obliged to do X? The appropriate answer is that the question is legally unsettled, and therefore, unless there is some kind of a default rule that applies here, the answer is 'no: P_1 is not legally obliged to X'. This is just as objective a matter as the conclusion about those cases which do fall under the category P without any doubts. Needless to say, the law can normally be changed so as to yield a specific outcome, typically, but not necessarily, by judicial decisions. Before such a change in the law takes place, however, it is objectively the case that the issue is not settled by the law.[22]

[20] See Chapter 3.

[21] Another source of legal gaps is one which is due to factual indeterminacy: the law may prescribe a legal standard which depends on the existence of certain facts, and it may well happen that those factual elements which would render the law applicable are not ascertainable under certain circumstances.

[22] Notably, indeterminacy is always from a particular point of view: an answer to a particular question can be objectively indeterminate from a legal point of view, for example, but it may have a determinate moral answer, and vice versa, of course.

It might be important to note that the possibility of legal gaps is compatible with the view which maintains the applicability of logical bivalence and the excluded middle to the legal domain. If there is any problem here, it stems from general logical concerns about vague concepts, and the question of whether vagueness is compatible with both bivalence and the excluded middle. From the vantage point of *legal* theory, however, the existence of a legal gap simply entails that it is determinately false that the law requires such and such, or that the law grants a certain right, etc. Legal gaps are not truth-value gaps. Statements about the law purport to describe authoritative resolutions. If the authority's prescription is for some reason objectively indeterminate, due to vagueness or for any other reason, then there is no authoritative resolution on the matter, which means that it is false that the law requires whatever it is that it might prescribe in the circumstances.[23]

LAW'S OBJECTIVE MERIT

Even if one concedes that there are objective answers to the questions about the identification of the law, one could still maintain that objectivity about the content of the law is highly suspect: we may know for sure what the law is on a given issue, but whether it is right or wrong is something that cannot be objectively determined. Now, is this just the familiar worry about the objectivity of moral values? Not necessarily. There is a jurisprudential issue here that must first be settled. The issue is whether legal norms' appraisals in terms of right or wrong necessarily reduces to moral worth. Or are there any *legal* standards of appraisal which are at least partly autonomous of moral or other evaluative concerns about the law?

It is undeniable that law, like other social institutions, affects people's lives in countless moral ways. Almost all but perhaps the most technical or declarative legal norms have some moral ramifications for some people. This does not entail, however, that legal norms can only be appreciated by moral standards. Nor do I think that many people have claimed that it is otherwise. Obviously, legal norms can be evaluated from other perspectives. Legal standards and arrangements can be more or less economically efficient, or intellectually intriguing, or internally coherent or elegant, and so on. Thus, the question is not whether the law can only be assessed by moral standards. There are two other questions which are far more important. First, there is a whole cluster of questions which pertains to the relations between the moral evaluations of the law and other types of human concerns. Should we hold, for example, that the moral perspective must prevail over all other concerns?

23 The law often deals with such gaps by a complex set of default rules, like the rules determining the burden of proof, presumptions, canons of construction, and the like.

Is it always relevant? To what extent do other evaluative perspectives, like economic efficiency, for example, derive from underlying moral principles? All these and similar questions are very contentious and extremely complex. Some of these questions pertain to the scope of morality itself.[24] In any case, I will have nothing to say here about these issues. My concern is with the second main question, namely, whether there is any distinctive *legal* set of standards for evaluating rightness or wrongness of legal norms and decisions. Is law, in other words, at least partly autonomous in its own standards of appraisal?

The idea that law is autonomous in its own standards of appraisal is often associated with the notorious Legal Formalism that was prevalent amongst American jurists at the turn of the previous century. Their idea of the 'inner logic' of the law is one of the main jurisprudential themes which were ridiculed by the American Legal Realists at the beginning of the last century, and then, later, by various 'critical' movements. This 'inner logic' of law, they claimed, is nothing but the ideology of those who make the law for us. Law has no 'inner logic', it has been argued, but only the logic of veiling up ideological biases and preferences in neutral and objective language. Against this historical background, it may seem that all talk about the autonomy of law would be reminiscent of Formalism, buried, we hoped, a long time ago. But I would like to urge some caution here. Those who completely deny the autonomy of legal discourse face a serious challenge as well. They must explain why legal discourse is so unlike what they claim that it actually is. After all, legal discourse *is not* simply moral-political discourse. It has its own distinctive features, its own language, its own standards of excellence and failure, and so on.[25] When lawyers criticize a legal decision, they often do so on distinctive legal grounds. It is not uncommon, for instance, to encounter criticisms of particular legal decisions as 'legally wrong, even if morally acceptable'. Is all this discourse sheer nonsense, then? We should seriously doubt it. Surely part of it might be nonsense. And it certainly does happen that lawyers and judges speak the language of law, when in fact it is only their moral or ideological preferences that they actually express. Yet the entire discourse cannot be so easily dismissed. So I think that we must try to explain how legal discourse actually comprises its own standards of appraisal, even if, needless to add, those standards are not exclusive of other, especially moral, evaluations of the law. Once we have such an account, we may go on to examine both its relation to the moral point of view and its potential objectivity.

Needless to say, the law is not unique in its relative autonomy. There is a great number of conventionally established practices which are just as autonomous as law is; in fact, typically much more so. The constitutive con-

[24] See, for example, Scheffler, *Human Morality*.
[25] See, for example, Fried, 'The Artificial Reason of the Law or: What Lawyers Know'.

ventions establishing such practices also establish some of the practices' own standards of appraisal. Consider, for instance, games like chess. A set of constitutive conventions determine what the game is. But these conventions and the practices emergent from them also determine, to a considerable extent, what it is to be a good or a bad chess player, what constitutes an elegant or a sloppy move, and so on. And the same is true, for example, of operas. As a distinct genre, opera is a conventional practice. Its standards of appraisal are partly autonomous. There are, of course, musical and dramatic standards of appraisal that we can apply to operas, irrespective of its distinctive genre-defining features. But these external standards are utterly incomplete. The conventions establishing the practice of operas also establish certain unique standards of excellence which are distinctively operatic.[26]

It is important to reiterate, however, that even autonomous practices, such as chess and opera, are closely related to external values and general human concerns which are independent of the conventions constituting the particular practice. Chess is a competitive game of a certain sort, and it is thus related to certain general concerns about playing games, winning and losing, intellectual superiority, and the like. Operas are probably even more closely related to general artistic values. In this respect opera might be closer to law than chess is. Law is clearly connected to, and largely guided by, general human concerns. Its autonomy is very limited. However, with respect to all these examples, including the law, some of the values they instantiate, and their standards of appraisal, are underdetermined by those external concerns and values to which they are closely related. Intellectual competitions can be conducted in an indefinite number of ways; similarly, musical and dramatic values can be instantiated in infinite ways. The game of chess, and the practice of opera, constitute particular and unique ways of instantiating these general human concerns. Only once there is a practice of operas does it make sense to speak of distinct operatic values, achievements, and so on. To a lesser extent this is also true with regard to the law. There are countless ways of doing right or wrong in various human affairs, regardless of law; the law creates, however, some of its own conceptions of right and wrong, in ways which are unique to law and dependent on its particular conventions. To give just one instructive example, consider the extremely complex relations between the law of contract and the moral concept of a promise. That these two concepts are closely linked is hardly disputable. But it is equally clear that even for those who maintain that Contract is basically the legal form of a promise, the former cannot be simply reduced to the latter. The legal forms of contract, and their various ramifications, create unique legal concerns that are not simply instantiations of general moral values.[27]

[26] See Chapter 1.
[27] See, for example, Raz's Book Review 'Promises in Morality and Law'.

Law is very much like opera. It is a conventionally established practice, closely related to, but underdetermined by, the general human concerns it is engaged with. The conventions establishing the law, and its emergent practices, partly create their own values and standards of appraisal. But it is crucial to note that these unique values and standards of appraisal are constituted by the conventions which are constitutive of the practice. Just as it makes no sense to say that distinct operatic values existed before operas were invented, so it would make no sense to speak of distinct legal values and standards of appraisal in the abstract, as if these were some Platonic or Rational standards law has to meet. The autonomous values are created by the constitutive conventions of the law and not followed, or emulated by it. They are created by those same conventions which create the law itself.[28]

Without too much commitment to established nomenclature, let me call these conventionally constituted values and standards the *legal culture* which is distinctive of different legal systems. It may be useful to distinguish two layers of such legal cultures: a superficial layer and a deeper one. At the superficial level we would find those aspects of legal culture which are analogous to the folkloristic aspects of general cultures. They would typically include accepted forms of legal argumentation, the conventions and practices of legal education, some canons of construction, ritualistic aspects of legal practices, and such. At the deeper level, we would find those aspects of a legal culture which partly constitute its unique basic norms of legitimacy. For example, the underlying social conventions of US constitutionalism, often described as America's 'civic religion', are undoubtedly, a deep cultural aspect of the US legal system. The underlying conventions of the Civil Law, or the Common Law, would provide another familiar example. Now one of the main differences between the superficial and deep aspects of legal culture consists in the fact that the latter are inextricably tied to questions of moral legitimacy. The superficial aspects of a legal culture would rarely have much moral significance. Consider, for example, textual or syntactical canons of construction in legal interpretation. These vary considerably between different legal systems, but their moral implications are very limited. And equally limited are the numerous ritualistic aspects of legal practices. Such conventions do define ways of going about practising law, and therefore they also constitute and define ways of going rightly or wrongly about it, but not in any morally significant way. The deep aspects of a legal culture, on the other hand, are to a considerable extent about conditions of legitimacy and moral-political acceptability. In Marxist terms, we could say that the deep aspects of legal culture constitute its unique ideological forms. Whether these ideologies are

[28] I do not intend to claim that the distinction between external and internal-autonomous values of such conventional practices is a clear-cut dichotomy. Such values, needs, and functions can be mixed, and they may exert pressures and modifications on each other.

indeed forms of false consciousness as Marxists would have it, or not, is a question I will not attempt to address here.

Let us return to the question of objectivity. With respect to those values and standards of appraisal which are unique to law, objectivity should not be so mysterious . If we thought that there were some distinct legal values which the law was there to follow, as it were, the objectivity of such values would be quite a mystery. But once we realize that the values which are distinctive of legal culture are only those which are in fact constituted by its own conventions, we can see that objectivity is rendered fairly mundane. To the extent that one can hold an objectivist stance about conventionally established practices, objectivity about the legally autonomous standards would make sense. So here, once again, I would advocate objectivity without realism. When we talk about legal right or wrong (that is, distinctly legal, as opposed to moral), there are objects we actually talk about, namely, constitutive conventions and practices emergent from them, and I see no reason to deny the possibility of ascribing determinate truth values to descriptions of such values.

The conclusion that there are objective *legal* values, established by the constitutive conventions of the law is a very modest one. Such values are internal to legal practice, and they are, of course, susceptible to external moral evaluation. Just as one could, for example, criticize specific operatic values on general artistic and aesthetic grounds, one could also criticize the autonomous values of the law on general moral grounds. The moral perspective is of crucial importance, particularly, as we have seen, with respect to the deep levels of legal cultures.

OBJECTIVITY, NEUTRALITY, AND EQUALITY

One of Marx's main insights about the law is the twofold claim that the law must present itself as an objective, unbiased arbitrator of disputes and that it systematically fails to meet this challenge. According to Marx and later Marxists, law's claim to objectivity in this respect is one of its main ideological aspects. More recent literature, be it in the feminist or other critical traditions, has provided ample evidence of the failure of law in maintaining objectivity between different classes, genders, races, and so on. I will not try to dispute any of these claims here. The question of whether the law can actually maintain objectivity or is bound to fail, is one I will not try to answer here. In view of considerable confusion about different concepts and ideas which prevail in this field, my only purpose here is to suggest some clarifications. In particular, I will try to clarify some essential distinctions between law's claim to objectivity, neutrality, and equality.

Undoubtedly, one important sense of 'objectivity' concerns the way in which we would expect arbitrators, judges, and other people or institutions who are in a position to resolve disputes to form their judgements. Let me call this sense of objectivity 'judicial objectivity', although it should be clear that the term is not confined to judges. Judicial objectivity is the opposite of bias, prejudice, one-sidedness, parochialism, bigotry, and such. Notably, it has an inherent moral component. Failure of judicial objectivity is a moral deficiency. However, judicial objectivity also has an epistemic counterpart which often results from a failure to see the other side's interests and concerns, from a failure to comprehend the complexity of the situation, and other similar epistemic distortions. Therefore, the judicial sense of objectivity is closely related to epistemic objectivity in general. Theoreticians and scientists, for example, may fail to be objective in a very similar sense when they are theoretically prejudiced, parochial, or one-sided.[29] Despite these similarities, however, I will confine myself here to an analysis of judicial objectivity in the strict, confined sense.

Judicial objectivity is often confused with neutrality. There is some overlap between these two ideas, but we should be cautious not to confuse them. Neutrality is a notoriously problematic concept. In its central sense, a stance manifests neutrality when it amounts to some form of non-interference in an existing dispute. We can say, for example, that Switzerland was neutral during the war by not taking sides, not participating in it. Note, however, that not all forms of non-interference in face of a conflict amount to neutrality. To begin with, neutrality is a *deliberate* abstention from interference. A would not manifest neutrality about the conflict between B and C, if A is unaware of the conflict or if A is in no position to take sides anyway.[30] Secondly, there must be some background expectation that A would naturally tend to take sides in the conflict. Neutrality must have a point. Thirdly, and this is one reason why the idea of neutrality is so problematic to apply in a variety of cases, neutrality must be an actual possibility. A third party is not always in a position which actually enables it not to take sides. It is sometimes the case that whatever you do or refrain from doing, you will end up assisting or hindering one of the parties involved.

The main problem with neutrality, however, is actually a moral one. Imagine, for example, that you encounter two children fighting in your neighbourhood, and that one is the neighbourhood bully and the other is a much weaker little boy. Assuming that the causes of the fight are neither here nor there, would you manifest neutrality by non-interference? This is far from clear. One can believe that neutrality requires not taking sides in the conflict, and thus one would also tend to conclude that behaving neutrally in such a case is morally wrong. Or one could think that neutrality has no clear application in such a case. Either way, it is at least clear that assisting the weak side

[29] See Raz, *Engaging Reason*.

[30] Taking sides need not be an action; it can also be a judgement or an opinion formed.

is not a neutral stance in such cases, although it may well be precisely the action which would be required of an objective adjudicator. I will return to this point shortly.

If we associate the central cases of neutrality with non-interference, with not taking sides in a dispute, the question that arises is whether we can apply the idea of neutrality to cases of adjudication or arbitration, which are initially meant to result in some form of interference. Can an adjudicator be expected to resolve a dispute in a neutral way? Perhaps, but then it should be clear that the term *neutrality* is being used in a very different sense. Neutrality in adjudication would simply mean something like judicial objectivity. Its violation would consist in the fact that the adjudicator has reached her decision by initially favouring one of the disputing parties or giving undue weight to the perspective or interests of one of the parties involved. In other words, when the concept of neutrality is applied to instances of adjudicative decisions, it is used as a synonym of what we have labelled judicial objectivity. The latter is quite different from the central cases of neutrality, which we typically apply to a stance of non-interference in a conflict between other parties.

The distinction between neutrality and judicial objectivity is not just a pedantic terminological matter. There is a substantial moral difference between judicial objectivity and neutrality as non-interference. The latter calls for much more substantial moral justification. Roughly, we could say that judicial objectivity is *prima facie* good, unless some deviation from it can be justified, whereas the opposite may be true of neutrality as non-interference. Deviations from judicial objectivity are justified, for instance, in cases of justified partiality. It is certainly arguable that there are cases in which we may favour one side in a dispute just because it is, somehow, *our* side. In such cases we explicitly forgo judicial objectivity in favour of some explicit partiality. Yet these cases are problematic and morally exceptional. On the other hand, I do not think that we are entitled to assume that neutrality as non-interference is a default moral position. Quite the contrary: neutrality is *often* the morally wrong stance to hold precisely because it violates judicial objectivity. Recall our example of the neighbourhood bully; objective reasons would call for interference on behalf of the weak party. Neutrality is typically the deliberate suppression of action on the basis of objective reasons. A deliberate stance of neutrality is, therefore, an instance of a decision to act on exclusionary reasons, that is, reasons not to act on the balance of objective reasons that apply to the case. It may well be the case, of course, that neutrality is justified in certain circumstances, but such justifications are definitely called for.

I conclude that neutrality in its central sense, viz., as non-interference, is quite irrelevant to the main concerns of the law. Law is there to intervene in disputes in order to resolve them. What would seem to be central to law's claim to objectivity, therefore, is not neutrality but the judicial sense of objectivity.

From an analytical vantage point, the main worry about the idea of judicial objectivity is whether it is doing any work at all. Of course we know all too well what would be clear instances of the violation of judicial objectivity. As we have noted earlier, bias, favouritism, one-sidedness, and such, clearly violate judicial objectivity. The worry about redundancy stems, however, from the question of whether there is anything more to judicial objectivity than the requirement that resolution of conflicts and disputes be *based on the right reasons*. In other words, the question is whether judicial objectivity simply reduces to the general requirement to base one's decisions on the right reasons which apply to the case.

Perhaps the worry about redundancy is not such a serious worry as it might seem. There are countless human interactions where partiality seems to be justified. All we have to assume here is that people may have reasons to behave partiality under certain circumstances. Would it not be the case then that we could face situations of conflict which would warrant a partial stance, thus not being judicially objective? After all, partiality, whether justified or not, is a clear violation of judicial objectivity. If I favour my neighbour just because she is my neighbour, objectivity is not a candidate for whatever justifies this stance. But now, if we assume that even morally justified instances of partiality would typically violate judicial objectivity, it may be worth asking why that is the case. Is it because partiality violates the principle of equal concern and respect? This is not an implausible position, and it may suggest that judicial objectivity in general is ultimately reducible to the deontic ideal of equal concern for people's needs, interests, and the like.

So now it seems that there are two redundancy questions we should consider. First, the question of whether judicial objectivity boils down, eventually, to the ideal of equal concern and respect. Secondly, the question of whether the latter is doing any work over and above the general requirement to base decisions and actions on the right reasons. Let me explore and defend the possibility that judicial objectivity is essentially an egalitarian concern, and that in this sense of equal concern it is not entirely redundant.

It is a truism, but an important one, that bias, one-sidedness, favouritism, and such familiar failures of judicial objectivity cannot be judged by the actual results of decisions and actions. The question is not whether one side in a conflict ended up favoured over the other, but whether such uneven results were justified by the right reasons which apply to the case. Violation of judicial objectivity is always an instance of *unjustified* favouritism. Judicial objectivity, therefore, is an essentially deontic concept; it concerns the question of how reasons were considered and weighted. This does not mean, of course, that consequentialist considerations cannot be the reasons favouring one decision over another. The likely effects of various decisions and actions may well be the reasons supporting them. Note, however, that even if the likely consequences are the *only* relevant reasons, judicial objectivity consists in the requirement to give those consequentialist reasons equal consideration with respect to the relevant parties. Suppose, for example, that a particular decision favouring A over B is justified because the likely benefits to A exceed the likely benefits to B (and suppose that there are no further considerations involved). The decision would satisfy judicial objectivity, however, only if A's and B's relevant benefits and burdens have been given equal consideration. Even the strictest consequentialist considerations must rely on a prior decision on how to weight costs and benefits *vis-à-vis* the different subjects involved. A prior commitment to equality is only one option. Consequentialist considerations must always rely on some idea about who counts in the calculus and, crucially, how much they count *vis-à-vis* one another. Consider, for example, a consequentialist position which maintains that the suffering of animals should be taken into account, but to a lesser extent than the comparable suffering of humans. Perhaps this position is wrong, but it is hardly incoherent.

Whether genuine partiality is ever justified on consequentialist grounds is a difficult and contested issue. In any event, a stance on this issue does not form part of my argument. Partiality, however, violates judicial objectivity, and it violates it precisely because it is a violation of the ideal of equal concern and respect. Partiality can be warranted by reasons. It may well be the case that under certain circumstances, the right course of action for me to pursue is one which deliberately favours the interests of my family members over the interests of others, and just because they are *my* family members. But then, of course, my course of action cannot follow from a decision which I could describe as judicially objective.

To sum up my argument so far: I suggest that judicial objectivity eventually boils down to an egalitarian concern. It consists in the requirement to give equal consideration and respect to the interests of all parties concerned. As such, judicial objectivity is a moral ideal, and one which does not necessarily have universal applicability. People are sometimes justified in violating this ideal as, for instance, in cases of justified partiality. Therefore, it also follows that judicial objectivity as the ideal of equal concern and respect is not conceptually redundant; it is not simply reducible to the requirement to base one's decisions on the right reasons. Under certain circumstances the right reasons may warrant a violation of equal concern, and therefore of judicial objectivity.

A possible objection should be mentioned here. Arguably, genuine partiality is not really an exception to judicial objectivity because it is not strictly speaking a *moral* concern. Morality, it may be thought, never warrants a genuinely partial position. Partiality, according to this view, is outside the scope of morality and to the extent that we act on partial considerations which are somehow warranted, these should be regarded as limits on the demands of morality, not instances of it. If this view is correct the redundancy charge could regain its force. One could then claim that judicial objectivity is simply the requirement to base decisions and actions on the right *moral* reasons, that is, as opposed to partial or other non-moral considerations. I find this view unconvincing, however. Morality does not have such well-defined boundaries as the argument under consideration would have it. The boundaries between morality, ethics, and other practical concerns of human conduct are much more fuzzy. As long as practical conclusions follow from reasons, it matters little how we classify the reasons in play.

It is very tempting to assume that the law, as such, must be committed to judicial objectivity throughout. Perhaps as an ideal it should be. There is a very plausible distinction to be drawn here between public and private reason. In the realm of private reason partiality is often justified. However, in the realm of public reason, we may hold the view that partiality is never warranted. Be this as it may, an interesting question is whether the law is *essentially* committed to judicial objectivity, or not. The answer is both yes and no. The negative aspect is obvious: There is nothing conceptually incoherent, though a great deal may be wrong, with a legal system which does not purport to treat *all* its subjects with equal concern and respect.[31] On the other hand, there is some level of judicial objectivity which is essential to the functioning of law. No legal system can be totally partial, or biased. Legal prescriptions must be issued at a certain level of generality. Therefore, even when the law is markedly partial it would favour some *class* of people as such. Suppose, for example, that the law is biased in favour of property owners by, say, granting property owners certain benefits which are denied to others. At least within the class of property owners, however, the law would exercise some level of judicial objectivity; it would grant the benefit to all Xs who happen to be property owners in the requisite sense. This, of course, is what makes the discernment of bias and prejudice so difficult in practice. Whether any given class of people as such is entitled to some preferential treatment always depends on the underlying reasons for it. Bias is rarely on the surface.

In sum, I have argued that judicial objectivity eventually boils down to the moral ideal of equal concern and respect. It is an ideal which we should expect the law to pursue as far as it can. But as a moral ideal, it is also susceptible to justified exceptions. Furthermore, although it would be safe to assume that few legal systems, if any, instantiate judicial objectivity to a desirable degree, no legal system can function without some level of such objectivity simply because the law must operate at certain levels of generality.

[31] It may be worth noting, however, that even in the most liberal of moods, most legal systems are much less committed to judicial objectivity than one would tend to assume. After all, most liberal legal systems adopt a great deal of explicit particularism favouring, for example, their own citizens to those of other countries.

METHODOLOGICAL OBJECTIVITY

Decisions and resolutions of conflict are not the only things which can be biased. Theories can be biased as well. It has become a recurrent theme in recent literature that legal theory is particularly prone to bias, since it aims to describe a social practice which is essentially normative. The standard claim is that legal theory cannot purport to be purely descriptive. Ultimately, legal theory relies on moral-evaluative views. Therefore, any attempt to present a theory of law which purports to be value free is an inevitable distortion. This is the claim I want to discuss here. My discussion will focus on two main arguments which have been offered to support this claim and I will try to show that neither is convincing. These arguments are not cast in the framework of objectivity. They do not aim to call into question the objectivity of legal theory, or any other kind of social explanation. Their main purpose is to prove that social explanations, like a theory of law, are inevitably value laden. They claim that there is no hope for a value-free, purely descriptive jurisprudence. Part of my argument here is, however, that the issue is really about the possibility of an objective, that is, non-biased description of social practices. We must confront the question of whether we can provide a description of social practices which is not tainted by our own moral values and other evaluative preconceptions.

The first argument is Dworkin's, and it is parallel to the argument discussed in Chapter 4 about the value dependence of interpretation. Essentially, the argument is based on two main premisses. The first premiss is that legal theory, as such, is a form of interpretation; jurisprudence is an interpretation of a social practice. The second premiss maintains that all interpretations are essentially value laden. Once we are in the business of interpretation evaluative judgements are necessarily part and parcel of what we are engaged in. Therefore, it follows, jurisprudence is necessarily value laden.

The second argument is Stephen Perry's, and it is best summarized in the following passage: 'Jurisprudence requires a conceptual framework. The difficulty is that the data can plausibly be conceptualized in more than one way, and choosing among conceptualizations seems to require the attribution to law of a point or function. This in turn involves not just evaluative considerations, but moral argument.'[32]

The argument from interpretation has a long history in the social sciences. Modern sociology and the other social sciences have largely evolved from early nineteenth-century Positivism. The latter was inspired by a pretty naive view which sought to develop the sciences in the social realm based on the model of the natural sciences, such as physics and biology (as those were

[32] Perry, 'Interpretation and Methodology', 123.

viewed at the time). Later founding fathers of sociology discarded such naive aspirations, but it has long remained an aspiration of the social sciences to disassociate themselves from morality, social criticism, and anything else which could not be considered 'scientific'. Sooner or later, this scientific aspiration was bound to come under attack, and this occurred on a large scale, particularly after the Second World War (mainly in response to the collapse of Colonialism). Much of this debate surrounded the question of whether the social sciences are forms of interpretation, rather than science, and the value-laden nature of the former. This debate has a long history, and its context is much broader than our present concern with legal theory.

The status of the social sciences, however, is not what we want to discuss here. Analytical legal philosophy, founded by H. L. A. Hart, had no 'scientific' aspirations, whatever those would be taken to be. Hart did express his view, however, that he regarded his own jurisprudential project as a piece of 'descriptive sociology', a view which he basically reiterated in his postscript. Descriptive it was certainly meant to be, and it is this descriptive aspiration which we want to examine here.

The immediate objection to this descriptive project is clearly apparent. After all, descriptions, *per se*, do not amount to a theory. The descriptions are to be assessed, somehow. No legal theory looks like a list of descriptions of various aspects of legal practice. (Think how long and tedious such a list would be!) At the very least, theorizing about the law, or anything else for that matter, must assume that certain aspects of it are more important than others. We would want to say, for example, that the fact that law purports to be authoritative is far more important than the fact that judges wear gowns.[33] Even such trivial judgements about relative importance of data, however, are evaluative.

One of Dworkin's most important insights about interpretation consists in the way he regards evaluations essential to any interpretative project. One cannot even begin to interpret any text, he claims, without first having an idea, that is, an evaluative judgement, about the values which are inherent in the genre to which the relevant text belongs. After all, how can I begin to form an interpretation of, say, a novel, without having a pretty good idea about what makes novels valuable, better than others, and the like. A certain vision of what the values inherent in the genre are is essential to any attempt to interpret texts which belong to it. Similarly, Dworkin could have claimed that interpretations must also rely on certain views about what makes some interpretations better than others. I do not wish to deny any of this. On the contrary: we should realize that this value dependence of interpretations is an essential feature of theorizing, as such. There is nothing unique to interpretations here. Any theory must rely on a host of evaluative judgements both

[33] I do not want to suggest that this fact is entirely without theoretical significance.

about its subject-matter and about the theorizing itself. No theory whatsoever can be descriptive throughout. Each and every type of theory, be it scientific, interpretative, or any other type of theory, must rely on certain evaluative conceptions about what makes such a theory successful, what would render it better than competing theories of the same subject matter, and so on. At the very least, each and every type of theory must have its own norms of success. Needless to say, no amount of description could lead us to any conclusions about such norms and their conditions of validity.

Still, Dworkin could claim that interpretation of works of art, social practices, and such, are unique in that their *subject-matter* is an evaluative enterprise. Therefore, Dworkin claims, in addition to any other evaluative aspects of theories as such, in cases of interpretation the interpreter must also form an evaluative judgement of her own about those values which are inherent in the practice she purports to interpret. Such judgements, Dworkin claims, are not essentially different from the evaluative judgements of the practitioners themselves.[34]

This last move, however, is not so smooth. There is a crucial difference between forming a view about values which are manifest in a certain practice, and having an evaluative judgement about them. An anthropologist may form the theoretical view that a certain rite is valuable for the people who practice it because it enhances their social cohesion, without having any particular judgement about the value of social cohesion which is somehow competitive with her subjects' evaluative judgements. Similarly, a legal theorist may come to the conclusion that the authoritative nature of law is much more essential to it than the law's ritualistic aspects, without having any particular judgement about the values of authority, social rites, or whatever. Forming a theoretical view about the values inherent in a given practice is not the same as forming an evaluative judgement about it, nor is the latter entailed by the former.

Let me emphasize that I do not wish to claim that a theoretician can form a judgement about values which are inherent in a social practice by mere description. Descriptions can only get us as far as having a list of observations. Any type of theorizing involves evaluations. But this is not the controversial issue. The question is this: what difference does it make to the type of evaluations involved in a theory that the subject-matter of the theory is itself an evaluative enterprise, namely, a social practice which instantiates certain values. Dworkin believes that it makes all the difference that renders interpretations unique, because it forces the theory to be involved in the assessment of those same values it purports to interpret. But again, this seems to ignore the crucial difference between grasping a value and having an evaluative judgement about it. People can comprehend the values held by others,

[34] *Law's Empire*, 64.

understand their point, their relevance, etc., without actually forming any judgement of their own about those values. I can easily understand, for instance, that the admiration of nature forms an essential value of a certain artistic genre, without admiring nature myself, or having any particular view about this.

Well, in one obvious sense this is not quite accurate. Our understanding of values is limited by our own past experience and conceptual-evaluative scheme. Sometimes people can come to understand new values by learning, but this is a relatively rare occurrence, it takes time and effort, and the learning may not succeed. Learning is based on past experience and personal capacities, and there is a limit to what we can learn afresh. Does this mean that there are values of alien cultures which we could never come to understand? Not necessarily.[35] It does mean, however, that learning new values is relative to what we already know and to the values we are already familiar with, and this certainly renders our ability to grasp values somewhat limited and relative to our own culture. Nevertheless, the distinction between grasping a value and having an evaluative judgement about it still holds. The fact that our ability to understand values or practices of other cultures is limited by our cultural-evaluative background does not entail that understanding necessarily collapses into judgement. And if this distinction holds, it becomes very difficult to understand why social theories are necessarily value laden in the way Dworkin suggests.

Let me try to sum up the point of disagreement here. There are two ways in which we should concede the value dependence of social theories, and one sense in which I want to deny it. First, it is true that any theory, as such, is value laden; there is no such thing as a purely descriptive theory. Mere descriptions never amount to a theory, they only form part of it. To begin with, any theory requires evaluative judgements about its own norms of success and failure. Furthermore, any theory, particularly in the social realm, involves assessments about what is more or less important in its subject matter, what is essential to it, and what are aspects of the subject-matter which need explaining as opposed to those aspects of it which can be taken for granted. All these aspects of theorizing, and many others, involve evaluative judgements. Secondly, we must realize that our ability to understand values is limited by the values we are already familiar with. The limit is not rigid. It can be overcome by learning, but our ability to learn is, of course, limited.

My argument purports to show, however, that there is nothing in the value dependence of social theory to justify Dworkin's conclusion that the normative nature of the practice requires any adequate explanation of it to be engaged in evaluative judgements which are somehow competitive with the judgements of the subjects themselves, the practitioners. Even if our under-

[35] See, for example, Raz, *Engaging Reason*.

standing, particularly in a theoretical form, depends on numerous evaluations, it is understanding we can aim at, not necessarily judgement. Dworkin, of course, denies this, since he insists that any understanding which he labels interpretative aims to present its subject-matter in its *best possible light*, that is, best all things considered. If we accept this argument, we would have to concede that any interpretative understanding collapses into judgement. But there are no good reasons to accept this last move. The arguments against the scope of Dworkin's 'constructive' model of interpretation are well known, and there is no need to repeat them here.[36] Suffice it to say that the kind of value dependence of legal theory that Dworkin has in mind entirely depends on it. That is, the whole argument depends on Dworkin's insistence that legal theory, like interpretation in general, must present its subject matter in its *best* possible light.

Does it not make any difference, however, that the practice we aim to explain is a normative one? It does indeed. A normative practice is one which gives rise to reasons for action and its theoretical explanation must take this fact into account. It is a truism, gravely misunderstood, however, that an explanation of a normative practice must take into account the participants' internal perspective. But we must be very precise about what this means. Basically, it means that an explanation of a normative practice must, *inter alia*, account for the ways in which the participants regard various components of their practice as reasons for their action. A reason for action necessarily assumes that something is valuable. A's reason to do X is based on the fact that X is valuable, either instrumentally or intrinsically. Therefore, under normal circumstances, A would believe that she has a reason to do X only if she believes that X is valuable. Note, however, that A's belief in a reason to do X does not render, by itself, X valuable. A may be wrong about the value of X. Even if A is wrong, however, her belief in the value of X explains why she would be inclined to pursue it.

Now suppose that we want to understand a social practice constituted by rules or conventions. Knowing the rules would not suffice to explain the practice. We must understand their point. For example, we cannot hope to explain the game of chess, without understanding what games are and what is their point. We must understand that the participants aim to win the game, which means that we must understand the complex value of winning a game (and such subtleties as winning it gracefully, or barely winning, etc.). This is part of what it means to understand a reason for action. In other words, it is certainly true that an understanding of a normative social practice, like law, games, etc., must comprise an understanding of its points, that is, of the values which would render the participants' beliefs in their reasons for action intelligible. Needless to say, these beliefs can be put to critical scrutiny. We

[36] For my own reservations, see *Interpretation and Legal Theory*, ch. 3.

may wish to say that the values are not worth pursuing, or that the practice may have had other, better values worth pursuing instead. But this kind of criticism is just an option which we may or may not decide to pursue.

It is overly simplistic to assume, however, that an account of a social practice's point or value can either be purely descriptive, in that it only aims to elucidate its participants' *beliefs* in their reasons for action, or else it is critical and evaluative, in that the theory takes up a critical-moral evaluation of those beliefs. Descriptive jurisprudence is not based on opinion polls. Consider, for example, a straightforward explanation of a social rule. Suppose we can show that the function, or rationale, of a social rule, say R, in a give society S, is to solve a recurrent coordination problem. Solving the putative coordination problem is what explains the rationale of following rule R in society S. Such an explanation would typically rely on certain propositions about matters of fact, like the nature of the situation, people's beliefs and preferences, and about the logic, or the rationality, of the rule in their practical deliberation, given those factual assumptions. I find it very difficult to see, however, where the moral argument is hidden here. The explanation need not contend that the coordination problem that rule R is there to solve is one which ought to be solved, or that it morally justifies following R. It only explains the rationality of R, given certain assumptions about social facts. Morality is largely about the values which are worth pursuing. A theory of a social practice, or any other type of a theory about practical reasoning, need not rely on any particular views about the desirability of the values which would make sense of a given practice.

This widespread assumption, that making sense of a normative practice is either a causal explanation or else it must be a moral evaluation, explains Stephen Perry's argument about the moral-value dependence of jurisprudence. The argument rests on this false dichotomy, namely, that an account of law's major functions in society is either part of a causal explanation, or else it must be 'moral in character: it is grounded in a certain understanding of the moral point or value of the institution of law.'[37] Take for example H. L. A. Hart's thesis, that one of law's most important functions is to guide human conduct *ex ante*, 'out of court', which forms the explicit target of Perry's argument. This is neither a causal explanation nor a moral evaluation. It is a complex thesis, based on certain assumptions about facts (e.g. that people typically know what the law is, that they actually employ such knowledge in their deliberations about their conduct, etc.) and about the roles of legal authority in practical reasoning. When we talk about the practical function, or rationale, of a social institution, it need not be a causal explanation, or a moral evaluation. Once again, we can make sense of a social practice, render its rationale intelligible, without forming a judgement about the merit of the values which render the practice rational for the participants.

[37] Perry, 'Intrpretation and Methodology', 114.

Perry would be right to complain that rationality is not a value-free concept. But we have already seen that theories are rarely, if ever, value free. Furthermore, Perry (unlike Dworkin, perhaps) is very careful to emphasize that it is *moral* evaluation that he ascribes to jurisprudence, not just theoretical evaluations in general. But this moral component seems to be lacking. Essentially, what Hart is saying is that law is a tool, and tools can be used for good or bad purposes alike. Descriptive jurisprudence, of the kind Hart had had in mind, aims to explain what kind of tool the law is, and how its various features figure in its putative functions. We can say what purposes tools can be used for, this is what it normally means to explain what kind of tool it is, yet at the same time we can remain entirely agnostic about the moral merit of such uses. To the extent that Hart has had certain views about the moral merit of such objectives, they are not essential to his theory.

Let me sum up the argument: descriptive jurisprudence is not value free. No theoretical explanation can be value free. Furthermore, since jurisprudence aims to explain a normative social practice, it must comprise an account of the possible values which render the practice intelligible for us by making sense of the participants' reasons for action. On the other hand, jurisprudence, like any other type of social explanation, need not engage in a moral evaluation of the values which render the practice intelligible. In this important sense, description and criticism can be kept apart. Admittedly, none of this secures the methodological objectivity of jurisprudence. There are countless ways in which theories can go wrong. Each and every evaluative aspect of a theory can be contestable. My purpose here was limited to showing that in one crucial sense jurisprudence need not rely on contestable moral views. We can make sense of a social practice and at the same time remain agnostic about the moral merit of the values which render the practice intelligible.

8
On the Objectivity of Values

Do we value things because they are valuable, or are things valuable only in so far as we value them? This is the basic dilemma between objectivist and subjectivist accounts of values. The subjectivist claims that it does not make sense to assume that things are intrinsically valuable in a way unrelated to the fact that there are human subjects who happen to have an attitude towards certain aspects of the world, and those attitudes are what we call 'valuing'. The objectivist remains unconvinced, mainly, I will suggest, because the subjectivist accounts leave the rational motivation for valuing unexplained: why should we value things unless they are indeed valuable?

The debate is, of course, far more complicated. In the first section, I will suggest a rough outline of an objective account of values, relying on the idea that values are analogous to relational properties. In the second section, I will consider in some detail four reasons for scepticism about values, arguing that none of them are compelling. Finally, I will discuss two influential attempts to construct a subjectivist account of values, suggesting that these alternatives to objectivism are much more problematic than the objectivism they aim to replace.

Before we proceed, however, it is essential to have a clearer picture of the problem. One way to see this is by reflecting on the immediate problems facing any simple-minded or naive version of subjectivism about values. A naive version of subjectivism would hold that valuing is simply an attitude, or preference, that we happen to entertain. 'We' meaning, let us assume, 'I, and those sufficiently like me', or something along these lines. Let us further grant to the naive subjectivist that the attitudes or preferences in question are, typically, second-order preferences. Roughly, then, 'X is valuable' means that one desires to desire X. Now, the immediate problem for the naive subjectivist is that most surface phenomena of evaluative discourse are strikingly at odds with this account. Let me mention, very briefly, the central cases.

1. *Intelligent disagreements*. Evaluative discourse lends itself to intelligent disagreements between individuals holding opposite, often straightforwardly conflicting evaluative judgements. A simple-minded theory of values which regards valuing as no more than expressed, or reported, subjective preferences seems futile to explain the phenomena of argument and disagreement.[1]

I am grateful to Charles Larmore, Alon Harel, Chaim Gans, David Heyd, David Enoch, and Meir Dan-Cohen for helpful comments on drafts of this chapter.

[1] Sophisticated forms of subjectivism distinguish between reports and expressions of preferences. Throughout this chapter, however, I will not be careful to distinguish the cognitive and non-cognitive versions of subjectivism, as I believe that the distinction does not affect my particular arguments.

When we express preferences which are obviously subjective we do not tend to argue about them, let alone demand that others share our preferences. We may sometimes hope that others share our own preferences, but if they do not, we typically find it easy to accept the fact that we just happen to have different preferences.[2]

Evaluative discourse is strikingly different. People are typically prone to argue about their evaluative views and strive to convince others who disagree with them that they are mistaken. We normally think that others should share the views we hold firmly. True, often evaluative arguments are not really about values but about matters of fact. Moral disagreements often stem from disagreement about factual assumptions underlying our moral views. But often enough the arguments are simply about the values we ought to pursue.[3] Thus, one well-known challenge any sensible subjectivist must meet is explicating the rationality of moral disagreement and moral argument. Even if the subjectivist concludes, however, that the phenomenon of moral argument in face of disagreement is, ultimately, irrational, any sensible subjectivism would still have to explain why we bother to engage in it; and why we bother to engage in it in certain types of preference-expressions discourse, such as morality and politics, and not in others, such as preferences about lifestyle, or food.

2. *General application.* Related, but not quite identical, to the first point is the conspicuous other-regarding nature of standard evaluative discourse. Compare, for example, instances of disgust with moral condemnation. Many people are disgusted by cockroaches, and I guess that most people would react with utter disgust to the suggestion that they eat cooked cockroaches. But at least upon reflection, disgust does not seem to involve an other-regarding preference. Being told that others eat cockroaches, I might feel disgust, and perhaps I could not imagine doing it myself, but I would not necessarily condemn those who do. I would not think that they ought to feel similarly disgusted, even if I cannot imagine how it is that they do not entertain similar feelings. Moral reasoning is quite the opposite. We typically conceive of our own evaluative views as instances of general reasons that apply to us, and *ipso facto*, to others as well.[4]

3. *Propositional language and Classical logic.* A related problem concerns the fact that evaluative discourse seems to adhere to propositional calculus. Desires do not logically entail other desires. Moral evaluations can entail

[2] Note that this is not only an interpersonal phenomenon. People often undergo considerable changes in their own tastes and preferences, and such changes are relatively easy to adapt to. Few people would be bothered by realizing that the tastes and subjective preferences they have entertained throughout their lives were on the whole inconsistent.

[3] R. M. Hare, *Moral Thinking*, 77.

[4] This is not tantamount to Hare's universalisability condition; the latter is a stronger version of the general idea mentioned here.

other moral evaluations and moral conclusions.[5] Consider the following inference, which is logically valid:

1. It is wrong to cause unnecessary pain.
2. If you kick a dog just for fun, you cause unnecessary pain.
3. Therefore, kicking a dog just for fun is wrong.

Any sensible version of subjectivism, therefore, must account for the fact, which is at least a surface phenomenon of evaluative discourse, that propositional logic seems to apply to it. Evaluative discourse is typically cast in propositional language, and at least on the surface, this propositional language seems to adhere to classical logic.

4. *Structures and constraints.* Anything can be an object of a subjective preference. Few people would actually prefer the moon to be green, but there is nothing extraordinary in the expression of such a preference. More importantly, expressions of subjective preferences do not constitute a highly structured type of discourse. This is not so with standard evaluative discourse, which is highly structured and constrained by elaborate conceptual schemes and interlocking language games.[6] Moral commitments affect each other, and we often realize that given certain evaluative views we have, others views can or cannot follow.

All these and other aspects of the surface phenomena of evaluative discourses show that naive subjectivism does not constitute a plausible philosophical explanation. A sensible form of subjectivism must be much more sophisticated. It must explain the differences between expressions of subjective preferences, easily recognized as such, and evaluations, which, at least on the surface, look quite different. The point here is not only that subjectivism necessarily entails some form of an error-theory, though that too. It goes deeper. The point is that subjectivism must also explain the rationale of such comprehensive errors, and it must explain the logical and conceptual structures of evaluative discourse. This chapter argues that subjectivism, sophisticated as it may be, is not capable of explaining all that. First, however, let us consider, at least in rough outline, the possibility of objectivity about values.

[5] This is called the Geach–Frege Problem. See Blackburn, 'Evaluations, Projections, and Quasi-Realism', 189.

[6] Consider, for example, the idea of hypocrisy. The typical hypocrite is one who tries to conceal subjective, or egoistic preferences by some pretence to high moral standards. But hypocrisy is not simply a lie. It is, typically, a very elaborate form of pretence, often involving considerable self-deceit, which is only rendered possible by making moves within a highly structured social language game.

REASONS, VALUES, AND RELATIONAL PROPERTIES

Something is intrinsically valuable if we value it for its own sake. Some of those things we value for their own sake, we value because they form part of, or instantiate, other things which we value for their own sake. Some things are of ultimate value, however, in that we value them for their own sake, regardless of any other things we may value.[7]

What exactly is the possible reference of a statement in the form: 'X is intrinsically valuable'? Is the value of X a quality that attaches to it, like the shape of a table or its colour? The colour analogy has caught the attention of some philosophers, suggesting the idea that values are like secondary qualities.[8] On the face of it, the analogy seems appealing because it would explain two things at once: why does valuing depend on human cognition but at the same time it also picks out a real, objective feature of the world? Colours of objects depend on perception, but they are not thus rendered any less real for that; colour perception does pick out real features of the world which can be explained by familiar scientific theories. Despite this appeal, however, the analogy between values and secondary qualities might be more misleading than helpful. The features of the world discerned by colour perception are there anyway, at least partly, regardless of human recognition. It is only the *subjective experience* of colour perception itself which depends on perception. Values might be different. It is far from clear that something can be valuable even if nobody could ever recognize it as such. I will return to this point shortly.

Even worse, however, is the perception analogy itself. As David Lewis rightly noted, valuing is not a reaction to samples.[9] To realize something's value often takes imagination, cognition, habituation, and learning. Consider a non-ethical example, like the values we find in works of art. People with no knowledge of the arts who just walk into an art gallery assuming that they will recognize the works' artistic values as they see the samples are most likely to be disappointed.[10] The appreciation of the values of a work of art is facilitated only by learning, imagination, and creative thought. The same is true of values in general. Perception, as a reaction to samples, forms only a small part of valuing. Recall that evaluative discourse includes disagreements, arguments, errors, and misconception.

Of course we have not yet answered the sceptic's question: in what sense can values be real, objective aspects of the world? If the secondary quality

[7] Raz, *The Morality of Freedom*, 200.

[8] See McDowell, 'Values and Secondary Qualities'.

[9] See Lewis, 'Dispositional Theories of Value'.

[10] Well, they may recognize certain aspects of the work's merit, but even if they think that they understand what makes the work valuable, such an understanding is bound to be very partial and limited, without a great deal of knowledge.

analogy does not prove very useful, what else is there? Let us depart from ontology for a moment and consider a few instances of valuing. In general, harm is intrinsically bad. The prospect of harming someone always counts against an action; avoiding harm is a reason for action. It is, however, overly simplistic to assume that harm reduces to an experience of suffering. People may not actually experience suffering from the harm caused to them, perhaps because they are not aware of the harm or lack the relevant dispositions. Here is an extreme example: suppose you could instantly reduce someone to such a level of stupidity that he would not even realize that something is wrong with him. You have obviously harmed him, even if he does not experience any suffering. Is it fair to say, then, that harm is something that happens, it takes place, as it were, but not necessarily in the minds of individuals? In one sense it must be true, and this is precisely the idea we have to make sense of. On the other hand, harm does seem to depend on the existence of the appropriate kind of creatures who can recognize it as such. A fish bitten by a shark is not humiliated, although it may suffer. Humiliation is only possible within certain social forms of life. Some forms of harm, or benefit, take an entire culture to sustain; others are more elemental and only depend on basic human (or other creatures') capacities and dispositions.

Consider another example: late nineteenth-century Impressionism changed, rather dramatically, the ways in which paintings were evaluated in European art. The Impressionists managed to create new values in art, hitherto unrecognized in Western culture. It was a cultural development that created new artistic values. As Raz carefully pointed out, values can be gained by innovation, cultural revolutions, and countless other ways, but they are never really lost. Values may, of course, lose their relevance or be forgotten. Values often become obsolete. But, in principle, it is always possible to understand what the value was and why it was relevant at the time. Values are somewhat like works of art: some of them withstand cultural changes over centuries and remain with us for a very long time; others are more parochial and may lose their significance as circumstances change.[11]

It is tempting to think that there is a dichotomy between creation and discovery. But this is not necessarily the case. Abstract painting created new artistic values by discovering that the structured composition of a painting need not be figurative. Non-figurative composition is both a discovery and a creation, and it is not particularly important which of these concepts we choose to describe the innovation. Similarly, the value of gender equality can be said to have been discovered in the last few decades as we have come to realize how harmful and unjustified patriarchalism has been (and unfortunately still is). This discovery is also a creative process. We come to see human relations in new lights, hitherto unknown.

[11] See Raz, *Engaging Reason*.

Granted all this, how can values be objective? The key element here is to realize that values are not qualities *of* objects, or aspects of the world; rather they are *conclusions* we draw from situations, from our interaction with certain aspects of the world.[12] In other words, there are situations in the world, or aspects of it, which *objectively deserve* certain evaluative descriptions or attitudes, although the same situation may deserve different evaluations by different creatures. By 'different creatures' I mean different types of subjects, or similar subjects situated in different environments. Note that this is an objectivist position which goes a long way in the direction of value relativism. Biological and cultural factors may determine the ways in which we ought to react to aspects of the world, and as these vary, values would vary as well. Consider, for example, the value of friendship. Friendship is valuable only for creatures who are psychologically and socially constituted in certain ways, and whose needs and aspirations in life render friendship valuable. As such biological and social circumstances change, so the value of friendship may change accordingly. Friendship is only a value *for us*, but then, of course it greatly depends on who 'us' are. Note that it is relativism, and not simply diversity, that I have in mind here. One and the same moral principle may easily require different application in different cultural environments. The latter differs from relativism which holds that as cultural or other circumstances vary, such variations determine the truths of the values appropriate for the relevant culture.

According to this view, then, evaluations are rendered true or false due to objective aspects of the world, though in a relative and relational manner. Note that such a view does not collapse into subjectivism if we are careful to avoid the assumption that evaluators are themselves the best judges of their appropriate evaluations. The assumption is certainly wrong. Impressionism deserved praise and admiration years before it was generally recognized as a valuable transformation of artistic conventions. People can be wrong about the values they hold. Nevertheless, aspects of the world may deserve different evaluations by different creatures, and that is why objectivity is not incompatible with relativism.

When we say that a situation, an action, or an aspect of the world *deserves* particular evaluative judgements, we must mean that there are certain *qualities* of the situation which warrant that evaluation. These qualities, however, are not identical to the intrinsic value of the situation; values are not natural or 'non-natural' *properties of* objects, actions, or situations. Values are best seen as analogous to relational properties of objects, situations, etc. The attribution of intrinsic value is a complex relational idea, meaning that the object has certain qualities which warrant the attribution of a certain value to it by

[12] The account that follows is greatly influenced by McDowell, 'Projection and Truth in Ethics', and Raz, *Engaging Reason*.

the kind of creatures confronting it. Note that *warrant* is used here as an epistemic concept. What I mean by it is that given the situation and the creatures confronting it, they would be mistaken if they failed to recognize the value in question.[13] But the mistake is not perceptual, as intuitionism would have it. Cruelty, for example, is not a quality of an action, any more than the fact that Sarah is 10 inches taller than John is a quality of John. Nevertheless, it is an objective fact *about* John that he is 10 inches shorter than Sarah. Similarly, it may be an objective fact about X that it is cruel. The fact that values are like relational properties, then, does not render them any less objective for that. Note that another analogy obtains here: without a taller Sarah around, John would not be 10 inches shorter than Sarah. Similarly, without, for example, human culture, actions could not be humiliating.[14]

The conclusion of the previous section is very limited but crucially important. The objectivist about values need not postulate 'non-natural qualities' of objects in order to make sense of the idea that there are situations in the world which objectively deserve certain evaluations. Values are not qualities that are somehow attached to objects, like the shape of a desk or the size of my shoes. The natural properties of a shoe, however, like its size, shape, elasticity, etc., make it useful for us. Being useful for us is not a 'non-natural property' of shoes, but it is objectively true about shoes that they are useful. (For human beings, of course; not for horses.) Note that the usefulness of shoes is both relational and relative to an environment. Shoes are only useful for humans, and they might lose their usefulness if the environment changes (e.g. if the surface turns sandy all around, or something of this nature). We may also discover new uses for shoes, and once discovered, they become objectively true about shoes, like their current use. Well, what does it mean to say that shoes are useful? It means that we relate to or interact with the objects in question in a certain way, and this use warrants the evaluative conclusion that shoes *are useful*, that is, valuable in a certain respect. Usefulness, as a value, is not a quality of certain artifacts, like shoes; it is a conclusion which follows from the situation, analogous to the way in which we conclude that John is 10 inches shorter than Sarah.

Consider another example: suppose you take a walk in the woods along a narrow track, and you suddenly encounter a fence blocking your way. The fence obstructs your progress. Being 'obstructive', however, is not a property of the fence. Nevertheless, it is objectively true about it that it obstructs your walk, or that of anybody else who might be similarly situated. Therefore, under the circumstances, the fence *is* obstructive; it blocks your way. Or actu-

[13] I believe that this view is consistent with Raz's idea that knowledge, in general, is path dependent. For his detailed account see *Engaging Reason*, ch. 6.

[14] It is not an essential part of my argument that animals cannot experience any form of humiliation. I do tend to think that only humans can experience humiliation, but for those who may think otherwise, I would change the example.

ally, it may not—you could turn out to be wrong about this. Perhaps you have not noticed that there is an easy way around it. In that case, the fence is not really as obstructive as you might have thought.

Does this mean that in order for something to be valuable, it must be valuable *for* someone? Generally speaking, yes, although it need not be valuable for someone in particular. Saying that something is valuable necessarily suggests that it is valuable for, say, humans, or humans situated in a particular way, or such. It is crucial to note, however, that this does not render all values instrumental. Things can be good for someone non-instrumentally. Consider knowledge, for example. We can say that knowledge is intrinsically valuable although it is only valuable for humans (and similar creatures). Knowledge is valuable for us even if it is not put to any particular use or otherwise serves any other purpose we may have. Knowledge may be a good in itself, even if it is only good for humans. Or consider, once again, the value of friendship. Friendship is intrinsically valuable. Friendly relationships between people have certain qualities which deserve our appreciation, regardless of anything else. But friendship is only a good for certain types of creatures, such humans and other creatures capable of friendship. Being good for someone does not necessarily entail that the good is instrumental.

The fact that values are basically conclusions drawn from certain aspects of the world and the way we relate to those aspects explains in what sense values can sometimes be discovered, or invented, and, of course, why people can be wrong about them. Just as we can discover or invent new uses of objects, we can discover or invent new values of things or actions. And once discovered they are there, as such, as long as our memory retains them. Similarly, things can lose their value if circumstances change, and thus they become obsolete or irrelevant. Often such changes take place during a transitional period, and it is typically during such transitional phases that people tend to be wrong about values on a large scale. Transition tends to be more difficult for some than for others. People differ in their capacities to adapt and recognize the need for change. Racial and gender equality are the examples that come to one's mind these days.

The fact that values are[15] relational and relative properties vindicates relativism to a considerable extent, but it also indicates the limits of value relativism. Such properties depend on circumstances and the environment. That much we have seen already. It is equally true, however, that relational and relative properties do not depend on the subjects' perception of them. Once again, let me invoke the analogy of usefulness. Whether something is useful or not depends on circumstances, but use can also be misidentified. Something can be useful even if nobody realizes it. Recognition, private or

[15] I am not sure whether values *are* relational properties, or *analogous* to relational properties. But I am not sure that much depends on this distinction either.

public, does not constitute the value of things. Therefore, the fact that values are relative to cultures does not entail the subjectivist conclusion that there is nothing more to values than the fact that people entertain certain attitudes or dispositions. People, even entire cultures, can be wrong about values. Cultural relativism is not tantamount to immunity from evaluative error, even on a large scale. On the other hand, it is true that a great many things may not be valuable for creatures who are incapable of recognizing certain aspects of the situation. This is not necessarily a form of error. In different societies things may have different values.

FOUR REASONS FOR DOUBT

It is impossible to enumerate all the reasons philosophers might have for doubting the objectivity of any particular realm. Scepticism comes in all forms and shapes and there is never any assurance that we have already encountered all the main reasons for doubting the objectivity of values. But the philosophical tradition is limited, and sceptical arguments, like others, tend to repeat themselves. I believe that the philosophical tradition reveals four main arguments underlying the scepticism about the objectivity of values. Let me take up these four arguments in turn.

1. *Objectivity involves dubious metaphysics.* This is probably the most widely shared argument amongst sceptics about values. As Mackie succinctly formulated the idea, 'if there were objective values, then they would be entities or qualities or relations of a very strange sort, utterly different from anything else in the universe.'[16]

The appeal of this argument is not difficult to grasp. The objectivist assumes that when we talk about values, we talk about something which is there anyway, independently of our attitudes and preferences. But how can values exist in this way? What kind of entities values are? Surely, values cannot be like chairs or atoms which are there anyway, even if nobody is watching. So it seems that when we talk about values we can only refer to ourselves; we can only talk about *our* attitudes and preferences. Nothing else is plausibly out there, existing independently of us. As Mackie sees it, the contrary assumption that values are objects of some kind requires philosophical mystification, postulating 'queer' entities.[17] As it stands, however, Mackie's argument seems to be missing its target. First, because the view about the objectivity of values I have sketched in the previous section does not accord values the status of 'entities', or 'qualities of entities' in the world. Second, it seems that the immediate target of Mackie's argument is metaphysical real-

[16] Mackie, *Ethics*, 38

[17] Mackie's argument from queerness is sometimes understood in combination with Hume's argument about moral motivation—see the discussion of Hume's argument below.

ism about values or, at least, it would be more convincing if it is understood in this way. As we have seen in detail in Chapter 6, however, objectivity is compatible with an anti-realist stance. Nevertheless, it is worth exploring Mackie's insights a bit further. Eventually, Mackie's view boils down to the claim that objectivity about values necessarily involves a metaphysics of values which is inconsistent with our scientific world view. In short, values are just not the kind of things which we can fit in the inventory of metaphysically respectable entities in the world.

Whether this is a serious worry is more difficult to ascertain than is typically assumed. First, this motivation for subjectivism seems to accord science a somewhat dubious foundational status.[18] Even if we assume (and note that I have not made this assumption) that values are not the kind of entities which would fit our scientific world-view, it is far from clear that science ought to be regarded as definitive of sound metaphysics. First of all, science itself is in constant flux about its own understandings of sound scientific ontology, and, more importantly, such self-understandings tend to be complementary to, and derivative of, the success of the theories which employ them. Entities of scientific theories are postulates which are needed to make sense of a particular scientific theory. Theories are then systematically verified in various ways, in terms of their predictive and explanatory power. If the theory turns out to be successful, it is rare that the theory is questioned on the basis of the dubious characterization of entities postulated by it. What eventually proved Newton's physics to be partially wrong is not the mysterious ontological nature of his postulate about gravitation (that Berkeley famously mocked at the time as queer and mysterious!), but the better predictive power and explanation of Einstein's theory of relativity. The latter is hardly more convincing on grounds of its more respectable or intuitive ontology.[19]

Second, we should bear in mind that scientific theories and generally our modern scientific world-view presuppose metaphysics which is not less problematic than the metaphysics of values. We need only to recall Hume's doubts about the ontology of causation to realize the pervasiveness of the problems of scientific ontology. To be sure, I do not want to doubt the achievements of modern science. These are extraordinary and their philosophical implications should not be overlooked. However, the intellectual achievement of modern science does not rest on its sound ontology, but rather on its forms of explanation, prediction, and verification procedures. What renders astronomy much more credible than astrology is not the nature of their respective ontologies, but the entire structure of explanation, predictive power, refutability, etc. Science may well have some foundational status with respect

[18] See, for example, Hampton, *The Authority of Reason*.

[19] See Berkeley, *The Principles of Human Knowledge*, sections 103, 106. It is a telling irony that Einstein's metaphysical qualms and reservations about Quantum Physics have been gracefully ignored.

to acceptable theorizing about nature, but it simply does not follow that it must also have a foundational status with respect to ontology and metaphysics in general.

Admittedly, none of this dispels the puzzle. There are genuine puzzles about the ontology of values, but they are not so easy to define. Consider, for example, the following question: can there be something valuable, even if nobody happens to value it? An affirmative answer is not implausible on any meta-ethical account. For example, gender equality may well have been valuable even at times when (almost) nobody thought so. This is a plausible position, because sexual inequality causes harm, and harm can be present even if people misidentify its exact nature, or its causes, or even if they fail to realize that the harm exists. Perhaps some forms of harm require awareness to become harm in the first place, but others may be present as harm even without awareness of their presence.

The more difficult question, however, is whether something can be valuable even if people are *incapable* of realizing it. It is not implausible to maintain that in order to be values in the first place, moral values do require some basic potential for human recognition.[20] Would this prove that values cannot be objective in the metaphysical sense? If we assume that some minimal potential for recognition is a necessary constituent of values, this might prove that metaphysical realism about values is untenable.[21] As we have seen in Chapter 6, however, anti-realism does not necessarily entail subjectivism. Perhaps it is true that this recognition constraint on the metaphysics of values is one which we do not normally associate with the ontology of scientific entities. But we are forced to admit this constraint in countless other contexts; numerous social constructs, besides values, that is, embody a similar constraint. There are countless social constructs such as states, games, cultural artefacts, and so on, whose existence depends on human capacity of recognizing such constructs with their epistemic faculties and conceptual schemes. Are cultural artefacts and the rest of our social world ontologically 'queer' or mysterious? Mystery is in the eyes of the beholder. The ontology of values does call for a philosophical explanation, but I think that little is gained by enfolding the explanandum with clouds of mystery.

In any case, it is crucial to bear in mind the distinction between realism and objectivity. It was not my intention to defend anything like metaphysical realism about values. There are domains which admit of metaphysical objectivity without realism. Values, and perhaps relational properties in general, may

[20] We should distinguish between the question I considered in the previous section, namely, whether something can be valuable even if there are no people, or similar creatures, for whom it could be valuable, and the question I consider here of whether the possibility of recognition is essential to values.

[21] That is, unless we consider something like Putnam's 'internal realism' as a form of realism as well.

well be objective aspects of the world even if their ontological status is not mind-independent as the realist would have it.

2. *Objectivity involves dubious epistemology.* Suppose that when we talk about values we talk about something which is there anyway. But how could we come to know this? How do we gain knowledge about values? Some philosophers assumed that this question about the epistemology of values boils down to the following: what epistemic faculty of the mind enables us to grasp the existence and nature of values? It was once fashionable to assume that we grasp values by *intuition*. Admittedly, such a postulate of a special value-detector faculty of the mind does sound very dubious indeed. Let us assume, then, that we do not have any special value detectors. Is this a serious worry for an epistemology of values?[22] It takes a very crude form of Empiricism to see any problem here. Early, eighteenth-century Empiricists assumed that all knowledge of the outside world derives from sense data. If we thought that this was true and insisted that values are out there as part of the external world, we would need some kind of value sensation to account for the epistemology of values. But this picture of knowledge is obviously too crude. Most of our knowledge of the external world does not derive from any straightforward sense data. We do not see or detect with any of our senses most of the objects we assume exist in the world. The existence of the vast majority of objects in our world-view is not observed, but assumed as part of the theories we entertain to account for observable data. Consider, for example, this headline I found in today's newspaper: 'Dr. Klein, the Director of the Israeli Central Bank announced that he intends to keep interest rates on their present high level to keep inflation under control. He predicts that the growth rate of the economy will gradually pick up, reaching a possible 4% in the year 2001.' Any average reader of a daily newspaper can understand what has been said here. Most of the concept words used in these two sentences, however, do not refer to observable data, nor are they reducible to such data in any straightforward sense. In order to explain how an average newspaper reader understands these sentences, we would have to tell a very complicated story. There is no reason to assume that an epistemology of values would be simpler. Values are not things we can observe, or feel with any of our senses. But the same is true about social constructs (e.g. 'Dr.', 'Bank', 'Israel', 'year 2001', etc.), theoretical concepts ('economy', 'inflation', 'growth rate'), and even, perhaps, arithmetic. If the failure of ad hoc intuitionism is a blow to the epistemology of values, it would be an equally fatal blow to most of our epistemology. Once again, none of this entails that there are no serious worries about the epistemology of values, but only that the fate of intuitionism is not one of them.

[22] It is worth noting that both Mackie and Blackburn thought that it is. See Mackie, *Ethics*, 38, and Blackburn, 'Evaluations, Projections, and Quasi-Realism', 182.

3. *The reason–passion distinction.* Like so many of the classical sceptical arguments, we owe this one to David Hume as well. Here's the relevant passage:

> Since morals, therefore, have an influence on the actions and affections, it follows that they cannot be deriv'd from reason; and that because reason alone . . . can never have any such influence. Morals excite passions, and produce or prevent actions. Reason of itself is utterly impotent in this particular. The rules of morality, therefore, are not conclusions of our reason.[23]

The upshot of Hume's argument is that reason alone cannot move us towards action, and therefore reason alone cannot account for moral motivation. Motivation for action always requires passion, namely, a subject's desire to attain, or avoid, some state of affairs. Any reason for action, Hume maintains, presupposes a subject's desire. Therefore reasons for action are ultimately subjective in nature since they always depend on the contingent desires of the subjects concerned.

There are two parallel ways of understanding Hume's argument. One standard interpretation concentrates on moral motivation as a problem for philosophy of action. On this reading, the problem for the moral objectivist is to explain how people can be moved to act in one way or another, without possessing a desire. Reason alone cannot move us towards any action. Morality, on the other hand, cannot be motivationally inert. Morality is essentially something which motivates behaviour, and only desires can do that.

The second interpretation of Hume's argument pertains to the concept of rationality. Hume in effect maintains that the only sensible concept of rationality is confined to instrumental reasoning. Reason can only prescribe that an object is desirable if that object is instrumental in the achievement of another object, which we happen to desire. Reason cannot prescribe ultimate values; ultimate values, or objectives, always require subjective desire.

Let me try to explain why I do not find Hume's scepticism convincing. Anything which counts in favour of doing something is, or forms part of, a reason for action. Reasons for action are rarely stated in their complete form; we normally take a host of factors for granted, or simply do not bother to render them explicit. Philosophically, however, Hume is right to insist that we must account for complete reasons for action. The Humean thesis is that a complete reason for action necessarily presupposes the subject's desire. Reason by itself cannot prescribe that you do anything, unless there is something you already desire. As we have already noted, one standard understanding of reason's motivational inertness consists in the thesis that rationality is confined to instrumental reasoning. There is, famously, an entire Empiricist tradition following Hume in this dismissal of any notion of rationality which is not strictly instrumental. It is all too often overlooked, how-

[23] Hume, *A Treatise of Human Nature*, 457.

ever, that this stance is incoherent: Instrumental rationality presupposes non-instrumental rationality.

Practical rationality is a normative concept. Rationality counts in favour of actions, and irrationality counts against them. We employ norms of rationality to prescribe actions, criticize or condemn them, etc. Had we assumed that rationality is restricted to pointing out instrumental relations, we would have had nothing to say against behaviour which defies instrumental reasoning. Rationality, even as predominantly instrumental, presupposes its own intrinsic value.[24]

Let us take a straightforward instance of instrumental reasoning which is instrumentally irrational. Say, for example, that S faces the option of either doing or avoiding X, knowing full well that X is a necessary step towards achieving P. Suppose S opts for avoiding X, as it is instrumental in his quest for Q. Now suppose that S actually prefers P over Q, and no other preferences are involved. Has S done something irrational? The Humean instrumentalist is quick to answer 'yes', since we have easily demonstrated that S's action is instrumentally irrational. But this only makes sense if we can also explain where the *norm* of instrumental rationality comes from. Why is it *really irrational* to behave in a way which simply defies instrumental reasoning? At the very least instrumental rationality itself must be assumed to be an intrinsic value, something we ought to pursue for its own sake. Otherwise we are left with no account of why the person who does not adopt his means to his ends is condemnable in any way.

Can the Humean instrumentalist simply deny the normative aspect of instrumental rationality, claiming that the means–ends relation is only a descriptive matter, having no normative bearing whatsoever? No other stance would be coherent. Either instrumental rationality is normative, in which case, it must be assumed, at the very least, that instrumental rationality is valuable in itself; or else rationality has no normative significance whatsoever. The problem with the latter option is that it flies in the face of the idea of reason to deny it any normative status. Not having any reason to be instrumentally rational would render instrumental rationality itself totally insignificant, like any other aspect of behaviour which neither counts in favour or against performing it.

The Humean instrumentalist may strive for this option: instrumental reasoning may simply stand for a desire people happen to have, like the passion for success, or sex, or whatever.[25] On this account, practical reason itself simply reduces to the desire to match means to an end, a desire one may, or may not, entertain. Needless to say, according to this version of the Humean

[24] Hampton, *The Authority of Reason*, and Korsgaard, *The Sources of Normativity*. I am not assuming here that intrinsic values are necessarily objective.

[25] There is some textual indication that Hume actually favoured this option, but we need not decide this interpretative question here.

position, instrumental rationality loses its normative aspect entirely. The rational person and the irrational one simply happen to have different desires. So here is the real dilemma we face: either instrumental rationality is normative, in which case it must be assumed that there is at least one thing in the world which is intrinsically valuable, namely, instrumental rationality itself; or else, we must concede that there is no normative aspect whatsoever to instrumental rationality; it is just another passion that some of us happen to have. To be consistent the Humean must opt for the latter. To make sense of our practical reasoning, we must opt for the former.

The problem with the Humean rationality thesis is even deeper. Humean instrumentalism takes desires for granted as something that simply happens to people. You like vanilla ice cream while I prefer the chocolate flavour, and there is not much else to say about it, except for the fact that we simply have different desires. (We may get a more accurate picture if we take second-order desires into account, but the idea remains essentially the same.) More often than not, however, desires people have are desires they would want to have, or to avoid, *for reasons*. My desire to write a good book (or, if we prefer, my desire to desire this) is not just something I happen to have, like a headache. It is a desire motivated by reason. It is motivated by my belief in the fact that good books are valuable, and that I have reasons to try to do valuable things in my life. After all, why would I desire to do, or to have, anything, unless I thought that it is, ultimately, valuable.[26] It is true, of course, that I cannot also translate everything I sincerely regard as valuable into a desire of mine. People often realize that they have a reason to do something although they cannot form the appropriate desire to perform it. Or they can form the desire but fail to act on it. Reason is, sometimes, motivationally inert. Generally, however, people's belief in a reason for action is precisely what makes sense of their relevant desires, and reasons for action necessarily assume that certain aspects of the world are valuable.[27]

There is a question about philosophical explanation lurking in the background of this debate. Hume probably thought of the relations between reason and desire in causal terms. At least as understood by Kant, Hume seems to have maintained that reason cannot be the mental cause of any desire. Reasons and passions are causally severed. Notably, this is a particularly perplexing position for Hume to hold, having raised serious doubts about the metaphysics of causal relations in general. Be this as it may, discovering causal relations is not what philosophers should be after, particularly in this context, as it is far from clear that we can ever employ mental concepts in a robust scientific causal explanation. At least those who maintain that the mental is reducible to or supervenient upon the physical, would want to keep

[26] Acting on a whim may be an exception. Note, however, that even whimsical behaviour is often motivated by the belief in such values as spontaneity or authenticity.

[27] Cf. Larmore, *The Morals of Modernity*, ch. 5.

the causal chain at the physical level anyway. The essential point is, however, that a philosophical account that reduces desires to aspects of our lives which just happen to us remains utterly unsatisfactory at the phenomenological level. Philosophically, the question is how best to make sense of our desires, our reasons for action, and the relations between them. The better explanation would be one which makes sense of the ways in which we think about our actions, aspirations, and projects in life. The fact is that we simply do not regard most of our desires as things that we just happen to have. People often realize, for example, that they have a desire which they ought not to have because there are reasons not to have it. Sometimes people may cultivate a desire because they believe that they have a reason to do so. All these reasons, of course, ultimately depend on what we regard as intrinsically valuable. Reasons for action, generally, depend on intrinsic values. Even the strictest instrumentalist, as we have seen, must at least assume that instrumental rationality is intrinsically valuable.

To conclude: objectivity about values, far from creating a problem for the explication of moral motivation, actually fairs better than the subjectivism Hume espouses. It is the subjectivist's account of moral motivation which leaves us without an explanation of motivation; after all, why would people desire anything unless they thought that the things they desire *are* valuable.

4. *Cultural relativism.* In popular thought cultural relativism has always been one of the driving forces of subjectivism about values. People just look around and realize how diverse and inconsistent the values of different cultures are. They then wonder whether it makes any sense for them to assume that there is more to their own values than the upshot of their cultural contingencies. From a philosophical perspective, however, this is the least convincing argument for subjectivism. As we have observed already, an objective stance about values may well be consistent with a great amount of cultural relativity. Second, any reasonable moral theory can entail that others are seriously mistaken. In fact, no theory of values is credible unless it explains *both* of these features of evaluative discourse, namely, that it admits of a considerable amount of cultural relativity, and that people can be wrong about values, even on a very large scale. Far from being mutually exclusive, both relativism and the possibility of error are essential elements of values.

There is, however, a radical form of cultural relativism, all too fashionable these days, which we can call *the displacement theory of values*. According to this theory, any value we hold can be explained, causally, that is, as a result of our contingent make-up and cultural upbringing. Allegedly, I only value the equality between the sexes, for example, because it is fashionable these days, and because I have been brought up to think in this way. The general structure of the argument always follows the form 'you only believe in . . . because you belong to this culture, you've been brought up this way, etc.'

Nagel was right to remark that as it stands, the displacement theory is inconclusive. A causal explanation of how one came to have a certain view about values simply does not entail anything about its truth or validity. Even if it is the case that all of our views about values stem from our contingent cultural background, they may nevertheless be true. However, Nagel also admits that there is a question of credibility here. After all, if all our values can be explained causally, as emanating from the biological and cultural factors that shaped our lives, insisting on their independent truths *qua* universally valid values is somehow not so credible. Nagel's own response to this challenge is based on a version of the 'open question' argument. The normative realm, Nagel claims, simply cannot be transcended by the descriptive. Whenever the descriptive explanation is exhausted, the normative question 'given all that, what should I do?' is still in order.[28]

Be this as it may, cultural relativity as a displacement theory is not necessarily confined to the realm of values. Beliefs about science, nature, or just about anything else, are susceptible to similar debunking explanations. Therefore, the debunking explanation may well be turned against those same theories it relies upon. If any of this entails subjectivism—which is far from clear—the debunking explanation would quickly turn out to be self-defeating. If it defeats anything, it also defeats the causal explanations it relies upon.[29]

The essential question is, therefore, whether there is anything unique to the realm of values which makes the latter more susceptible to such debunking explanations. Now it seems that it is here, at this point, that the facts about cultural relativity would be brought into the picture. The subjectivist relies on the assumption that the considerable inconsistency of moral cultures strongly indicates that values are somehow more contingent than other domains of thought. In other words, displacement theories of value would seem to be on much firmer ground if combined with strong assumptions about relativism. Therefore, one crucial question is how strong, and yet still plausible, such assumptions about cultural relativity may be. In particular, we must be very cautious about two main assumptions that such a strong version of relativism would have to maintain. First, it must be assumed that values held by people in one culture are not only different, but also substantially at odds with the values held in other cultures. Relativism would be sufficiently strong only if it assumes the mutual exclusivity of evaluative schemes held by different cultures. Secondly, it must also be assumed that people from one culture cannot come to appreciate the values of other cultures, even if given the relevant knowledge and opportunity to learn. Whether it is plausible to defend these two theses is a difficult question, and there are many reasons to doubt it. Cultural diversity is something we can normally come to understand. Even

[28] Nagel, *The Last Word*, ch. 6.

[29] This self-defeating nature of such strong forms of relativism has been observed by Plato, if not earlier.

when faced with the values of the most alien cultures to us, we can typically understand the differences in our respective situations, and if we make an effort, we can come to realize the point of their values.[30] Consider child labour, for example. Contemporary Western cultures observe with disdain the norms of child labour and exploitation of children in some poor third-world communities. The more we become acquainted with such cultures (and perhaps the history of our own), however, and learn about their economic constraints, religious beliefs, cultural heritage, and the like, the easier it becomes to understand their acceptance of child labour, and to realize why they do not, and perhaps cannot yet, recognize such practices as unacceptably exploitative and abhorrent. This process of learning and developing new sensitivities is potentially symmetrical. Just as we can come to learn their constraints, they can learn and develop ours. Moral sensibilities are not just given; they can be acquired and developed by learning.

Cultural relativism is undoubtedly a fact. To a great extent, cultural contingencies affect the values people hold and, potentially, the values they ought to hold. The main mistake of the naive relativist is to assume that relativism is tantamount to immunity from cultural error. No such conclusion follows, however. Even if it is true that values themselves vary with cultural or other changes in the environment, it simply does not follow that those who occupy the relevant environment cannot be mistaken about values. Our suggestion to regard values as analogous to relational properties may well account for both of these features of the realm of values; it explains how it is the case that values are, at least partly, relative to culture, and at the same time, why people, perhaps even entire cultures, can be wrong about the values they hold.

DISPOSITIONAL THEORIES OF VALUES

Let us now consider two sophisticated and influential subjectivist theories of value. Both share the view that, roughly, values are what we are disposed to value. David Lewis's theory, however, works out the details of this idea in a way which strives to account for the facts of sensible disagreements and errors within evaluative discourse. Simon Blackburn's emphasis, on the other hand, concerns the question of how to bring such a dispositional account of values in line with classical logic. Blackburn's main challenge is to explain how subjectivism is compatible with the propositional features of evaluative language.[31] Note, however, that it is not my purpose here to present a detailed critique of these two theories. My main concern here is with a certain line of

[30] See Raz, *Engaging Reason*.

[31] There is an important difference between these two dispositional theories, that I will largely ignore here: Lewis's theory is a form of cognitivism, whereas Blackburn's account is a non-cognitivist one.

reasoning which seems initially appealing, rather than with the details of these particular theories of value.

Let us begin with Lewis's definition: 'Something of the appropriate category is a value if and only if we would be disposed, under ideal conditions, to value it.'[32] Why the addition of 'ideal conditions'? Normally, we would think about ideal conditions not for valuing, but for the purpose of balancing values. When circumstances arise where we have to choose between competing values it would seem sensible to try to avoid bias and other distractions, and one way to do this is by trying to idealize the epistemic conditions under which balancing would have to be carried out. But this is quite explicitly not Lewis's idea here, since he is interested in valuing and not in balancing. Therefore, when he elaborates on what conditions are ideal, we learn that they do not consist of the availability of information or the elimination of distractions. Conditions are ideal when they enable the 'fullest possible imaginative acquaintance'. Furthermore, this is a directional, progressive sequence. 'For in learning how to imagine X, you gain abilities; later you have all the relevant imaginative abilities you had before, and more besides . . . by and large, the process resists reversal.'[33]

Admittedly, imagination is crucially important for any theory of values. The simple- minded subjectivist takes valuing to be essentially passive, a reaction to the world we happen to encounter. But Lewis is right to maintain that valuing is not simply a reaction to samples. People often value things that they have never encountered. People have views about values, and they can often elaborate on those views. Most importantly, people can be convinced to change their minds about values, by means of rational or irrational arguments. Imagination is crucial to all these aspects of valuing. After all, how would I know whether I am disposed to favour X, unless I can imagine what would it be like to have X. The least we can say is that imaginative acquaintance is often indispensable for valuing. Let us grant, further, that for the more complicated cases, imaginative acquaintance is crucially important. But it still leaves the difficult questions unanswered. Some of them fare better than others.

Let us take the issues of disagreement and error first. One standard charge levelled at dispositional theories of value is that such theories render values

[32] Lewis, 'Dispositional Theories of Value', 113. Charles Larmore pointed out to me that Lewis's definition seems on the face of it to be circular, since the notion of *'ideal'* conditions cannot be but an evaluative concept: whatever makes something an ideal condition for valuing is itself a matter of evaluation. Therefore the definition of what is valuable crucially relies on evaluative judgements about what is an ideal condition for valuing. I must admit, however, that I am not entirely convinced by Larmore's criticism. It is not clear to me that all forms of 'ideal' conditions are necessarily evaluative. Often we use idealized conditions as standards of measurement (as in observation standards), and those are hardly evaluative in the sense Larmore has in mind. Perhaps Lewis erred here, but the error does not strike me as so obvious as Larmore suggests.

[33] Lewis, 'Dispositional Theories of Value', 122–3.

relative to each individual's constitution and preferences. Even worse, since we have no reason to assume that individuals' constitution and preferences remain constant across time and varying circumstances, values would turn out to be as fickle and subjective as one's preferences about ice cream flavours. When a speaker says that X is valuable, she could only mean that 'X is what *I* am disposed to value as I happen to be right now, and I'm not so sure about tomorrow'. But then why would she see any point in arguing with another speaker, who is disposed to value X differently? Now you might think that the addition of idealized conditions solves this problem. Perhaps one speaker would complain that the other values as she does, only because she is not valuing as she would under ideal conditions, that is, under conditions of the fullest imaginative acquaintance possible. But this does not take us far enough. The ideal condition requirement can be employed to account for one rather limited sense in which we can attribute error to another's values. It still leaves the motivation for argument entirely unexplained. If it is the case that even under ideal conditions of valuing, people can be differently disposed towards the same object under similar circumstances, and that people can realize this, then there does not seem to be any point in arguing about values. The interlocutor could always retort 'So what if I'm wrong? Even if I had thought about my dispositions under ideal conditions, we could still end up with the opposite results.' Wouldn't you think that they would stop arguing at this point? Not necessarily, Lewis contends, as they might assume that 'whatever relativity there is, it won't matter in *this* conversation'.[34] So moral disagreement proceeds under the initial assumption that we—perhaps all mankind—are disposed to value similarly under ideal conditions; we assume absolutism for the sake of the argument and try to see whether we can get away with it. If our assumptions prove wrong as we proceed, we may be forced to narrow down our claim about who 'we' are; such narrowing down may well eventually take us to the 'I, here and right now', but there is a long way to go before we are forced to reach that point. So each moral argument is '*conditionally relative*', Lewis claims: 'relative if need be, but absolute otherwise'.[35]

Is this an adequate reply to the question of motivation? Let us try to get a clearer picture about a more profound aspect of motivation, namely, the motivation *for valuing*. Lewis describes valuing as a canonical exercise in which we try to imagine whether we would be disposed to value X under ideal conditions of the fullest possible imaginative acquaintance. But what is the initial motivation for undertaking the canonical exercise itself, if it is clearly *not* the case that it aims to discover what values there are? Consider, for comparison's sake, other attitudes we have with respect to aspects of the world, besides valuing, that is. Let us return to the example of disgust for a moment.

[34] Ibid. 128. [35] Ibid. 129.

We can easily construct a comparable canonical exercise about the attitude of disgust. But that would seem to be pointless. There is no need to imagine what we/I would be disgusted by under ideal conditions of the fullest possible imaginative acquaintance. Such an exercise would be radically under-motivated because we do not think that there is anything philosophically interesting to discover by it. Aspects of the world do not seem *to deserve* an attitude of disgust; the latter is just something that happens to us (due to, let us assume, evolutionary causes which have shaped our species and culture). Similarly, valuing would be radically under-motivated if we assumed that it is just something that happens to us. Valuing is different from disgust, however, because we assume the opposite. We assume that aspects of the world deserve certain reactions and attitudes. Cruelty, for example, merits condemnation because it is harmful and bad. An attempt to figure out our attitudes and dispositions under ideal conditions may well facilitate our awareness and sensitivities to these aspects of the world. But that can be so only if we seek to discover what is valuable, anyway.

To put this argument another way: idealized conditions, of any kind, only make sense as theoretical devices aiming to avoid some kinds of distortion or bias. But the suspected distortions must be distortions of something; it takes an externalist assumption to make sense of such a theoretical device. The device of idealized conditions must be motivated by seeking knowledge of something which is there anyway; it can only be justified as indicative of truths we would like to discover.[36] If there is nothing to discover, it makes no sense to be worried about distortions. Unless, of course, valuing is only an exercise in self-knowledge. But then there is no point in arguing about it as part of interpersonal discourse.

The fact that evaluative discourse is essentially interpersonal, mostly propositional, and semantically descriptive, is taken very seriously by Simon Blackburn's version of a dispositional theory of values. Like Lewis, Blackburn also asserts that evaluations are essentially expressions of dispositions (or, as he prefers to call it, sensibilities). When we assert an evaluative judgement, we simply project our dispositions and attitudes onto the world, as it were. But, and this is Blackburn's quintessential point, we do it in a special way, namely, by transforming the semantics of evaluation from dispositional to propositional language. This transformative semantics is what Blackburn calls projectivism, and it forms a major part of his 'quasi-realism' about values. The expressions of our dispositions are transformed in standard ethical discourse into semantics of a quasi-propositional language, that is, by expressing attitudes, dispositions and the like, *as if* they were propositional statements describing aspects of the world.[37]

[36] Cf. my brief discussion of internal realism in Chapter 7.

[37] Blackburn, 'Evaluations, Projections, and Quasi-Realism'. See also, his *Essays in Quasi-Realism*.

This form of semantic transformation is actually familiar from contexts in which there is no doubt that something like projectivism takes place. People often say, for example, that 'X *is* disgusting'. This sounds like a standard propositional assertion describing a feature of X. In fact, though, it is easy to concede that something else is going on here. Disgust is more plausibly accounted for as a propensity to react to certain features of the world in a typical way, and expressions of this reaction only take the superficial form of a proposition; in fact, they are only projections of the relevant propensity onto the world, *as if* X 'is' disgusting. Thus a statement of the form 'X *is* disgusting' actually means 'I tend to react to X with an attitude of disgust'.

Blackburn claims that this transformational semantics applies across the board in evaluative discourse. And it is a good thing too, because it enables us to bring evaluative discourse within the confines of classical logic. It enables us to treat the expressions of dispositions as if they were propositions and apply standard propositional calculus to the discourse. Blackburn pays very little attention, however, to the question of why quasi-realism is limited to evaluations, as opposed to other types of expressions of dispositions. After all, we have not adopted this transformational semantics indiscriminately. A great deal of dispositional language remains subjective on the surface or, at least, would be conceded as such upon immediate reflection. Very often we simply express attitudes, dispositions, and sensibilities without projecting them onto the world; such expressions remain transparently subjective. Is there anything in Blackburn's theory to account for this discrimination? I will return to this shortly. First we need to see how he treats the notion of truth in evaluative discourse.

Blackburn concedes that quasi-realism faces a problem about the idea of truth which would apply to evaluative assertions. A standard correspondence theory of truth would not do. Quasi-realism is not an error theory. It purports to account for the rationale of evaluative discourse, not to render it philosophically mistaken throughout. If evaluative assertions are only projections of sensibilities onto the world, they cannot be rendered true or false by anything like a standard Tarski-model of truth.[38]

Blackburn's solution is to avoid the correspondence theory of truth altogether and to assume that evaluative discourse employs a constructive notion

[38] Note, by the way, that the disquotational formula (which is not equivalent to correspondence) would lead to embarrassing results. Take a standard evaluative assertion on the quasi-realist model, say, 'X is F', asserted by a speaker S in circumstance C, where f stands for an evaluative term. On the quasi-realist model, it translates to 'S has a propensity to react to X with the attitude F', which is typically expressed as the assertion 'X is an F'. Now, let us call 'X is an F' 'P', and 'S has a propensity to react to X . . .' we can call 'Q'. The quasi-realist asserts the equivalence of 'P' = 'Q'. According to the disquotational formula, 'P' is true if and only if P, and similarly, 'Q' is true if and only if Q. Now 'P' would always turn out to be false, because, *ex hypothesi*, X is not the kind of thing which can have the property F, and therefore, it is not the case that P. On the other hand, given certain assumptions about conditions of sincerity, Q would always turn out to be true. The disquotational formula does not work here.

of truth. Basically, Blackburn suggests a set-theoretical notion of truth, whereby truth means membership in a set. According to this formula—

'P' is true, if and only if, *P* is a member of M
where 'P' is the evaluative assertion and *P* is the attitude expressed by 'P'.

Accordingly, Blackburn maintains, we get two notions of falsehood:

'P' is weakly false = it is not the case that *P* is a member of M
'P' is strongly false = 'not-*P*' is a member of M

Whether the distinction between weak and strong falsehood is still compatible with the excluded middle is a difficult question I will not try to pursue here. The more obvious worry for now is to have an idea about the relevant set. Unless we can find a well-defined set which would be relevant for evaluative discourse, a set-theoretical notion of truth will remain utterly pointless. Anything can be a member of an arbitrarily chosen set. Now, a natural suggestion would be the following: let us assume that the relevant set is the largest possible set of attitudes people actually have which is still logically consistent. This is structurally close to Rawls's 'reflective equilibrium', and as Rawls rightly remarked, we have no assurance that only one set would fit the demand. Possibly we can have several, perhaps overlapping sets, each the largest internally consistent set of attitudes. It is not surprising that relativism is the price we have to pay for quasi-realism, and Blackburn goes to some lengths to show that this price is not too high.

It is far from clear, however, that relativism is the highest price we have to pay for the endorsement of this quasi-realist project. Other problems are more pressing. To begin with, a theoretical account of the motivation underlying the quest for coherence is badly needed. Coherence is self-evident when it is taken as an indication of truth. An incoherent theory cannot be true. But why should we seek the largest possible set of consistent evaluations, if those are not meant to be true in any straightforward sense. People often have inconsistent preferences and attitudes, and we normally don't worry about the inconsistency as such, as long as we can get away with it in practice. Nobody is particularly troubled by inconsistencies in her attitudes of disgust, for example, as long as those enable her to lead her life as she pleases. Inconsistency is worrying only when it forms part of an objectivist framework. The quasi-realist seems to be left without a convincing explanation of why we should worry about inconsistency at all. In other words, as soon as we realize that our evaluations are only projections of our attitudes onto the world, we seem to lose an interest in their truth, however that truth is defined.[39]

More importantly, however, quasi-realism leaves two closely related questions unanswered. First, why do we project certain attitudes onto the world,

[39] But see Gibbard, *Wise Choices, Apt Feelings.*

while we easily recognize (at least upon reflection) many others as subjective dispositions? If we are somehow doomed to projectivism, why do we discriminate between overtly subjective attitudes and values? The problem is that quasi-realism rules out the obvious answer, namely, that this discrimination is not due to sheer luck, but something that is called upon by the relevant features of the situation. Certain situations deserve certain attitudes. Indignation in the face of cruelty is not just an attitude we happen to have, but something that deserves this attitude because cruelty is wrong. Second, quasi-realism fails as an *explanation* of evaluation even in the simplest cases, as it leaves the motivation for projection entirely unaccounted for. If the only objective feature of cruelty is that it evinces a certain propensity in our psyche, why not leave it at that?

Finally, and perhaps most importantly, quasi-realism fails in its implicit reduction. McDowell rightly claimed that the idea of something being, for example, comic resists any attempt to reduce it to subjective attitudes, like a propensity to laugh. An inclination to laugh is not a satisfactory answer to what makes a situation comic. Laughter can be a response to other things, which are not comic but, say, embarrassing, and vice versa; some comic situations are not necessarily accompanied by an inclination to laugh.[40] Similarly, cruelty is not reducible to any particular attitude of indignation. One may observe, or even cause, an act of cruelty and tell oneself 'I wish I did not enjoy this . . . because it is so cruel'. There is a clear distinction between how one perceives the situation and one's attitude towards it. There is an important distinction between how things are and how we tend to react to them, and the attempt made by quasi-realism to reduce the former to the latter seems unavailing in countless occasions.

McDowell is also correct to point out that quasi-realism and dispositional theories of value in general are reactions to a false dichotomy: either we endorse Platonic realism about values, which would render them ontologically mysterious, or else we are forced to accept subjectivism.[41] As we have seen all along, the alternative to subjectivism is objectivity, not Value-Platonism.

[40] McDowell, 'Projection and Truth in Ethics'. [41] Ibid.

Bibliography

ALEXANDER, LARRY, and KRESS, KENNETH, 'Against Legal Principles', in A. Marmor (ed.), *Law and Interpretation* (Oxford, 1995), 279.

AUSTIN, JOHN, *The Province of Jurisprudence Determined* (first published 1832; London, 1954).

BERKELEY, GEORGE., *The Principles of Human Knowledge* (first published 1710), (ed. Engle and Taylor, California, 1968).

BLACKBURN, SIMON, 'Evaluations, Projections, and Quasi-Realism', in his *Spreading the Word (*Oxford, 1984), ch. 6.

——*Essays in Quasi-Realism* (Oxford, 1993).

BRINK, DAVID, *Moral Realism and the Foundation of Ethics* (Cambridge, 1989).

BURGE, TYLER, 'On Knowledge and Convention', 84 *Philosophical Rev.* (1975), 249.

COLEMAN, JULES, 'Incorporationism, Conventionality, and the Practical Difference Thesis', 4 *Legal Theory (*1998), 381.

——'Second Thoughts and Other First Impressions', in B. Bix (ed.), *Analysing Law: New Essays in Legal Theory* (Oxford, 1998), 257.

——and LEITER, BRIAN, 'Determinacy, Objectivity, and Authority', in A. Marmor (ed.), *Law and Interpretation* (Oxford, 1995), 203.

DAN-COHEN, MEIR, 'Law, Community, and Communication' (1989) *Duke LJ* 1654.

DAVIDSON, DONALD, *Inquiries into Truth and Interpretation* (Oxford, 1984).

DESCARTES, R., *Meditations on First Philosophy* (1641), trans. L. J. Laflens (London, 1960).

DWORKIN, RONALD, *Taking Rights Seriously* (London, 1977).

——'A Reply to Critics', in Cohen (ed.), *Ronald Dworkin and Contemporary Jurisprudence* (London, 1984), 247.

——*Law's Empire* (London, 1986).

——'Objectivity and Truth: You'd Better Believe It', 25 *Philosophy and Public Affairs* (1996), 87.

DUMMETT, MICHAEL, *Truth and Other Enigmas* (London, 1978).

——*The Interpretation of Frege's Philosophy* (London, 1981).

ELLICKSON, ROBERT, *Order without Law* (Cambridge, Mass., 1991).

FINNIS, JOHN, *Natural Law and Natural Rights* (Oxford, 1980).

FISH, STANLEY, *Is there a Text in this Class* (Cambridge, Mass., 1980).

——'Working in a Chain Gang: Interpretation in Law and Literature', in W. J. T. Mitchell (ed.), *The Politics of Interpretation* (Chicago, 1983), 271.

FRANKFURT, HARRY, *The Importance of what we Care About* (Cambridge, 1988).

FRIED, CHARLES, 'The Artificial Reason of the Law or: What Lawyers Know', 60 *Texas LR* (1981), 85.

GANS, CHAIM, *Philosophical Anarchism and Political Disobedience* (Cambridge, 1992).

GIBBARD, ALLAN, W*ise Choices, Apt Feelings* (Cambridge, Mass., 1990).

GILBERT, MARGARET, *On Social Facts* (London, 1989).

GREEN, LESLIE, 'Law, Co-ordination, and the Common Good', 3 *Oxford Journal of Legal Studies* (1983), 299.

——'The Concept of Law Revisited', 94 *Michigan Law Rev.* (1996), 1687.

——'Positivism and Conventionalism', 12 *Canadian Journal of Law and Jurisprudence* (1999), 35.
HAMPTON JEAN, *Hobbes and the Social Contract Theory* (Cambridge, 1990).
——*The Authority of Reason* (Cambridge, 1998).
HARE, RICHARD, *Moral Thinking* (Oxford, 1981).
HART, H. L. A., *The Concept of Law* (Oxford, 1961); 2nd edn. with Postscript, ed. Raz and Bulloch (Oxford, 1994).
——*Essays on Bentham, Studies in Jurisprudence and Political Theory* (Oxford, 1982).
HIMMA, KENNETH, 'Incorporationism and the Objectivity of Moral Norms', 5 *Legal Theory* (1999), 415.
HIRSCH, ERIC D. JR., *Validity in Interpretation* (New Haven, 1967).
HOLMES, OLIVER WENDELL, 'The Path of Law', 10 *Harvard Law Review* (1897), 457.
HUME, DAVID, *A Treatise of Human Nature* (first published 1739), 2nd edn. ed. Nidditch (Oxford, 1978).
KELSEN, HANS, *General Theory of Law and State* trans. Wedberg (New York, 1945, 1961).
KORSGAARD, CHRISTINE, *The Sources of Normativity* (Cambridge, 1996).
LARMORE, CHARLES, *The Morals of Modernity* (Cambridge, 1996).
LEITER, BRIAN, 'Book Review: Objectivity and the Problems of Jurisprudence', 72 *Texas LR* (1993), 187.
——'Realism, Hard Positivism, and Conceptual Analysis', 4 *Legal Theory* (1998), 533.
LEWIS, DAVID, *Convention: A Philosophical Study* (Oxford, 1968).
——'Dispositional Theories of Value', *Proceedings of the Aristotelian Society, Supplementary Volume*, no. 62 (1989), 114.
MCDOWELL, JOHN, 'Values and Secondary Qualities', in T. Honderich (ed.), *Morality and Objectivity* (Routledge, 1985), 110.
——'Projection and Truth in Ethics', in S. Darwall, A. Gibbard, P. Railton (eds.), *Moral Discourse and Practice* (Oxford, 1997), 215.
MACKIE, JOHN, *Ethics, Inventing Right and Wrong* ((London, 1977).
MARGOLIS, JOSEPH., *Art and Philosophy* (Brighton, 1980).
MARMOR, ANDREI, *Interpretation and Legal Theory* (Oxford, 1992).
——'On Convention', 107 *Synthese* (1996), 349.
MOORE, MICHAEL, 'Interpreting Interpretation', in A. Marmor (ed.), *Law and Interpretation* (Oxford, 1995), 1.
NAGEL, THOMAS, *The Last Word* (Oxford, 1997).
NOZICK, ROBERT, *Anarchy, State, and Utopia* (New York, 1974).
PERRY, STEPHEN, 'Interpretation and Methodology', in A. Marmor (ed.), *Law and Interpretation* (Oxford, 1995), 97.
——'Two Models of Legal Principles', 82 *Iowa Law Rev.* (1997), 787.
POSTEMA, GERALD, 'Coordination and Convention at the Foundations of Law', 11 *Journal of Legal Studies* (1982), 165.
PUTNAM, HILARY, *Reason, Truth, and History* (Cambridge, 1981).
——*Realism and Reason* (Cambridge, 1983).
——The Dewey Lectures: 'Sense, Nonsense, and the Senses: An Inquiry into the Powers of the Human Mind', 91 *Journal of Philosophy* (1994).
RAZ, JOSEPH, *Practical Reason and Norms* (London, 1975).

RAZ, JOSEPH, 'Reasons for Action, Decisions, and Norms', in Raz (ed.), *Practical Reasoning* (Oxford, 1978), 129.
——'Legal Principles and the Limits of Law', in M. Cohen (ed.), *Ronald Dworkin and Contemporary Jurisprudence* (London, 1984), 73.
——*The Authority of Law* (Oxford, 1979).
——'Promises in Morality and Law, Book Review', 95 *Harvard LR* (1982), 916.
——*The Morality of Freedom* (Oxford, 1986).
——'*Facing up*: A Reply', 62 *Southern California LR* (1989), 1153.
——'Authority, Law and Morality', in his *Ethics in the Public Domain* (Oxford, 1994), ch. 9.
——*Ethics in the Public Domain* (Oxford, 1994).
——'Moral Change and Social Relativism', 11 *Social Philosophy and Policy* (1994), 139.
——'Interpretation without Retrieval', in A. Marmor (ed.), *Law and Interpretation* (Oxford, 1995), 155.
——*Engaging Reason* (Oxford, 1999).
SCHAUER, FREDERICK, 'Prescriptions in Three Dimensions', 82 *Iowa L. Rev.* (1997), 911.
SCHEFFLER, SAMUEL, *Human Morality* (Oxford, 1992).
SCHIFFER, STEPHEN, *Remnants of Meaning* (Cambridge, Mass., 1989).
SCHWYZER, HUBERT, 'Rules and Practices', 78 *Philosophical Rev.* (1969), 451.
SEARLE, JOHN, 'Literal Meaning', 13 *Erkenntnis* (1978), 207.
——*Speech Acts* (Cambridge, 1969).
SHAPIRO, SCOTT, 'The Difference that Rules Make', in B. Bix (ed.), *Analysing Law: New Essays in Legal Theory* (Oxford, 1998), 33.
SIMMONS, JOHN, *The Lockean Theory of Rights* (Cambridge, 1992).
TUSHNET, MARK, 'An Essay on Rights', 62 *Texas Law Rev.* (1984), 1363.
WALDRON, JEREMY, *Law and Disagreement* (Oxford, 1999).
——*The Dignity of Legislation* (Cambridge, 1999).
WALUCHOW, WIL, *Inclusive Legal Positivism* (Oxford, 1994).
WARNOCK, GEOFFREY, *The Object of Morality* (London, 1971).
WIGGINS, DAVID, 'Moral Cognitivism, Moral Relativism, and Motivating Moral Beliefs', *Proceedings of the Aristotelian Society* (Fall, 1991), 61.
WILLIAMSON, TIMOTHY, *Vagueness* (London, 1994).
WITTGENSTEIN, LUDWIG, *Philosophical Investigations* ed. Anscombe (Oxford, 1958).
WOLFF, ROBERT PAUL, *In Defense of Anarchism* (London, 1970).
WOLLEHEIM, RICHARD, 'A Paradox in the Theory of Democracy', in P. Laslett and W. G. Runciman (eds.) *Philosophy, Politics and Society* (Oxford, 1969), 75.
WRIGHT, CRISPIN, *Truth and Objectivity* (Cambridge, Mass., 1992).

Index